DISPLACEES AND HEALTH: ISSUES AND CHALLENGES

NORVY PAUL

Notion Press

No.8, 3rd Cross Street,
CIT Colony, Mylapore,
Chennai, Tamil Nadu – 600004

First Published by Notion Press 2021
Copyright © Norvy Paul 2021
All Rights Reserved.

ISBN: 978-1-63806-669-9

Contents

Acknowledgements 5

List of Abbreviation 7

1. Introduction 11

2. Forced Displacement and Racism: A Global Public Health Concern
   Veronica Fynn Bruey 25

3. Internally Displaced People and Mental Health Issues
   Lucy Njarui Njiru 65

4. Sustainable Development Goals and Refugees,
   Poverty and Health Issues
   Puranjoy Ghosh 85

5. Right to Fair Compensation and Transparency in
   Land Acquisition, Rehabilitation and Resettlement Act 2013
   and Marginalisation of Oustees in India
   Norvy Paul 98

6. A Gender-Based Perspective on the Internal
   Migrants' Issue Associated with COVID-19 Pandemic
   Anupama Haridas 123

7. Health Service Delivery for Internally Displaced
   People: Issues and Challenges in India
   Pinki Kumari & Pushpalatha N 147

8. Creating Harmony Among the Internally Displacees Through
   Narrative Performance: A Case of Gulu Uganda
   Lucy Nabukonde 164

9. Challenges of Refugees in an Integration
Challenged Community: Refugees in the USA
Henry Poduthase & Genevieve Sabala.................................. 188

10. Social Support to Adolescent Mothers' for School
Re-Entry: Kakuma Refugee Camp-Kenya
Charity Kola 213

11. The Human Cost of Development: Displacement
and Resettlement Experiences from India
Shreya Mitra.. 232

12. Internal Migration and Women's Health in India:
Understanding the Vulnerabilities and Way Forward
Subrata S Satapathy.. 256

13. Where do we Stand among the Marginalized
in a Foreign Country?
Henry Poduthase & Lisa Garza 271

14. The Transit from the Land Acquisition Act 1894 to RFCTLARR
Act 2013 in India – Evaluation of Impact on People Affected
Binod Chandra Mishra 284

Acknowledgements

This book is a continuous effort by a group of academicians and practitioners to disseminate knowledge and share the uncoloured life of displacees, refugees and migrants and their struggles to address health and related concerns. Appreciating unreckonable struggles undertaken by the authors to bring the best out of the subject matter they have dealt with, I salute their commitment to the cause of displacees, refugees and migrants. I am privileged to extend my sincere gratitude to those who assisted and encouraged me in this endeavour, including my friends and family members, and especially my professional colleagues, Lucy Nabukonde and Johnson Mavole. I sincerely thank Notion Press Publishers for publishing and distributing the book. I dedicate this book to my loving parents.

List of Abbreviation

ACT	Access to COVID-19 Tools
ASCI	Administrative Staff College of India
APA	American Psychological Association
AePS	Aadhaar enabled Payment System
BCS	Bethany Christian Services
CBT	Cognitive Behavioural Therapy
CEPI	Coalition for Epidemic Preparedness Innovations
CIAL	Cochin International Airport Limited
CPRs	Common Property Resources
CPT	Cognitive processing therapy
CMIE	Centre for Monitoring Indian Economy Pvt. Ltd.
CWS	Church World Services
CEDAW	Committee on the Elimination of Discrimination against Women
DBT	Direct Benefit Transfers
DST	Department of Science and Technology
DFID	Department for International Development
EMDP	Eye Movement Desensitisation Processing
ECDC	Ethiopian Community Development Council
EMM	Episcopal Migration Ministries
ESL	English as a Second Language

EU	European Union
FRA	Forests Rights Act
HIAS	Hebrew Immigrant Aid Society
ICTT	International Container Tranship Terminal Limited, Vallarpadam
IIM	International Institute of Minnesota
IRC	International Rescue Committee
IDP	Internally Displaced People
IDMC	Internal Displacement Monitoring Centre
ILO	International Labour Organization
IOM	International Organisation of Migration
GAVI	Global Vaccine Alliance
GDP	Gross Development Product
HIV	Human Immunodeficiency Virus
JERS	Journey's End Refugee Services
KCPA	Kenya Counsellors and Psychologists Association
LAA	Land Acquisition Act
LGBT	Lesbian, Gay, Bisexual and Transgender
LRA	Lord's Resistance Army
LARR	Land Acquisition, Rehabilitation and Resettlement
LIRS	Lutheran Immigration and Refugee Services
MPI	Migration Policy Institute
MCL	Mahanadi Coalfield Limited
MDGs	Millenium Development Goals
MERS	Middle East Respiratory Syndrome Coronavirus

MED	Microenterprise Development
MGNREGS	Mahatma Gandhi Employment Guarantee Scheme
NDA	National Democratic Alliance
NFSA	National Food Security Act
NFHS	National Family Health Survey
NGO	Non-Government Organization
ORR	Office of Refugee Resettlement
PAP	Project Affected People
PDS	Public Distribution System
PE	Prolonged Exposure
PESA	Panchayat Provisions Extension to Scheduled Areas
PTSD	Post-Traumatic Stress Disorder
PPP	Public-Private Partnership
PMDKY	Pradhan Mantri Gareeb Kalyan Yojana
PNU	People's Movement in Uganda
POSCO	Pohang Steel Company
RA	Resettlement Agency
R&R	Rehabilitation and Resettlement
RBI	Reserve Bank of India
RFCTLARRA	Right to Fair Compensation and Transparency in Land Acquisition, Rehabilitation and Resettlement Act
RPDAC	Rehabilitation and Periphery Development Advisory Committees
RTAP	Refugee Technical Assistance Programme
RWTP	Rural Women Technology Park

SAIL	Steel Authority of India Limited
SARS	Severe Acute Respiratory Syndrome
SDO	Sub Divisional Officer
SETSPL	Tata Steel & Sasol Joint Venture project
SAMHSA	Substance Abuse and Mental Health Services Administration
SDGs	Sustainable Development Goals
SEZs	Special Economic Zones
SIA	Social Impact Assessment
SIT	Stress Inoculation Therapy
SPSS	Statistical Package for Social Sciences
SWAN	Stranded Workers Action Network
TSP	Technology Solution Providers
UNHCR	United Nations High Commissioner for Refugees' Convention
USCRI	United States Committee for Refugees and Immigrants
UDHR	Universal Declaration of Human Rights
UPA	United Progressive Alliance
USCCB	United States Conference of Catholic Bishops
USCIS	United States Citizenship and Immigration Services
UNFPA	United Nations Population Fund.
WHO	World Health Organization
WR	World Relief
WW I	World War I

Introduction

Displacees, a contesting terminology needs to be defined in the wake of current developments, evident in Europe, Middle East (Palestine and Turkey), Asian (Bangladesh, India, Burma, and in the African countries (Congo, Sudan, Kenya, Somalia etc.). Despite the fact that the UN Refugee Agency's effort to identify and define issues related to internal displacement, refugees and rehabilitation, the growing magnitude of the issue continues to disturb the human mind, human living and human settlement irrespective of culture, continents and development in spite of the declaration of the Jubilee celebrations of the UN Guidelines on Internal Displacement. Often, refugee-related problems or issues are generated from the culture of silence and the besetting process of recognising the issue. These issues range from unauthorized violation of human rights, concerns of refugees' economic rights, adequacy of shelter and protection of life, refugee asylums to all sorts of disasters. The attempts to address resettlement, rehabilitation, and mainstreaming among citizens are not found sporadically.

Refugees or internally displaced people are faced with multiple crises from local to international levels in the arena of detention, deportation, fragility, sexual orientation, gender identity, out place experience, armed non-state actors, HIV/AIDS, security, conflict, climate change, education of future generation, ethical concerns, human rights, disability etc. All these issues spur from the fundamental question of life close to the living conditions and life as human beings. This seems to challenge man's health as a refugee or displacee irrespective of gender, class, and citizenship. Considering the above a set of scholars both academicians and practitioners committed to the cause of refugees, internal displacees, and migrants and their life is trying to explore refugees' lives or internally displaced with specific reference to the health and life and the aftermath of status. The book is keen to bring to board refugee workers, policymakers, administrators, displacement studies experts, and academicians into one platform to reflect on the experiences and knowledge of communities and individuals directly affected to contribute towards the realization of the welfare of internal displacees. The wellness ought to commence from recognition to rehabilitation mooted not with a political agenda but in humanitarian understanding as declared by the United Nations in 1948.

The displacement induced by any paradigms cause human living and forces people to move from their land of origin and gradually become an alien to the country/place of their origin and the newly settled area. The quality of life of displacees is at stake though promises are made by the governments of the respective countries and international bodies. The sudden erupt of violence due to various reasons, forceful eviction for development projects, abrupt implementation of administrative policies and natural calamities forces human beings to make a trajectory to the unknown places and unknown host communities. This forces them to be victims of landlessness, placelessness and homelessness, which gradually transition from comfort zones to uncomfortable zones which makes downward mobility in the quality of life. This vulnerability leads them to be excluded from society's mainstreams and become marginalised in various life segments or become part of society's outskirts. Therefore, the displaced or refugees or migrants' workers are inflicted with life challenges that are not faced in mainstream society. The primary challenge is closely related to the quality of life and living standards, which intrinsically contribute to the individuals' healthy living. It is presented in the book by various authors by sketching their expertise blended with research skills in the daily living of the displacees, migrants and refugees of America, Africa and Asia.

Veronica argues that whether forcibly or voluntarily, humans have always migrated in search of food, safety, security, and shelter. To preserve life, survival instinct compels us to prevent death or dying by leaving harmful or dangerous places to sustain life. Historically, host cultures and communities have always welcomed and protected us as strangers seeking refuge. Notwithstanding, a common thread runs through cataclysmic events such as colonisation, slavery, the Great War, and the Total War of modernity: systemic racism. The author deems that recent protests against police brutality in the United States call for the declaration of racism as a serious public health concern. It is against this backdrop the scholar examines the history of racial discrimination against displaced people of colour from the Global South by white people in the Global North and calls to action for public health practitioners, scholars, and researchers to rethink primary prevention ensuring health to all migrants seriously.

Lucy Njiru states that mental health impacts on global development goals have led to mental health inclusion in the Sustainable Development Goals. Despite the high number of individuals needing mental health care services, access to these services remain a challenge in many low and middle-income countries. The author argues that evidence has shown that the situation is worse among internally displaced people (IDPs) than their counterparts. Effective treatment for mental, psychological, and emotional problems is minimally costed. Despite this, treatment coverage for these illnesses remains low across all populations. Her writing provides a brief overview of mental health concerns among IDPs. Clinical presentation of common psychiatric conditions among IDPs is examined to provide readers with an enhanced foundation for understanding these conditions. Assessment in mental health is a crucial component since it lays a basis for treatment and intervention planning. In addition, main risk and protective factors for post-traumatic stress disorder (PTSD) have been examined to help plan for effective prevention programmes. The final part of the article deals with some of the most effective treatment modalities for post-traumatic stress disorder that can be used in managing PTSD among IDPs.

The strength of public health policy, public health care services, combined efforts of the health institutions and its professions that pledged for the care, preservation and protection of the valuable resources (read human) of the state, have been well-experimented with the outbreak of infectious covid-19. Puranjoy Ghosh argues in the wake of the pandemic we are challenged currently that even being matured and convinced in realizing the uncertainty and unpredictability of this infectious zoonotic virus the initiatives in implementing the protective measures in the light of disaster management by the enforcement agencies along with its coordinating-contributory agencies have evoked incertitude, inter alia: 1) the accuracy of the information, being aired and its trustworthiness; 2) the trustworthiness upon the governance machinery about the public health emergencies.

The survival instinct of the living creature, irrefutably, predominates the behavioural pattern and while in a predicament it becomes violent even. In an ordered society like human being where the behavioural pattern has been conditioned adaptively by the normative frameworks prioritizing thereof the humanity as an integral part of formal living – any maladaptive responses in the society like ill and misleading medical ordinances by the endorsed health care agencies, the defiance by small social groups in complying preventive norms of the pandemic, hoarding and stockpiling of essential resources, marriage ceremony of the son of peoples' representative in Karnataka during the nation-wide lockdown, transportation of migrants, etc. Are healthy response of lack of social responsibility, social cohesion or solidarity and integrity. However, those indications measure the strength of democracy but bespeak the scapegoating conditions orchestrated to pursue 'the rule of law' and 'equality' for the mass myriad. What is more, painstaking is a preferential and discriminatory approach to implementing agencies in a nation warranted by cooperative federalism principles. In the present discourse, an endeavour is undertaken to critically analyse India's public health policy and its impact upon the psycho-social relationships and mental health of the citizens in such social emergency when the free movement for the greater interest of the society has been suspended.

India is a predominant developing country of Asia; its development strategies and projects require land to realise the goal marching towards a developed nation. Being the second-largest populated country, population density is high, and any projects for development require moving people forcefully from their living area to another. Such acquiring is guided by Right to Fair Compensation and Transparency in Land Acquisition, Rehabilitation and Resettlement Act 2013. Understanding the forceful eviction of people using RFCTLARRA, 2013 in India Norvy Paul argues that the Act needs to be read from sustainable challenges put forward by SDGs that aim at leaving no one behind. The Act primarily enlists areas that vent to land acquisition for development under the precept of primaeval hegemony of public purpose and eminent domain understanding prescriptive norms of compensation and devoid of the context of decision making of economic and non-economic asset loss, especially of natural and social capitals compelling them to be willing sellers. The requiring body often applies the sub silent doctrine of Social Impact Assessment forgetting social, psychological and physical aspects of life, under the pretext of the public hearing that force free consent obtained by an abusive process of the majority led by political regime though offered solatium of market value but not equal to the social value which often produces frustration against strive of welfare state due to the deprivation at heights and advantages at an abyss. Since the law attempts to follow proportional equality with a hollow heart, the SIA assured in the law concentrate social returns and not social costs that lead to the marginalisation of oustees of displacement at economic, social, psychological and political life. This could have been avoided if the acquisition had not taken place, and if it happened with social licensing, that opens space for dialogue and participation in decision making. Marginalisation sprouted and can never be overcome if space-time-place continuum has not reckoned adequately while designing resettlement action plans facilitated by social licensing that include reintegration via intervention and reclaim of social and individual identity. The author thus attempts to understand marginalisation of oustees in India on the background of Right to Fair Compensation and Transparency in Land Acquisition, Rehabilitation and Resettlement Act 2013 and recent displacement occurred in the country considering its provision of land acquisition, Social Impact Assessment, compensation provisions offered to Internally Displaced People of the country.

Since India's first case on 30 January 2020 the COVID-19 pandemic is the most disproportionately affected health crisis in recent times. The subsequent lockdown to curb the virus's spread has caused severe economic devastation and almost crushed informal workers' livelihood, small scale entrepreneurs and farmers and a significant chunk are the Internal Migrants. Forty million internal migrants have been impacted by lockdown, even losing their lives in the process of reaching their native. Under such a crisis, the women affected are either wives of migrant workers or low paid or informal sector workers like domestic workers, daily waged building workers. Wives of migrant workers don the hat of familial heads in their villages and depend on their husbands' remittance to run families. Anupama Haridas sketches women as informal sector workers facing the mental trauma of abandonment by their employers, coupled with their domestic responsibilities to make ends meet. The author delves into women's crisis under such circumstances, like loss of livelihood, vulnerability to domestic violence, improper menstrual hygiene, and reproductive health that requires concerns to be addressed.

Henry Poduthase and Genevieve Sabala focus on how US Federal and State agencies collaborate with voluntary agencies (VLOAG) to implement the refugee resettlement process to integrate into the community. The authors depend on the premise that failure to recognize refugees' credentials, in addition to individual and institutional barriers, contribute to economic and integration challenges. However, change in societal attitudes, and economic empowerment programmes show that adapting innovative hands-on practices, from sustainable employment to unlocking entrepreneurial potential, is transformative. They narrate an in-depth perspective of the refugee community's economic and integration challenges in the US, which affect the healthy living of the refugees. The study uses recent and relevant research about refugee settlement and challenges faced, focusing on the United States. Integrating relevant theories and empirical research, the authors depict the refugee community's social and economic reality in the country. The authors explore empowerment programmes by VOLAGs, including Journey's End Refugee Services in Buffalo NY, Peace of Thread in Clarkson GA, International Institute of Minnesota, and Global Talent Boise, ID to substantiate their argument. The findings show that refugees in the country are predominantly located into urban areas and relocating to new locations are discouraged by the US refugee policy based on a perceived challenge of secondary migration and community integration. However, there is a disconnect between US resettlement policy and refugee secondary migration where the refugees move to various rural locations for employment opportunities, welfare benefits, reunification with relatives, and a more congenial climate. Later, in achieving economic stability, refugees must face challenges like language skills, mental health, individual challenges, whereas recognition of qualifications and negative cultural bias/discrimination are common institutional challenges. Failure to recognize refugees' qualifications and previous work experiences, limited language skills, societal and cultural biases, and regulatory barriers in the host country affect refugees' ability to achieve economic sustainability, pointing to healthy living. The importance of recognizing the impact of both individual and institutional challenges on refugees' economic success must be underscored during the resettlement process. Ultimately, using the strengths and empowerment approach to support and promote entrepreneurship, is an alternative to employment among refugees, increases economic, healthy living and social benefits for the host country.

Pinki Kumari and Pushpalatha after scanning the existing literature and documents suggest that despite the increasing magnitude of internally displaced persons, there is still no universal legal definition to define them, and hence, it remains a contesting terminology. Nevertheless, unlike refugees, they do not cross the country borders. As they present their study, they describe that internally displaced persons (IDPs) in any country can be categorised majorly into three groups: people displaced due to conflict, people displaced due to natural disasters and people displaced due to developmental projects. Worldwide there are over 40 million IDPs, out of which 80% are women and children, and in India, the number was 2.4 million in 2016. The displacees have to face multiple problems as they are ousted from their original places such as social exclusion, marginalisation, poverty, and unemployment, which significantly impact their health. The absence of access to proper food, shelter, clean drinking water and sanitation results in several health problems and directly related to the physical, mental and reproductive health of displacees and even suffer from the disease, disability, injury, malnutrition, trauma, depression and anxiety. 19th principle of the United Nations Guiding Principles on Internal Displacement focuses on IDPs' health care provisions. The scholars argue that providing health care facilities to the displaced population is a challenging issue in India as there is an acute shortage of health care facilities. Health care workers face complex challenges in providing care to displaced people. Lack of access to health care facilities, services, and supplies, including medicines, increases the problem's gravity. Responding to the IDPs' health care needs a multi-pronged approach from the state, NGO sector, and civil society. They need to take proactive steps to make health services available and accessible to IDPs that provide culturally appropriate and financially feasible intervention plans.

Displacees are earth-born who tend to tell they are natural events to their companions in asylums. This is because every human being is synonymous with the human narrative. Therefore, an oral narrative is senescent through which displacees express their fears, aspirations, hopes and dreams. Lucy Nabukonda looking into Ugandan displacement experiences discusses that when displacees reckon their personal experiences, they create personal stamina and some upshots in their mental representation to sustain life. The study sought Narrative performance to exploring their total experiences in displacement focusing on: the harmony created through narratives existing among the internally displacees in Gulu; the relationship between the harmony and the human emotions expressed in narratives of displacees in Gulu and the perception of displacement in the narrative among the internally displacees in Gulu. Displacees expressed their new environment's comprehension and revealed that the configuring of narratives by the internally displacees reunites, regenerates and harmonies their experiences.

Charity Kola's work on teenage pregnancy brings forth refugee adolescent mothers and numerous health issues associated. Refugee adolescent mothers are exposed to a wide range of distress, including poverty that forces them out of school. Adolescent mothers are influenced by their social contexts and understanding the relationship between these contexts and their enrollment in school, retention, and transition is paramount. This chapter highlights the degree to which social support, including family, school, peer, and community, is accorded to adolescent mothers returning to school in Kakuma Refugee camp Kenya. The researcher employed a mixed-method study approach, and a descriptive survey was utilized to collect quantitative data while phenomenology design was used to collect qualitative data. The author argues that refugee adolescent mothers received little support from their families, schools, communities, and local schools for school re-entry. Their relationship with their peers changed due to pregnancy and parenthood, but peer groups remained an outstanding support group for refugee adolescent mothers. The author suggests that school guidance and counselling departments need to be well established in learning institutions while the community and the local government administration should take collective action and embrace girl child education, ensuring re-entry of adolescent mothers to school, facilitating a healthy life adolescent refugee mothers.

India's land rich natural resource base makes them a potential site for establishing development projects and industries. While these development projects can significantly benefit society, these projects often come at human costs, where the poor and the indigenous people are the victims and have a social-economic impact on the lives of the poor; the loss of traditional livelihood, culture, food security, ownership rights over resources, and land alienation are the most prominent among other issues they face. India has experiences where displacement and resettlement issues have taken a violent turn and increased mass protests and movements. Shreya Mitra critically appraises the consequences of development-induced displacement in India through secondary data analysis to determine the issues and challenges related to displacement, reallocation, and resettlement to be addressed to attain inclusive development. The author suggests that displacement and resettlement pose enormous risks for the poor who are uprooted from their native places and put into a new place with limited or no ownership of resources and lack access to basic amenities like health, sanitation, education and secure livelihood. Displacement must be done with informed choice and consent of the communities. Resettlement mechanism should not restricted to compensation and allocation of housing but focus on the specific needs of various communities, cultures, and ecosystems and ensure a sustainable livelihood for the displaced.

Internal migration, the movement of people within a country, results in a more efficient allocation of human resources to sectors and regions where they are better utilized. In India, as in most countries, there are generally no restrictions on internal movement. Subrata Satapathy referring to the number of internal migrants in India was 450 million (Census, 2011) argues that this exceeds the population growth rate of 18% across 2001-2011making an increase from 30% in 2001 to 37% in 2011 and among them that women form almost 70 per cent. The author argues that women migrants, in particular, suffer the consequences of being a woman and a migrant. They remain mostly discriminated in the workforce and invariably suffer economic exclusion. In addition to low pay and inhuman working conditions, low-skilled women migrants often get work that is saddled with health hazards like "respiratory illness, tuberculosis, ergonomic problems like back pain, mental health problems such as depression and reproductive health issues. Thus, the author attempts to throw light on India's women's internal migrants' various post-migration health vulnerabilities.

Henry Poduthase and Lisa Garza's work investigates refugees' systematic marginalization in a well-developed social class hierarchy in the United States of America. Furthermore, the chapter would discuss the effect of social hierarchy on refugees' social, economic, and political experiences. Discussing social hierarchy's theories, the authors explore recent and relevant research on marginalization and social hierarchies examining secondary data on refugees' marginalization in the United States. They adopted theoretical, cultural, empirical perspectives on refugees' adaptation to a new country and their challenges in an existing social hierarchy. The study examines various programs and organizations at the state, federal, and charitable level to bridge the marginalisation gap in assimilation and social integration into the mainstream society. Social cohesion among similar refugees is atypical of any minority group behaviour existing within the context of a majority social group. The authors pointed out that social, economic, and political marginalization is accepted, to an extent, by the refugees in the process of establishing themselves in their new world of already existing social hierarchy. Refugees provide invaluable services and play vital roles in the livelihood of our communities. Every day, refugees work difficult jobs such as providing food to a nation – often putting their health and families' health at risk.

Mahatma Gandhi's vision who advocated Panchayati Raj as the foundation of India's political system, Binod Misra was looking at RFCTLARR Act 2013 and attempted to discuss how Indian administration is moving towards power to people though not power decentralization is realised in its real sense. The author discusses the impact of power on people through the RFCTLARR Act over its journey for the last five years with a scope to address the livelihood issue and displacement issue by repealing the old Land Acquisition Act of 1984 provide a healthy living for the people displaced for the project. The livelihood of the displacees is the foundation stone for the expected oustees to improve the quality of life, which generally not addressed in the Indian scenario.

Reflecting upon the authors' perspectives inspires to state that refugees or displacees or migrants are challenged to face marginality and vulnerability, which are cross-regional and cross-disciplinary concerns. It often addressed with a problematic approach which is incomparable and complex to global actors to act upon who never operate in isolation. Because displacement on any variants is mooted by political actions having shared values of politics of colonisation. This calls for decolonisation and establishment of belongingness because internal displacement is a glaring global reality. Decolonisation of modern times urges to change the meaning of colonisation and change in tunes that draw boundaries between mainstream and outskirts. The decolonisation, therefore, is pushing out the edges of cultural and geographical divides that define margins and mainstreams. The pushing out of boundaries or melting the narrowed but strong division is possible but requires engagement and discourse between academia and practitioners. The reflections of this engagement and discourse on the structured realities of life need imminent critical interventions in the politics of culture, geography and governance due to prolonged stay in the same status as displacees and refugees. Such a structured political life of displacees marginalises the privileges of legal status. The apparent status of refugees forces them to fight for a place and space generated from homelessness and placelessness.

The decolonisation of displacement understanding shall assume that displacement is irreversible. The possible reality has scope for advocacy and policy formulation based on the justice realisation footed in the human right approach. Often politics of displacement or decolonisation sprout from the politics of home and relationality of migration and displacement. Mostly this relationality cause marginality or creation of margins who are always victims. The agents who propose the proactive policy that promote both local and global agents are against colonisation-dominance politics. This empirical advancement is primarily possible by avoiding naming, classification and categorisation by making the disconnect to connect. Such sporadic epitomes are possible and able to display when refugees become victorious than victims. The agitations against Citizen's Amendment Act, Farmers strike in Delhi against the newly enacted Farmers' Act in India, Rohingya events in Myanmar are examples. It becomes a movement to ensure the realisation of human rights. To understand or recognise victims as victorious demands pan-national neo perspectives that prevent selective or oppressive actions from sending them to invisibility. Therefore, it demands restructure policy, polity and society perspective that detour bordered life of human living or gentrification of marginality pushing to practice neo-colonisation within government or nation. Therefore, it demands a new understanding of displacees, refugees and migrants that primarily aspires to realise human rights recognising uniqueness and individuality, which can prevent social, cultural and political spheres in the neo-colonised world. Therefore, the concern is to realise healthy living irrespective of living standards pushing the boarders of margins that include the margins into the mainstream.

Displacement or involuntary migration irrespective of countries of any nature or people of any culture, people of any class or creed or any criteria cost human living. It uproots the umbilical code of one's existence, leading to homelessness and placelessness, which challenges the displacees or migrants to start their life afresh. The governance and welfare need to accord systems that support their living though not realised as expected and envisaged. It needs commitment and passion for safeguarding and promoting a decent living with dignity in society to effect decolonisation. Therefore, it is imperative to think that man does not want to lose the inherent identity unless it brings upward mobility that comforts life compared to the previous status. The welfare of individual needs to be reflected from the perspectives of quality of life and standard of living as we progress in science and services. Displacees, refugees, and migrants involuntarily moved do not enjoy the quality of life and standard of living as paramount to the remaining mainstream society as they are most marginalised and pushed to society's outskirts. It is primarily reflected in the healthy living of displacees, refugees and migrants as they are always challenged to cope with new situations that nobody wants to be. Coping such challenge to health is possible when there are policies and programmes, especially Resettlement Action Plan reflected to bring the economics of recovery, forcing them to be development partners and beneficiaries than victims at the altar of development, governance, natural and manmade disasters and violence.

Norvy Paul
Nairobi
22.01.2021

Forced Displacement and Racism: A Global Public Health Concern

Veronica Fynn Bruey[1]

Abstract

Whether forcibly or voluntarily, humans have always migrated in search of food, safety, security, and shelter. To preserve life, survival instinct compels us to prevent death or dying by leaving harmful or dangerous places so as to sustain life. Historically, host cultures and communities have always welcomed and protected us as strangers seeking refuge. Notwithstanding, a common thread runs through cataclysmic events such as colonisation, slavery, the Great War, and the Total War of modernity: systemic racism. Recent protests against police brutality in the United States are calling for the declaration of racism as a serious public health concern. It is against this backdrop that this chapter examines the history of racial discrimination against displaced people of colour from the Global South by white people in the Global North. The chapter concludes with a call to action for public health practitioners, scholars, and researchers to seriously rethink primary prevention in ensuring health to all migrants.

Keywords: Displaced People, Refugees, Public Health, Racism, Yemen, COVID-19

Introduction: A Brief History of the Origins of Displaced Peoples and Refugees

One was always a refugee – that is the name one was given, a sort of nickname (sobriquet). One was left with nothing, ruined, and

---

1 Editor-in-Chief, Journal of Internal Displacement, veronica.fynn@tuki-tumarankeh.org

> that is how people carried on talking about 'the refugee. We were
> not real people any more…we long to become people once again.
> A Belgian refugee survivor of the Great War (Gatrell, 2013, p. 49).

Several scientific theories are explaining how humans evolved and populated planet earth. Using human genome/DNA sequencing, evolutionary biologists affirm that *Homo sapiens* and the First Peoples began migrating from Africa to populate parts of Asia and Europe 35,000 and 65,000 years ago (Greshko, 2018; Thompson, 2016; Wells, 2002). Others reached the Americas *via* a land bridge created by the Pleistocene Ice Age (Brown, 2015; Hogenboom, 2017). Thus, whether forcibly or voluntarily, humans have always migrated in search of food, safety, security, and shelter.

Our natural inclination for self-preservation *vis-à-vis* survival instinct compels us to prevent death or dying by leaving harmful or dangerous places to sustain life. Strangers who sought asylum, a place of refuge, or a sanctuary were welcome, protected, and earned the right not to be seized (Cohen, 2019, p. 48). Such hospitality is proverbialised in the Niger-Congo Swahili language as *Kariba menu, likin gumweed macho* interpreted as "invite the stranger but do no scrutinise him" (Cohen, 2019, p. 47). In the Sene-Gambian Wolof expression, tuki tumarankeh means "it is the traveller who faces the most difficulty" (Fynn Bruey, Bruey, & Bender, 2017).

Research shows that around 1000 AD, development in long-distance travel brought Australia-Polynesia to Malagasy (present-day Madagascar) (Castles, Haas, & Miller, 2020, p. 2). The Muslim conquest in North Africa connected the Maghreb region with the Middle East, resulting in North Africa's Arabisation (Castles et al., 2020, p. 2). The movement of Arabs to North Africa mark the flight of the Bedouins fleeing "traumatic exogenous natural disasters – like floods or extensive droughts, human-made political calamities" (Castles et al., 2020, p. 2).

Between the fifth and seventh century, the slave trade expanded from tropical Africa, spreading towards the Mediterranean and Arabia as conquering kingdoms sold male captives to North African and Europeans traders for labour (Castles et al., 2020, p. 2). By the 13th century, forced migration drove the consolidation of the Bafour, Ghana, Benin and Lunda

Empires in Africa (Milner, 2009, p. 18). The French word *"réfugié"*, which later became "refugee' in English, is rooted in the escape of over one million Huguenots (reformed protestants) who fled religious prosecution in France's Catholic monarchy in the 17th century across Europe (particularly in England), African, and other parts of the world (Gatrell, 2013, p. 2; Hornak, 2017).

Barely two hundred years after the Huguenots persecution in France, the world experience the Great War, popularly known as World War I (WWI). In 1914, Russia occupation of East Prussia and Germany's aggressive control of Belgian, northern France, Poland and Lithuania ejected millions from their homes. A "total war" ensued at the dissolution of international boundaries – the refugee crisis of displaced populations was born (Gatrell, 2013, p. 26). During the First World War, an estimated 10 million people were uprooted and displaced internally (mostly within European countries) and internationally (Gatrell, 2013, p. 3).

Despite issues related to deportation, revolts, punitive resettlement, and forced labour, with a "free to migrate concept," the resettlement refugees across Europe, Australia, Canada, and America were considered more peaceful as hospitable host nations received displaced peoples fleeing from war and violence. For example, the United States immigrant population grew from 10.3 in 1900, to 13.5 in 1910, and 13.9 in 1920, 86 per cent of which were born in Europe (Gibson & Jung, 2006, p. 43). Over the same timeframe, 3.4 million immigrants landed in Canada, more than 50 per cent of whom were born in the British Isle (Statistics Canada, 2016).

In Australia, early migrants (1788-1900) were colonists, convicts, and bounty immigrants who encroached upon Native lands to flourish as a "White Only" colony. Six months after the Federation of Australia was established (*Australian Constitution* 1901), an act of Parliament, the *Immigration Restriction Act* 1901, stopped and prevented non-European immigrants from entering the country. Having little or no regard for Aboriginal Australians, the European born population in Australia swelled from 2.9 million in 1901 to 3.7 million in 1911, and 4.9 million in 1921 with British and Irish immigrants making up more than 75 per cent of all overseas born-Australians (Australian Bureau of Statistics, 2019).

Fast forward to the second World War, once British colonists succeeded in dispossessing Natives of their land in Canada, United States, and Australia, the perception that refugees are national security threat was born (Gatrell, 2013, p. 2). The Greatest War's impact was a grave public health disaster given the magnitude of deaths, starvation, and disease. Some 60-78 million casualties, 9.8-10.4 million were murdered because of their political affiliation or racial identity (Kesternich, Siflinger, Smith, & Winter, 2014, p. 5; Weinberg, 1995, p. 894, 2014, p. 241). Approximately 60 million people, mostly in Europe, fled genocide, massacres, ethnic cleansing, invasion, and violent military attacks (Gatrell, 2013, p. 3; Weinberg, 1995, p. 894).

The increasing hatred for displaced peoples prompted by Nazi Germany's extermination of six million Jews (Hilberg, 1985), created enough sympathy to resettle those fleeing into the Canada, United States, Australia, and other countries around the world. Interestingly, with much of their population wiped out by Nazi Germany, the relocation of some 1.95 million Jews to Palestine since 1948 has resulted in ongoing violent conflict, dehumanisation, forced eviction, and mass displacement of 5.1 million Palestinians (Gaba, 2015; Tolts, 2010).

Although insanely irrational, this cyclical prejudice and its affinity to sustain violent conflict and forced displacement somehow guide international law's conceptual underpinnings intended to protect displacement peoples. For example, the exclusion of displaced peoples outside of Europe from the United Nations High Commissioner for Refugees' *Convention Relating to the Status of Refugees* 1951 (hereafter, the *UNHCR Refugee Convention 1951*) caused chronic public health problems as noted above. Apart from the millions of lives lost in both the first and the second wars, many were maimed, diseased, homeless, malnourished, and mentally traumatised for the remainder of their lives, not just in Europe but other parts of the world.

Prior to drafting the UNHCR's Refugee Convention 1951, refugees and displaced persons existed outside of Europe. For instance, the Arab-Israeli conflict 1948, resulted in the displacement of some 700,000 Palestinians (Mayblin, 2010, 2014, p. 427); 1-5 million people were displaced during the *Korean War* 1950-53 (Gaba, 2015; Hickey, 2011) and millions more created by the partitioning of India (Mayblin, 2014, p. 427). Yet, Article

1 of the *UNHCR Refugee Convention* 1951 restricted protection to "events in Europe before 1 January; or events occurring in Europe or elsewhere before 1 January 1951."

Labelled "the myth of difference (the idea that great dissimilarities characterised refugee flows in Europe and the Third World)" (Chimni, 1998), the geopolitical and temporal limitations of the *UNHCR Refugee Convention* 1951 demanded a revision 16 years later. The universality of the *UNHCR Refugee Convention* 1951 was somehow invalid until 1967 when the *Protocol Relating to the Status of Refugees* removed the geographical boundaries and temporal limitations (V. P. Fynn, 2011, p. 10).

Having realised the Eurocentric nature of the *UNHCR Refugee Convention* 1951 failure to address the refugee crises in Africa, the OAU developed the *Convention Governing the Specific Aspects of Refugee Problems* 1969. Another 29 years would elapse before the first soft law (non-binding instrument) to protect internally displaced people (IDPs) emerged – the *Guiding Principles on Internal Displacement* 1998. The *African Union Convention for the Protection and Assistance of Internally Displaced Persons in Africa* 2012 is the only international law providing for IDPs' protection.

Displaced peoples have come a long way since the First and Second World Wars. Albeit, the negative perceptions held in Western countries in the Global North about new commons from the Global South have increasingly morphed into a tighter closed-border mentality, fear-mongering, xenophobia, crim-migration, securitisation, and outright racism against refugees and migrants. Yet, violent conflicts and wars in Israel/Palestine, Afghanistan, Iraq, Iran, Democratic Republic of Congo, Somalia, Syria, and Libya (to name a few) have elevated the number of displaced peoples to a record 79.5 million by the end 2019 (Internal Displacement Monitoring Group, 2020; The United Nations High Commissioner for Refugees, 2020).

Starting with critical definitions and conceptual framework the chapter unfolds in four distinct but intersecting layers: 1) a historical background on the origins of 'displaced peoples'; 2) the law as an apparatus or oppression based on race and social group membership; 3) systemic racism as a serious public health concern, and 4) negative perceptions and media representation of displaced peoples from the Global South in Global North.

The chapter concludes with highlighting challenges and opportunities in charting a way forward to address systemic racism against displaced people of colour using interventions based on public health principles.

1. Concepts, Theories, and Definitions

The Global South

In this chapter, the phrase The Global South refers to low-income countries in Asia, Africa, Latin America, and Oceania. Emphasising geopolitical power-relations, the term is derogatory. It subtly implies primitive, Third World, marginalised societies outside of advanced First World countries of the Global North in Europe and North America (Australia and New Zealand included) (Dados & Connell, 2012, p. 12). In 1964, the Group of 77 (G-77), the largest intergovernmental organisation of developing countries in the United Nations, was established by a Joint Declaration of the Seventy-Seven Developing Countries (Pal, 2020).

The aim of the G-77, whose membership has increased to 134 countries, is to "articulate and promote their collective economic interests and enhance their joint negotiating capacity on all major international economic issues within the United Nations system, and promote South-South cooperation for development" (G-77, 2020). The phrase's significance to this chapter highlights the racial distinction entre people from The Global South, who happen to be displaced migrants seeking refuge in the Global North. The reverse journey, i.e., migrants from the Global North to the Global South, is not the same but encumbered with Ross Coggins characterisation of the "Development Set" (Coggins, 1978, p. 80).

Oppressive/Discriminatory Laws

It seems counterintuitive, but so far this research evidence in this chapter affirms that the law is created mostly by (white) men, therefore are inherently discriminatory. It is naïve to claim that the law is objective in dispensing justice for all (Manuel & Derrickson, 2017). Think about the demographics, geopolitical locations, and racial identity of dead migrants from Africa lying on the shores of the Mediterranean, those detained at the US-Mexican borders (Taggart, Aleaziz, & Leopold, 2020), the intercepted

"Boat People" locked up in off-shore detention centres by the Australian government (Leach, 2003), and the death rates of those dying from COVID-19 (Reeves, 2020).

Yes, indeed, as an instrument of oppression, the law can discriminate based on race and social group (Fynn Bruey, 2016, p. 44; Rendel, 1975). This chapter argues that the *United States Constitution* 1789, *Canada British North America Act* 1867, the *Australia Constitution* 1901, and a host of immigration acts and specific acts of parliament and legislations are discriminatory laws (see below) insofar as they exclude and lack equal protection of the First Peoples, Black African slaves, women, and other displaced peoples. The argument here is that these nations' inherent racist foundations calcify and sustain ongoing systemic and institutional racism against displaced people, necessitating a public health pandemic declaration.

Displaced Peoples

The Guiding Principles on Internal Displacement (hereafter the Guiding Principles), 1998 defines internally displaced persons (IDPs) as

> "persons or groups of persons who have been forced or obliged to flee or to leave their homes or places of habitual residence, in particular as a result of or in order to avoid the effects of armed conflict, situations of generalised violence, violations of human rights or natural or human-made disasters, and who have not crossed an internationally recognised state border" (Deng, 1998, para. 2).

In this chapter, a composite description of displaced persons replaces a modified version of the Guiding Principles' definition of IDPs. It reads,

> displaced persons or groups of persons who have been forced or obliged to flee or to leave their homes or places of habitual residence, in particular as a result of or in order to avoid the effects of armed conflict, situations of generalised violence, violations of human rights or natural or human-made disasters, irrespective of whether they have not crossed an internationally recognised state border or not.

To be clear, the phrase "displaced peoples" is an amalgamated term encompassing various populations that are forcibly and coercively displaced under colonial violence (e.g., land dispossession), systemic racism, war and conflict, sexual and gender-based violence, corporate development, gentrification (resettlement or integration, harsh environmental or Climate change conditions, and health crises, such as the COVID-19 pandemic (Fynn Bruey, 2016, pp. 77–80, 2019, pp. 1–25; V. Fynn, 2011, pp. 47–46; V. P. Fynn, 2011, pp. 63–67; Greenhill, 2010, pp. 12–24; Skretteberg & Skjeflo, 2020).

This collective group of people include, but not limited to, internally displaced peoples (IDPs), refugees (including UNHCR *bona fide*, humanitarian, climate change, and economic refugees), asylum seekers, undocumented migrants, trafficked and smuggled persons, Indigenous Peoples, homeless peoples, and unaccompanied minors (Fynn Bruey, 2018). Displaced peoples in this chapter are not confused with those who volunteered and permanent migrants, whose travel are regulated by some legally recognised documents (Organisation for Economic Co-operation and Development, 2020).

2. (Systemic/Structural) Racism

Since there is only one human race, racism as an ideology is "a made-up social construct, and not an actual biological fact" (Gannon, 2015). The entire machinery and fabrication of colonialism, slavery, the holocaust, and apartheid were all based on racist ideas that vilify Africans and Indigenous Peoples as "savages" in need of "white saviours" to civilise them (Boly, 2018; Kendi, 2019, p. 13; Mutua, 2001, pp. 201–203). Racism is about one group (e.g., elite White people) having the power to carry out systematic discrimination through the institutional policies and practices of the society and shape the cultural beliefs and values that support those racist policies and practices (dRworks, 2020). Systemic, structural, or institutional racism is the intersection of racist and discriminatory practices that creates advantages (overtly or covertly) for the White group while impeding access for people/communities of colour (dRworks, 2020).

Racism invokes the "lesser than human" mentality. David Livingston Smith describes the ideology as dehumanising, demeaning, and cruel (Smith, 2011, pp. 6–14) in so far as it reflects the consequential act of violence, forced displacement, and mass murder of human beings rising well above the level of a grave global public health pandemic. The cruelty of racism is camouflaged and operationalised in the genocidal acts of the trans-Atlantic slave trade, anti-Semitism, and ethnic cleansing (to name a few). For approximately 374 years, between 1574-1875, a total of 34,087 voyages forcibly migrated 12,521,337 Black Peoples in chains from across the heart of Africa to the Americas *via* the trans-Atlantic slave trade (Fynn Bruey, 2016, p. 237).

According to Smith, much of what is known about the dehumanisation of slaves in North America is taken from Morgan Godwyn's writings, a missionary who later became an Anglican minister for white parishioners in Barbados (Smith, 2011, p. 122). Godwyn justifies the perception that "Africans were sub-human, uncivilised, and inferior to the Europeans in every way" (Racist Ideas, n.d.), asserting that,

> the Negros, though in their Figure they carry some resemblances of Manhood, yet are indeed no men and advocated 'Hellish Principles... that Negros are Creatures Destitute of Souls, to be ranked among Brute Beasts and treated accordingly' (Godwyn, 1680, p. Preface and Introduction; Smith, 2011, p. 122).

Sir Richard Blackmore, a British physician and writer, continued,

> As Man, who approaches nearest to the lowest Class of Celestial Spirits... so the Ape or Monkey, which bears the greatest Similitude to Man, is the next Order of Animals below him. Nor is the Disagreement between the basest Individuals of our Species and the Ape or Monkey so great, but that the latter were endow'd with the Faculty of Speech, they might perhaps as justly claim the Rank and Dignity of the Human Race, as the savage Hottentot or stupid Native of *Nova Zemblu* (Smith, 2011, p. 121).

Nazi Germany hatred for Jews exterminated over six million of them between 1939-1945, forcing thousands to flee and seek refuge across

Europe and the world. The Nazis saw "Jews, Gypsies, and the others as dangerous, disease-carrying rats that were enemies of civilisation, represented as parasitic organisms—as leeches, lice, bacteria, or vectors of contagion…the ferment of decomposition of peoples and states, just as it was in antiquity. It will remain that way as long as peoples do not find the strength to get rid of the virus" (Smith, 2011, p. 20). Similarly, ethnic cleansing, the expulsion and mass massacre of members of a particular Indigenous group was evident in the Rwanda Genocide. Referring to Tutsis as cockroaches, the Hutus murders 800,000 Tutsis in 100 days (*Mugesera v Canada*, 2005, paras. 48 and 65).

Australia's history of systemic racism against non-white immigrants began at its founding in 1901 as noted above (Fynn Bruey, 2016, p. 78; Szoke, 2012). The twisted idea of white supremacy arms James Cowles Prichard and many other white people, believing that Africans and Aboriginal Peoples in Australia are sub-humans, inferior and barbaric. James Cowles Pritchard claims that,

> Negroes, Hottentots, Esquimaux, and Australians are not, in fact, men in the full sense of the term, or beings endowed with mental faculties similar to our own. These and other barbarous tribes are inferior in their original endowments to the proper human family, … they are separated by an 'impassable barrier' from the race which displays in the highest degree all the attributes of humanity, and can never be raised to an equality with it…(Prichard, 1847, p. 151)

So-called 'great' white men (e.g. Winston Churchill, Abraham Lincoln, and Thomas Jefferson) also espoused ideas of white supremacy and racism against Indigenous Peoples in Australia and Africa (Ellis, 2020; Long, 1774; Pruitt, 2020; The Staff Reporter, 2002). According to Tom Heyden, "[i]n Churchill's view, Protestant Christians were at the top, above white Catholics, whilst Indians were higher than Africans…[he] saw himself and Britain as being the winners in a social Darwinian hierarchy" (Heyden, 2015).

Similar to Australia's founding and White Only policy scheme, the Canadian *British North America Act* 1867 was a White supremacy document designed to systematically disenfranchise Indigenous, Blacks, and Asian Peoples (Manuel, 2017). Up until 1978, Immigration Acts in Canada granted Cabinet the power to prohibit immigrants of any race from entering the country as the growing number of European immigrants "expressed concern that these immigrants threatened the preservation of Anglo-Saxon norms and were incapable of assimilating" (Gagnon et al., 2020).

While the *Immigration Acts* of 1869, 1906, and 1910 expanded a long list of deporting undesirable migrants (e.g., impoverish people and prostitutes) from Canada, in 1923, the Asian race was prohibited from entering Canada. By 1953, admission to Canada was limited to the United Kingdom, Australia, New Zealand, South Africa, Ireland, the United States, and France (Matas, 1985, p. 8). It is worth noting that before the above immigration acts, the arrival of 12,519 "dirty Irish" emigrants escaping the great famine "all of them sick, poor, starved and hopeless" (Fraiman, 2019).

In the United States, following the death of George Floyd (Bennett, Lee, & Cahlan, 2020), several cities (e.g., the City of Columbus City Council and Franklin) and states (e.g., Wisconsin and Michigan) have all declared racism a public health crisis (Columbus City Council, 2020; Ghose, 2020; Hazzard, 2020). It has taken more than three centuries to see an entrenched racial disparity in the United States knowing full well (or not) that its founding and existence are predicated on dispossessing Native Americans of their ancestral lands (V. Fynn, 2011; History.com Editors, 2009; Saunt, 2020; Spence, 2000), dehumanising the forcibly displaced enslaved Africans (Sweet, 2003), and persistently racialising new immigrants to their deaths (Taggart et al., 2020).

In 1776, when Thomas Jefferson wrote the American Declaration of Independence, a landmark document that epitomises freedom, equality, and justice for all men, the colony had more than 500,000 Black Africans enslaved with Jefferson and George Washington owning at least 100 each (Constitutional Rights Foundation, 2006). "We the people of the United States," written in the Preamble of the *United States Constitution* 1789 did not include women, Native Americans, and Black Africans (Facing History, 2020). In fact, Black African slaves were counted as three-fifths of a person while *Dred Scott v Sanford* 1857 confirms that they had "no rights which the white man was bound to respect", hence were not entitled to citizenship (also *see* the *Naturalisation Act* 1790 where citizenship was restricted to free Whites).

The irony of the mockery of justice displayed in United States Constitution 1789 is swallowed up in Emma Lazarus's The New Colossus, 1883:

> ...A mighty woman with a torch, whose flame
> Is the imprisoned lightning, and her name
> Mother of Exiles. From her beacon-hand
> Glows world-wide welcome; her mild eyes command
> The air-bridged harbour that twin cities frame.
> "Keep, ancient lands, your storied pomp!" cries she
> With silent lips. "Give me your tired, your poor,
> Your huddled masses yearning to breathe free,
> The wretched refuse of your teeming shore.
> Send these, the homeless, tempest-toast to me...

Three years before Lazarus's defining moment exalted the Statute of Liberty, the United States Congress passed the Indian Removal Act 1830, which legalised the forced relocation of thousands of Native Americans from 25 million acres of their fertile ancestral lands for white settlers in Georgia, Florida, North Carolina, Tennessee, Alabama, Mississippi, and Arkansas to farm (History.com Editors, 2009; National Geographic Society, 2020). Called the Trail of Tears, the forced displacement of Native Americans under the Indian Removal Act marked the birth of the "Indian Territory" (Saunt, 2020, p. 40). The Chinese Exclusion Act 1882, suspended immigration of Chines for ten years and denied them naturalisation rights. By 1902, Chinese immigration became permanently illegal (Adams, 2013, p. 3H).

Given such a depressing track recording elaborated above, public health and race relations experts argue that racism is a serious public health crisis (Yuko, 2020), others say it is an epidemic or a pandemic. Why should racism be addressed as a major public health concern? Racism as a disease affecting the wider population of displaced peoples meets the four criteria needed to identify a public health problem. That is, racism: 1) places an increasingly large burden on society; 2) affects displaced peoples of colour more than White nationals; 3) persists due to little or no implementation of intervention programs to eliminate risks factors associated with racialising displaced peoples; and 4) continues to persist due to the lack of holistic prevention or primary care programs (Devakumar et al., 2020; Yuko, 2020).

A systematic review of 138 empirical quantitative population-based studies on self-reported racism and health shows an association between self-reported racism and ill-health for oppressed racial groups. The most robust and most consistent findings are negative for mental health outcomes and health-related behaviours (Paradies, 2006, p. 888). More recently, the global COVID-19 pandemic attests to the strong correlation between racism and ill-health pertinent to a racial minority group (BBC News, 2020a; Doumas et al., 2020; Kirby, 2020; Reeves, 2020; Soucheray & 2020, 2020).

Perceived as racial discrimination (Keaten, 2020), on 14 April 2020, the United States suspended its contributions to the World Health Organization because, according to President Donald Trump, the organisation, *inter alia*, "...failed to adequately obtain, vet and share information in a timely and transparent fashion" (BBC News, 2020b) concerning the COVID-19 outbreak (Trump, 2020). By 6 July 2020, the United States began formally withdrawing from the WHO despite opposition from some 750 scholars and experts in global public health, US constitutional law, and international law and relations.

3. Public Health Principles and Approaches

Public health is the science and the art of preventing disease, prolonging life, and promoting physical health...the organisation of preventive treatment of disease, and the development of the social machinery which will ensure to every individual in the community a standard of living adequate for the maintenance of health (Schneider & Schneider, 2017, p. 4).

The overall mission of public health is to prevent ill-health and disease, decrease health disparities in the entire population and improve health (Goldsteen, Goldsteen, & Dwelle, 2015, p. 4). To this end, there are three principles and approaches in public health that are relevant for protecting displaced populations against racism. They are prevention, social determinants of health, and the social justice theory of public health. There are three types of prevention in public health: primary, secondary and tertiary. Primary prevention or primary care is about identifying and eliminating any exposure to risks factors to prevent a disease's occurrence (e.g., racism) (Goldsteen et al., 2015, p. 6; Schneider & Schneider, 2017, p. 10).

Secondary prevention focuses on detecting and treating the early stage to lessen the disease's severity (Goldsteen et al., 2015, p. 6; Schneider & Schneider, 2017, p. 10). Tertiary prevention works on moderating the disability via medical care and rehabilitation services to arrest the disease's progress (Goldsteen et al., 2015, p. 6; Schneider & Schneider, 2017, p. 11). Systemic racism is considered a disease in this chapter because of its ability to cause death, disability, and ill-health (Feagin & Bennefield, 2014). Although secondary and tertiary preventions are necessary for addressing racial discrimination already existing, the chapter emphasises the importance of primary prevention to effectively reduce the incidence and prevalence of racism against displaced peoples.

The social determinant of health is a public health principle which states that the conditions in which people are born, live, work, grow, and age, are shaped by the distribution of a host of social factors that each impact the physical, mental and spiritual health of the individual (Fynn Bruey, 2016, p. 44). The culture and society do not only influence these social conditions, but they also determine the "standard of living adequate for health and well-being" (V. Fynn, 2010, p. 5). Throughout this chapter, race as a determinant of displaced persons of colour, health is examined through the lens of social justice and rights-based approaches to public health.

A social justice theory of public health draws on the rights-based approach embedded in the *Universal Declaration of Human Rights* 1948 (hereafter UDHR) and other human rights instruments to assert that all persons are equally entitled to the necessary minimum standard of health (Beauchamp, 2013, p. 15; Donohoe, 2012, p. xiii). In advocating the social justice approach, it is crucial to assess the accessibility, availability, and affordability of quality public health for marginalised groups, such as displaced peoples (Donohoe, 2012, p. xiii). To this end, the *Alma-Ata*

Declaration 1978 emerges as a "major milestone of the twentieth century in the field of public health, and identify primary health care as the key to the attainment of the goal of Health for All [including displaced peoples]" (World Health Organization, 2020).

To ensure displaced people right to health necessitates their right to move freely within and beyond their state border (Article 13, UDHR) as well as their "...right to seek and to enjoy in other countries asylum from persecution" (Article 14, UDHR). In a similar vein, Article 25 of the UDHR states that "everyone has the right to a standard of living adequate for the health and well-being of himself and his family, including food, clothing, housing, medical care and necessary social services...or other lack of livelihood in the circumstances beyond his[/her] control."

As an aspirational document, the progressive realisation of Articles 13, 14 and 25 of the UDHR with respect to displaced peoples' right to health, is subject to a state's economic, social, and cultural situation. The application of a social justice model in guaranteeing displaced peoples the enjoyment of the highest attainable standard of physical/mental health is fundamental to the health and human rights-based approach and critical in preventing and eliminating the risks of racism to promote the health and well-being of displaced peoples.

4. Global Trends of Displaced Peoples

The years of 2010-2019 is considered the decade of displacement as some 100 million people were forcibly displaced with little or no protection (The United Nations High Commissioner for Refugees, 2020, p. 4). According to the United Nations High Commissioner for Refugees, in 2019, 79.5 million people were forcibly displaced worldwide as a result of violence, conflict, persecution, human rights abuses, and other disturbing public order (The United Nations High Commissioner for Refugees, 2020, p. 2).

Of the 79.5 million forcibly displaced peoples, 26 million (20.4 million under UNHCR mandate and 5.6 million Palestine refugees under United Nations Relief and Works Agency's Mandate) were refugees;

4.2 million asylum-seekers, 4.2 million asylum seekers; 3.6 million Venezuelans displaced abroad; and 45.7 million internally displaced people (The United Nations High Commissioner for Refugees, 2020, p. 2). In addition to the 45.7 million forcibly internally displaced peoples, 5.1 million are displaced due to disasters (Internal Displacement Monitoring Group, 2020, p. 2).

Five countries in the Global South produced 68 per cent (16.3 million) of all refugees worldwide. They are: – Syrian Arab Republic (6.6 million), Venezuela (3.7 million), Afghanistan (2.7 million), South Sudan (2.2 million), and Myanmar (1.1 million) (The United Nations High Commissioner for Refugees, 2020, p. 3). Similarly, five countries in the Global South produce 53 per cent (24.2 million) of people displaced by conflict and violence. They are: – Syria (6.5 million), Colombia (5.6 million), Democratic Republic of Congo (5.5 million), Yemen (3.6 million); and Afghanistan (3.0 million) (Internal Displacement Monitoring Group, 2020, p. 2).

The UNHCR submitted 81,600 refugees to States for resettlement. Notwithstanding, 26 countries worldwide admitted 107,800 refugees for resettlement with or without UNHCR's help (Internal Displacement Monitoring Group, 2020, p. 2). If not all, the majority of the 45.7 million IDPs and 400,000 unaccompanied and separated children will never be able to cross international borders to enjoy the relative stability of being a documented immigrant (The United Nations High Commissioner for Refugees, 2020, p. 4). Unfortunately, many of the few brave ones who venture on the path of irregular migration will end up raped, abused or dead – either washed up on the shores of beaches, murdered during their perilous journeys (Fynn Bruey, 2017).

Overall, developing countries hosted 85 per cent of the world's 26 million refugees in 2019 (The United Nations High Commissioner for Refugees, 2020, p. 2). The top ten hosts of refugees in 2019 were countries in the Global South except Germany. They are Turkey (3.6 million), Colombia (1.8 million), Pakistan (1.4 million), Uganda (1.4 million), Germany (1.1 million), Sudan (1.1. million), Islamic

Republic of Iran (1.1), Lebanon (0.9 million), Peru (0.5 million), and United States (0.3 million) (Internal Displacement Monitoring Group, 2020, pp. 3, 9).

For example, in 2018, 85 per cent of all refugees (720,000) from the Democratic Republic of Congo, then the seventh-largest refugee production nation, were hosted by surrounding neighbouring countries, while 94 per cent remained in sub-Saharan Africa (The United Nations High Commissioner for Refugees, 2019, p. 15). In a similar vein, in 2019, 53 per cent of Venezuelans displaced abroad remained in neighbouring countries (Internal Displacement Monitoring Group, 2020, p. 22).

The gap between refugees' needs for protection and resettlement opportunities as a supposedly durable solution has widened over 2010-2019. In this period, European countries approximately 144,000 refugees were admitted by European countries (The United Nations High Commissioner for Refugees, 2020, p. 52), which is twenty-one times more than the number of refugees (3.6 million) Turkey hosted with the single year of 2019.

In 2019, more than three quarters (76 per cent) of the 81,600 UNHCR assisted refugees were survivors (52 per cent of whom are children) of torture and violence, in dire need of legal and physical protection (The United Nations High Commissioner for Refugees, 2020, p. 51). The top three countries to resettle the highest number of refugees with or without UNHCR assistance were Canada (30,100); the United States (27,500); and Australia (18,000) (The United Nations High Commissioner for Refugees, 2020, p. 52) with the United Kingdom (5,800) and France (5,600) holding fourth and fifth positions in 2018 (The United Nations High Commissioner for Refugees, 2020, p. 52).

Together, France, Germany, Norway, Sweden and the United Kingdom were five of 20 countries to resettled 22,000 of the 33,838 UNHCR refugees in 2019 (United Nations High commissioner for Refugees, 2019, p. 1). It is against this backdrop that the situation of displaced racial minority groups in Canada, the United States, and Australia are showcased and highlighted.

5. Perceptions and Media Representation of Migrants from the Global South: Canada, United States and Australia

5.1 Canada

With ideals of multiculturalism and mosaic society, Canadians take pride in being a country built by immigrants, thus embracing its growing diversity (Parkin & Mendelsohn, 2003, pp. 2–5). Multicultural society in Canada is either descriptive (a sociological fact that refers to the presence of people from diverse racial and ethnic backgrounds), prescriptive (an ideology celebrating cultural diversity), or political (a law or policy formally managing diversity) (Bannerji, 2020, p. 328; Brosseau & Dewing, 2009, p. 1).

As the second country in the world with the largest proportion of migrants (i.e., 21 per cent of the population is foreign-born), Canada migrant population increased to 300,000 per year between 2015 and 2019 (BBC News, 2019b). In spite of Canada's multiculturalism, diversity, and perceived acceptance of newcomers, racism against displaced peoples is more covertly systemic, institutional, or structural (Gerami, 2020). For example, a study showed that a 15-year trend (1995-2010) of the low-income rate of roughly 50 percent was more evident among immigrants from Asia, Africa, and southern and eastern Europe than Canadian born (Picot & Hou, 2016, pp. 179–181).

Despite Prime Minister Justin Trudeau tweets of 28 January 2017: "To those fleeing persecution, terror & war, Canadians will welcome you, regardless of your faith. Diversity is our strength #WelcomeToCanada" (Trudeau, 2017), negative media representation of displaced peoples in Canada thrives.

A study examined 102 articles published in six Canadian newspapers six months before and after Tamil refugees' arrival by ship in Canada in August 2010 (Lawlor & Tolley, 2017). The research reveals that "...before the event refugees were portrayed more in terms of false claims for refugee status, [and] after the event refugees were portrayed more in terms of being either criminals and terrorists or victims (Medianu, Sutter, & Esses, 2015). For example, a Global News poll found that "51 per cent of Canadians said they agree that there are 'terrorists pretending to be refugees who will enter Canada to cause violence and destruction," while 32 per cent disagrees (Russell & Rocca, 2017).

5.2 United States of America

As indicated above, racism against displaced peoples in the United States did not end with the Trump administration (Boswell, 2003; Krogstad, 2019). For four hundred years between the 1600s and 2000s, ancestors of Africans and the people of African descent have endured the largest cross-continental forced migration – the trans-Atlantic slavery. Though not a voluntary migration, African-Americans find themselves at the centre of systemic racism in the United States.

In a historic step, the United Nations Human Rights Council adopts a resolution by a unanimous consensus (without a vote) strongly condemning racially discriminatory and violent practices perpetrated by law enforcement against Africans and people of African descent. The resolution that follows a rare Urgent Debate in the Human Rights Council was requested by the African group of nations, following George Floyd's death in Minnesota, United States of America (UN News, 2020).

Today, due to no fault of their own, many displaced people (e.g., forced migrants and refugees) fleeing violence and persecution are compelled to leave their homes searching for asylum and protection. Many traverse perilous journeys to arrive at the United-States-Mexican border. But since President Trump took office in 2016, racial discrimination against displaced people, threatening their protection and safety in the United States, have disturbingly increased exponentially (Austin-Hillery, 2018; Gladstone & Sugiyama, 2018; Southern Poverty Law Center, 2020).

> When Mexico sends its people, they're not sending their best. They're not sending you. They're not sending you. They're sending people that have lots of problems, and they're bringing those problems with us. They're bringing drugs. They're bringing crime. They're rapists. And some, I assume, are good people (Lee, 2015).

On 15 July 2019, President Trump was accused of racism when he attacked democratically elected Congresswomen, including Somali-born US citizen Ilhan Omar, who came to the US from as a refugee aged 12:

So interesting to see 'Progressive' Democrat Congresswomen, who originally came from countries whose governments are a complete and total catastrophe, the worst, most corrupt and inept anywhere in the world (if they even have a functioning government at all), now loudly... and viciously telling the people of the United States, the greatest and most powerful Nation on earth, how our government is to be run,... [w]hy don't they go back and help fix the totally broken and crime infested places from which they came. Then come back and show us how... it is done, ... [t]hese places need your help badly, you can't leave fast enough...(BBC News, 2019a)

The Trump administrations disdain for migrants of colour arriving at the United States-Mexican border led to his successful election in 2016 as his supporters chant: "build the wall" (Devereaux, 2020). The trauma, pain, and suffering caused by Trump's racist immigration policy and overtly racist comments are indelible even as hundreds of thousands of children are detained and separated from their parents (Flagg & Calderon, 2020).

5.3 Australia

Australia is the most diverse country globally with the largest foreign-born population at 30 per cent and a migrant population totalling more than 7.5 million (Australian Bureau of Statistics, 2020; BBC News, 2019b). One would expect such a diverse culture to be relatively accepting towards displaced peoples, especially given its founding history. On the contrary, the Australian psyche is replete with racially vilifying displaced people (Klocker & Dunn, 2003; Tsiolkas, 2013). Negative sentiments about Indigenous Peoples, migrants, and refugees can sometimes be overwhelmingly shocking as evidence in the documentary-series "Go Back to Where You Came From" (Special Broadcasting Service, 2020) and "First Contact" (Special Broadcasting Service, 2016).

For years the United Nations has called out Australia for its racist immigration policy in violation of international law (Office of the High Commissioner for Human Rights, 2018; United Nations High Commissioner for Refugees, 2018; Zhou, 2018). Regularly intercepted at seas and detained on off-shore detention centres in Papua New Guinea, Nauru, and Manus Islands; so-called "queue jumpers" who arrive undocumented are not allowed to enter Australia (Martin, 2020). Mostly from Afghanistan, Iraq, and Iran, displaced people arriving by boat in Australia are subjected continuously to adverse media scrutiny which has taken a toll on their health and wellbeing (Ware, 2012) (e.g., Reza Barati) (Griffiths, 2014).

6. Displacement and COVID-19 Pandemic: Public Health Challenges in Yemen

Racism is at the core of the many public health challenges facing displaced peoples. In particular, displaced people's public health situation, especially for those fleeing from war, violent conflict, and natural disaster, is certainly terrifying and worrisome. During and after the crisis, forcibly displaced peoples often find themselves in make-shift displaced camps that are overcrowded in poor sanitation conditions with lack of safe drinking water, which make them vulnerable to blood-borne, air-borne, water-borne, vector-borne communicable diseases such as malaria, HIV-AIDS, Ebola, and COVID-19 (WHO EMRO, 2020).

The protracted living condition of displaced peoples in transition, accentuated by additional lack of access to basic health, food, clothing, safe housing, education, and employment; exacerbates their susceptibility to non-communicable (e.g., Post-traumatic stress disorder) and vaccine-preventable diseases during displacement (Owoaje, Uchendu, Ajayi, & Cadmus, 2016, pp. 162, 168–169). This chapter would be incomplete without providing a context to displaced peoples' access to the newly developed COVID-19 vaccine regarding vaccine-preventable diseases. First, a relevant but successful case in point is worth noting.

Today, we celebrate the eradication of smallpox virus, which evidence shows has been with humankind since the 3rd Century BCE. Although the smallpox vaccine was discovered in the early 1800s, it took some 176 years to completely control the virus in 1977 (i.e., when the last case was diagnosed in treated). Success of the smallpox eradication is owed to the World Health Organization's initiation and intensification of an eradication program plan in 1959 and 1967, respectfully (Center for Disease Control and Prevention, 2019). Equipped with the above experience, the WHO, along with the Coalition for Epidemic Preparedness Innovations (CEPI) and GAVI – a global Vaccine Alliance – has once again issued a pandemic eradication plan, COVAX.

Launched in April 2020, COVAX is one of three pillars of the Access to COVID-19 Tools (ACT) Accelerator whose aim is to guarantee rapid, fair, and equitable access to COVID-19 vaccines for everyone (World Health Organization, 2020a). Unfortunately, the phrase, "...for all/everyone" is now a "dirty word" commonly overused by the United Nations to justify that some actions have been taken to address global injustice and unfairness. Notwithstanding the aforementioned, in his remarks to the media on 8 January 2021, Tedros Adhanom Ghebreyesus, Director General of the WHO, said:

> COVAX – set up by GAVI, CEPI and WHO in April last year – has now secured contracts of 2 billion doses of safe and effective COVID-19 vaccines, which we are ready to rollout as soon as the vaccines are delivered. However, this is where the current challenge is. Rich countries have bought up the majority of the supply of multiple vaccines. Going forward, I want to see manufacturers prioritise supply and rollout through COVAX (World Health Organization, 2021).

Ghebreyesus' concern is an urgent call to action in ensuring that everyone has equal and fair access to the COVID-19 vaccines, including displaced peoples in war-ravaged Yemen (for example) (Karasapan, 2020; Nasser, 2020). At present, no amount of anger (Torjesen, 2020; Zabludovsky, 2020) is good enough to stop Canada (Aiello, 2020), the United States (Lupkin, 2020), Australia (Australian Government Department of Health, 2020), or the United Kingdom (BBC News, 2020d) from pre-purchasing and stockpiling the COVID-19 vaccines while Yemeni displaced peoples struggle with the "faster, wider, and deadlier consequences" of the Coronavirus daily (BBC News, 2020b).

Conclusion: Opportunities and Challenges in Moving Forward

In 1945, at the end of the Second World War, the United Nations, a progeny of the League of Nations, was created in part, to respond to the stench of racism against Jewish people by Nazi Germany. Following the war, a catalogue of international human rights instruments was established to "save succeeding generations from the scourge of war" (Preamble, *United Nations Charter* 1945). One such human rights document is the *Convention on the Elimination of All Forms of Racial Discrimination* 1969.

State parties ongoing struggle to condemn and pursue appropriate means to eliminate all forms of racial discrimination necessitated the Durban Declaration in 2001. Nearly two decades ago, the world converged in Durban, South Africa for the World Conference against Racism, Racial Discrimination, Xenophobia and Related Tolerance, 2001 (hereafter the Durban Declaration). The Durban Declaration affirms that,

> ...racism, racial discrimination, xenophobia and related intolerance, where they amount to racism and racial discrimination, constitute serious violations of and obstacles to the full enjoyment of all human rights and deny the self-evident truth that all human beings are born free and equal in dignity and rights, are an obstacle to friendly and peaceful relations among peoples and nations, and are among the root causes of many internal and international conflicts, including armed conflicts, and the consequent forced displacement of populations.

Research evidence has shown over and again, the migrants and displaced peoples are a strength rather than a burden to their host communities. Yet, negative sentiments based on race and membership to a particular group (e.g., refugees, migrants, asylum seekers) remain. The racial divide between the Global North and the Global South pertinent to forcibly displaced people is a grave public health concern that must be declared as a global pandemic in order to solicit appropriate intervention.

At this juncture, readers are invited to deeply reflect on the gloomy history of systemic racism against Indigenous Peoples, Black African slaves and migrants of colour from the Global South. The failure of international and domestic law to protect displaced peoples against all manner of racial discrimination by White people in the Global North demands a solemn call to action for public health practitioners, scholars, and researchers to seriously rethink primary prevention to ensure health all migrants.

Reference

Adams, M. (Ed.). (2013). *Readings for Diversity and Social Justice* (Third). New York, NY: Routledge Taylor & Franacis Group.

Aiello, R. (2020, December 17). If Canada has excess COVID-19 vaccines they "absolutely" will be shared: PM. *CTVNews*. Retrieved from https://www.ctvnews.ca/politics/if-canada-has-excess-covid-19-vaccines-they-absolutely-will-be-shared-pm-1.5236745

Austin-Hillery, N. (2018, May 22). Trump's racist language serves abusive immigration policies [Private Advocacy]. Retrieved November 7, 2020, from Human Rights Watch website: https://www.hrw.org/news/2018/05/22/trumps-racist-language-serves-abusive-immigration-policies

Australian Bureau of Statistics. (2019, April 18). Historical population, 2016 [Government]. Retrieved November 2, 2020, from People/Population website: https://www.abs.gov.au/statistics/people/population/historical-population/latest-release

Australian Bureau of Statistics. (2020). *Migration, Australia, 2018-19 | Australian Bureau of Statistics*. Canberra, ACT: Australian Bureau of Statistics. Retrieved from Australian Bureau of Statistics website: https://www.abs.gov.au/statistics/people/population/migration-australia/latest-release

Australian Government Department of Health. (2020, October 23). Australia's vaccine agreements [Text]. Retrieved January 15, 2021, from Australian Government Department of Health website: https://www.health.gov.au/initiatives-and-programs/covid-19-vaccines/about-covid-19-vaccines/australias-vaccine-agreements

Bannerji, H. (2020). *The Ideological Condition: Selected Essays on History, Race and Gender*. Leiden, The Netherlands: Brill Nijhoff. https://doi.org/10.1163/9789004441620

BBC News. (2019a, July 15). Trump to congresswomen of colour: Leave the US. *BBC News*. Retrieved from https://www.bbc.com/news/world-us-canada-48982172

BBC News. (2019b, October 17). Is Canada taking more migrants than other Western nations? *BBC News*. Retrieved from https://www.bbc.com/news/50061529

BBC News. (2020a, June 2). Coronavirus: Risk of death is higher for ethnic minorities—BBC News. *BBC News*. Retrieved from https://www.bbc.com/news/health-52889106

BBC News. (2020b, June 20). Coronavirus: Five reasons why it is so bad in Yemen. *BBC News*. Retrieved from https://www.bbc.com/news/world-middle-east-53106164

BBC News. (2020c, July 8). Coronavirus: What are President Trump's charges against the WHO? *BBC News*, p. Online.

BBC News. (2020d, August 14). Coronavirus vaccine: UK signs deals for 90 million virus vaccine doses. *BBC News*. Retrieved from https://www.bbc.com/news/health-53772650

Beauchamp, D. E. (2013). Public health as social justice. In M. Donohoe (Ed.), *Public Health and Social Justice* (p. 658). Jossey-Bass Reader/Wiley.

Bennett, D., Lee, J. S., & Cahlan, S. (2020, May 30). The death of George Floyd: What video and other records show about his final minutes. *Washington Post*. Retrieved from https://www.washingtonpost.com/nation/2020/05/30/video-timeline-george-floyd-death/

Boly, R. (2018). Development and racism ideology [Academic]. Retrieved November 7, 2020, from Berkeley Master of Development Practice website: https://mdp.berkeley.edu/development-and-racism-ideology/

Boswell, R. A. (2003). Racism and U.S. immigration law: Prospects for reform after "9/11?" *Journal of Gender*, *7*, 315–356.

Brosseau, L., & Dewing, M. (2009). *Canadian Multiculturalism*. Legal and Social Affairs Division, Parliamentary Information and Research Service. Retrieved from https://lop.parl.ca/sites/PublicWebsite/default/en_CA/ResearchPublications/200920E

Brown, N. (2015). *First Peoples* [Video Recording]. Boston, MA: PBS. Retrieved from https://www.pbs.org/show/first-peoples/

Castles, S., Haas, H. de, & Miller, M. J. (2020). Migration shaping African history. In *The Age of Migration: International Population Movements in the Modern World* (pp. 1–5). Basingstoke, UK: Palgrave MacMillan. Retrieved from http://www.age-of-migration.com/resources/casestudies/2020/Migrations%20Shaping%20African%20History.pdf

Center for Disease Control and Prevention. (2019, February 15). History of Smallpox [Health]. Retrieved January 13, 2021, from Government website: https://www.cdc.gov/smallpox/history/history.html

Chimni, B. (1998). The geopolitics of refugee studies: A view from the South. *Journal of Refugee Studies, 11*(4), 350–374.

Coggins, R. (1978). The Development Set. *Journal of Communication, 28*(1), 80–80. https://doi.org/10.1111/j.1460-2466.1978.tb01566.x

Cohen, R. (2019). Strangers and migrants in the making of African societies: A conceptual and historical review. *Fudan Journal of Humanities and Social Sciences, 12*, 45–59.

Columbus City Council. (2020, June 2). Resolution Declaring Racism a Public Health Crisis in Columbus [Public]. Retrieved November 4, 2020, from News Releases website: https://www.columbus.gov/racismresolution/

Constitutional Rights Foundation. (2006). Constitutional Rights Foundation [Educational]. Retrieved November 4, 2020, from Black History Month: The Constitution and Slavery website: https://www.crf-usa.org/black-history-month/the-constitution-and-slavery

Dados, N., & Connell, R. (2012). The Global South. *Contexts, 11*(1), 12–13. https://doi.org/10.1177/1536504212436479

Deng, F. M. (1998). *Report of the Representative of the Secretary-General: Guiding Principles on Internal Displacement* (Economic and Social Council Report No. E/CN.4/1998/53/Add.2; p. 14). New York, NY: Office of the United Nations High Commissioner for Human Rights.

Devakumar, D., Selvarajah, S., Shannon, G., Muraya, K., Lasoye, S., Corona, S., ... Achiume, E. T. (2020). Racism, the public health crisis we can no longer ignore. *The Lancet, 395*(10242), e112–e113. https://doi.org/10.1016/S0140-6736(20)31371-4

Devereaux, R. (2020, October 31). A monument to stupidity: The trauma of Trump's border wall [Private Blog]. Retrieved November 7, 2020, from The Intercept website: https://theintercept.com/2020/10/31/trump-border-wall-legacy/

Donohoe, M. (Ed.). (2012). *Public Health and Social Justice: A Jossey-Bass Reader* (1ˢᵗ ed.) [Electronic resource]. San Francisco, CA: Jossey-Bass/John Wiley & Sons.

Doumas, M., Patoulias, D., Katsimardou, A., Stavropoulos, K., Imprialos, K., & Karagiannis, A. (2020). COVID19 and increased mortality in African Americans: Socioeconomic differences or does the renin angiotensin system also contribute? *Journal of Human Hypertension.* https://doi.org/10.1038/s41371-020-0380-y

dRworks. (2020). Racism Defined: What is Racism? [Educational]. Retrieved November 7, 2020, from Dismantling Racism Works Web Workbook website: https://www.dismantlingracism.org/racism-defined.html

Ellis, J. J. (2020). Thomas Jefferson—Slavery and Racism. In *Encyclopedia Britannica.* Retrieved from https://www.britannica.com/biography/Thomas-Jefferson

Facing History. (2020). We the People in the United States [Educational]. Retrieved November 4, 2020, from Facing History and Ourselves website: https://www.facinghistory.org/holocaust-and-human-behavior/chapter-2/we-people-united-states

Feagin, J., & Bennefield, Z. (2014). Systemic racism and U.S. health care. *Social Science & Medicine (1982), 103,* 7–14. https://doi.org/10.1016/j.socscimed.2013.09.006

Fraiman, M. (2019, August 2). The long history of "go back to where you came from" in Canada. *Maclean's.* Retrieved from https://www.macleans.ca/history/the-long-history-of-go-back-to-where-you-came-from-in-canada/

Fynn Bruey, V. (2016). *Systematic Gender Violence and the Rule of Law: Aboriginal Communities in Australia and Post-War Liberia* (PhD Thesis, The Australian National University). The Australian National

University, Canberra, ACT. Retrieved from https://openresearch-repository.anu.edu.au/handle/1885/159520

Fynn Bruey, V. (2017). Deadly voyage: Africans Crossing the Mediterranean. In Y. Gilpin-Jackson, S. J. Owusu, & J. Okonkwo (Eds.), *We Will Lead Africa* (pp. 70–77). Vancouver, BC: Create Space Independent Publishing Platform.

Fynn Bruey, V. (2018). Displaced Peoples: Welcome [Collaborative Research Network]. Retrieved October 30, 2020, from Displaced Peoples website: https://displacedpeoples.net/

Fynn Bruey, V. (2019). Development-induced displacement and homelessness in Seattle, Washington. *Artha: Journal of Social Sciences*, *18*(2), 1–25.

Fynn Bruey, V., Bruey, D., & Bender, S. (2017, April 16). About [Non-profit]. Retrieved October 31, 2020, from Tuki Tumarankeh website: https://tuki-tumarankeh.org/about/

Fynn, V. (2010). *Is the law a social determinant of health?* Health Digest, Toronto, ON.

Fynn, V. (2011). Around the fringes of internal displacement. *Journal of Internal Displacement*, *1*(1), 47–76.

Fynn, V. P. (2011). *Legal Discrepancies: Internal Displacement of Women and Children in Africa*. Kusterdingen, Germany: Flowers Books. Retrieved from https://www.amazon.com/Legal-Discrepancies-Internal-Displacement-Children/dp/1453873414

G-77. (2020). About the Group of 77 [UN]. Retrieved November 5, 2020, from The Group of 77 at the United Nations website: https://www.g77.org/doc/

Gaba, G. Z., Liam Moloney, Jovi Juan, Dan. (2015, September 22). Migrant crisis: A history of displacement. *WSJ*, p. Online.

Gagnon, E., Raska, J., Van Dyk, L., MacDonald, M., Obradovic, S., & Schwinghamer, S. (2020). Immigration Act, 1906—Pier 21 [Education].

Retrieved November 4, 2020, from Canadian Museum of Immigration at Pier 21 website: https://pier21.ca/research/immigration-history/immigration-act-1906

Gaikwad, N., & Nellis, G. (2020). Do Politicians Discriminate Against Internal Migrants? Evidence from Nationwide Field Experiments in India. *American Journal of Political Science*, ajps.12548. https://doi.org/10.1111/ajps.12548

Gannon, M. (2015, February 5). Race Is a Social Construct, Scientists Argue. *Scientific American*. Retrieved from https://www.scientificamerican.com/article/race-is-a-social-construct-scientists-argue/

Gatrell, P. (2013). *The Making of the Modern Refugee* (First). Oxford, UK: Oxford University Press.

Gerami, A. (2020, June 24). How Canadian immigrants are affected by racism [Law Firm]. Retrieved November 7, 2020, from Gerami Law: Canadian Immigration Lawyers website: https://www.geramilaw.com/blog/canadas-anti-racism-strategy-and-its-implication-on-racialized-immigrants.html

Ghose, C. (2020, June 2). Columbus City Council declares racism a public health crisis – will state follow? Retrieved November 4, 2020, from Columbus Business First website: https://www.bizjournals.com/columbus/news/2020/06/02/columbus-city-council-declares-racism-a-public-hea.html

Gibson, C., & Jung, K. (2006). *Historical Census Statistics on the Foreign-born Population of the United States: 1850—2000* (No. 81; p. 119). Washington, DC: United States Census Bureau. Retrieved from United States Census Bureau website: https://www.census.gov/content/dam/Census/library/working-papers/2006/demo/POP-twps0081.pdf

Gladstone, R., & Sugiyama, S. (2018, July 1). Trump's Travel Ban: How it works and who is affected. *The New York Times*. Retrieved from https://www.nytimes.com/2018/07/01/world/americas/travel-ban-trump-how-it-works.html

Godwyn, M. (1680). *The Negro's and Indians Advocate, Suing for their Admission into the Church*. London, UK. Retrieved from https://books.googleusercontent. com/books/content?req=AKW5QaebdEyF28TGN9RbW2xKo8BJT1_ HIUsP5f7VZuWWAdcjQsX2-Tt4LFr_1cR4l9VekAoVzl3kUSxQu j3jynZnHadB_ICLiDomHpk-Q9PB2EBzmNCOmRHeP3ohh5bI bLNZg5aMp_lLGI91OY5KFA36RXs62i5egJoQQjA5[rd]CgEEEr_r- t4gLHWUgc1yElRj31dZaVIIU49eTCwl_JA3kLHM3nEOpfEs9wMaUEe94 xbQtPS0c3WmPq3v2nFu5iEZF8mkAw4kwweJEUMSN55u3wwp_5GIe-Jw

Goldsteen, R. L., Goldsteen, K., & Dwelle, T. (2015). *Introduction to Public Health: Promises and Practices* (Second). New York, NY: Springer Publishing Company, LLC.

Greenhill, K. M. (2010). *Weapons of Mass Migration: Forced Displacement, Coercion, and Foreign Policy*. Ithaca, NY: Cornell University Press.

Greshko, M. (2018, November 8). What ancient DNA reveals about the first humans in the Americas [Educational]. Retrieved November 2, 2020, from National Geography website: https://www.nationalgeographic. com/science/2018/11/ancient-dna-reveals-complex-migrations- first-americans/

Griffiths, E. (2014, December 11). Deadly violence on Manus Island foreseeable, Senate report says. *ABC News*. Retrieved from https:// www.abc.net.au/news/2014-12-11/violence-at-manus-eminently- foreseeable-senate-report/5960752

Hazzard, A. (2020, August 25). Why racism was declared a public health crisis. *Southwest Journal*. Retrieved from https://www. southwestjournal.com/news/2020/08/why-racism-was-declared-a- public-health-crisis/

Heyden, T. (2015, January 21). The 10 greatest controversies of Winston Churchill's career. *BBC News*. PPToV-c1492. Retrieved from http:// www.bbc.com/news/magazine-29701767

Hickey, M. (2011, March 21). World Wars: The Korean War—An Overview. *BBC*. Retrieved from http://www.bbc.co.uk/history/worldwars/ coldwar/korea_hickey_01.shtml

Hilberg, R. (1985). *The Destruction of the European Jews* (Student). New York, NY: Holmes & Meier.

History.com Editors. (2009, November 9). Trail of Tears [Educational]. Retrieved November 4, 2020, from History website: https://www.history.com/topics/native-american-history/trail-of-tears

Hogenboom, M. (2017, March 30). The first people who populated the Americas [Educational]. Retrieved November 2, 2020, from BBC: Origins/Ancient Humans website: http://www.bbc.com/earth/story/20170328-the-first-people-who-populated-the-americas

Hornak, L. (2017, February 20). The word "refugee" has a surprising origin. Retrieved October 31, 2020, from The World from PRX website: https://www.pri.org/stories/2017-02-20/word-refugee-has-surprising-origin

Internal Displacement Monitoring Group. (2020). *Global Report on Internal Displacement* (p. 136). Geneva, Switzerland: Internal Displacement Monitoring Centre of the Norwegian Refugee Council. Retrieved from Internal Displacement Monitoring Centre of the Norwegian Refugee Council website: https://www.internal-displacement.org/sites/default/files/publications/documents/2019-IDMC-GRID.pdf

Karasapan, O. (2020, June 15). Yemen and COVID-19: The pandemic exacts its devastating toll [Academic]. Retrieved January 15, 2021, from Brookings website: https://www.brookings.edu/blog/future-development/2020/06/15/yemen-and-covid-19-the-pandemic-exacts-its-devastating-toll/

Keaten, J. (2020, April 8). UN health agency on defensive after Trump slams it on virus. *Associated Press*. Retrieved from https://apnews.com/article/e5b79d1a26063997c0dda8abcea67a41

Kendi, I. X. (2019). *How to be an antiracist* (First). New York, NY: One World.

Kesternich, I., Siflinger, B., Smith, J. P., & Winter, J. K. (2014). The effects of World War II on economic and health outcomes across Europe. *Review of Economics and Statistics, 96*(1), 103–118. https://doi.org/10.1162/REST_a_00353

Kirby, T. (2020). Evidence mounts on the disproportionate effect of COVID-19 on ethnic minorities. *The Lancet Respiratory Medicine, 8*(6), 547–548. https://doi.org/10.1016/S2213-2600(20)30228-9

Klocker, N., & Dunn, K. (2003). Who's driving the asylum debate? : Newspaper and government representations of asylum seekers. *Media International Australia, 109*, 71–92.

Krogstad, J. M. (2019). *Key facts about refugees to the U.S.* (p. 10). Washington, DC: Pew Research Center. Retrieved from Pew Research Center website: https://www.pewresearch.org/fact-tank/2019/10/07/key-facts-about-refugees-to-the-u-s/

Lawlor, A., & Tolley, E. (2017). Deciding who's legitimate: News media framing of immigrants and refugees. *International Journal of Communication, 11*, 967–991.

Leach, M. (2003). "Disturbing Practices": Dehumanizing asylum seekers in the refugee "Crisis" in Australia, 2001–2002. *Refuge: Canada's Journal on Refugees, 21*(3), 25–33. https://doi.org/10.25071/1920-7336.21301

Lee, M. Y. H. (2015, June 8). Donald Trump's false comments connecting Mexican immigrants and crime. *Washington Post*. Retrieved from https://www.washingtonpost.com/news/fact-checker/wp/2015/07/08/donald-trumps-false-comments-connecting-mexican-immigrants-and-crime/

Long, E. (1774). *History of Jamaica. Or, General Survey of the Ancient and Modern State of that Island: With Reflections on Its Situation, Settlements, Inhabitants, Climate, Products, Commerce, Laws, and Government.* Fleet-Street, UK: Oxford University. PPT0V-a1890. Retrieved from http://books.googleusercontent.com/books/content?req=AKW5Qadfavo5XVmZMOIa29Jhw680STcnX-qvy3MXHVY1bmEQtuQf8rTGI2i2SvaelLCMHMXVN9IK97JpJv5Da7tIw435FR_w5Y6DUjyryN-fpwbcn_jgrlFdTImmK6Iy-aicjCU1tWpSPlqkO1wcKfKLRL9_4kTdAJ6wAPkWSIre54RZCDJ4e9P2euWTHYQXG5Q3HZ53SIX7ufWHblwsYNJeIP75DsPVp_HzycMCZQICrg5cE-Dv2JSHH28jhF_VW8ldYMFlpejy

Lupkin, S. (2020, December 23). U.S. Government To Buy Additional 100 Million Doses Of Pfizer COVID-19 Vaccine. *NPR.Org*. Retrieved from https://www.npr.org/2020/12/23/949751699/u-s-government-to-buy-additional-100-million-doses-of-pfizer-covid-19-vaccine

Manuel, A. (2017, October 26). In Canada, white supremacy is the law of the land. *NOW Magazine*. Retrieved from https://nowtoronto.com/news/white-supremacy-is-the-law-of-the-land

Manuel, A., & Derrickson, R. M. (2017). *The Reconciliation Manifesto: Recovering the Land, Rebuilding the Economy*. Toronto, ON: James Lorimer Publishers.

Marouan, M., & Simmons, M. (Eds.). (2013). *Race and Displacement: Nation, Migration, and Identity in the Twenty-first Century*. Tuscaloosa, AB: The University of Alabama Press.

Martin, C. A. (2020). Jumping the queue? The queue-jumping metaphor in Australian press discourse on asylum seekers. *Journal of Sociology*, 144078332090565. https://doi.org/10.1177/1440783320905657

Matas, D. (1985). Racism in Canadian Immigration Policy. *Refuge: Canada's Journal on Refugees*, 8–9. https://doi.org/10.25071/1920-7336.21485

Mayblin, L. (2010, March 28). Historically European, Morally Universal? The 1951 Geneva Convention on the Status of Refugees [Public]. Retrieved November 5, 2020, from E-International Relations website: https://www.e-ir.info/2010/03/28/historically-european-morally-universal-the-1951-geneva-convention-on-the-status-of-refugees/

Mayblin, L. (2014). Colonialism, decolonisation, and the right to be human: Britain and the 1951 Geneva Convention on the Status of Refugees: Colonialism, decolonisation, and the right to be human. *Journal of Historical Sociology*, *27*(3), 423–441. https://doi.org/10.1111/johs.12053

Medianu, S., Sutter, A., & Esses, V. (2015). The portrayal of refugees in Canadian newspapers: The impact of the arrival of Tamil refugees by sea in 2010. *IdeAs, Fall/Winter*(6), 1–15. https://doi.org/10.4000/ideas.1199

Milner, J. (2009). *Refugees, the State and the Politics of Asylum in Africa.* Basingstoke, UK: Palgrave Macmillan ; in association with St. Antony's College. Retrieved from http://public.ebookcentral.proquest.com/choice/publicfullrecord.aspx?p=578893

Mugesera v Canada. , 2 Supreme Court Reporter 40 (Supreme Court of Canada 2005).

Mutua, M. (2001). Savages, victims and saviors: The metaphor of human rights. *Harvard International Law Journal, 42*(1), 201–209.

Nasser, A. (2020). War and COVID-19 in Yemen. *Istituto Affari Internazionali, 20*(74), 1–6.

National Geographic Society. (2020, April 6). Indian Removal Act [Educational]. Retrieved November 5, 2020, from This Day in Georgraphic History website: http://www.nationalgeographic.org/thisday/may28/indian-removal-act/

Nellis, G., & Gaikwad, N. (2017). The majority-minority Divide in attitudes toward Internal Migration: Evidence from Mumbai [Data set]. *American Journal of Political Science*, Vol. 61, pp. 456–472. https://doi.org/10.7910/DVN/WOI8EU

Office of the High Commissioner for Human Rights. (2018, September 10). 39th session of the Human Rights Council [United Nations]. Retrieved November 7, 2020, from Opening Statement by the UN High Commissioner for Human Rights Michele Bachelet website: https://www.ohchr.org/EN/NewsEvents/Pages/DisplayNews.aspx?NewsID=23518

Organisation for Economic Co-operation and Development. (2020). *International Migration Outlook 2020.* Paris, France: OECD. https://doi.org/10.1787/ec98f531-en

Owoaje, E. T., Uchendu, O. C., Ajayi, T. O., & Cadmus, E. O. (2016). A review of the health problems of the internally displaced persons in Africa. *Nigerian Postgraduate Medical Journal, 23*(4), 161. https://doi.org/10.4103/1117-1936.196242

Pal, S. (2020). The Group of 77 in a changing world [UN]. Retrieved November 5, 2020, from United Nations: UN Chronicl website: https://www.un.org/en/chronicle/article/group-77-changing-world

Paradies, Y. (2006). A systematic review of empirical research on self-reported racism and health. *International Journal of Epidemiology*, *35*(4), 888–901. https://doi.org/10.1093/ije/dyl056

Parkin, A., & Mendelsohn, M. (2003). *A New Canada: An Identity Shaped by Diversity* (p. 24). Centre for Research and Information on Canada. Retrieved from Centre for Research and Information on Canada website: file:///Users/veronicafynn/Desktop/cric-gmnc-03-not_000.pdf

Picot, G., & Hou, F. (2016). Immigration, Poverty and Income Inequality in Canada. In D. A. Green, W. C. Riddell, & F. St-Hilaire (Eds.), *Income inequality: The Canadian story* (pp. 175–211). Montreal, QC: Institute for Research on Public Policy.

Prichard, J. C. (1847). The physical and national history of mankind. *The British and Foreign Medical Journal of Practical Medicine and Surgery*, *XXIV*(IV), 49–80. PPToV-a1705. Retrieved from PPToV-a1705.

Pruitt, S. (2020, September 21). What Abraham Lincoln Thought About Slavery [Educational]. Retrieved November 4, 2020, from History website: https://www.history.com/news/5-things-you-may-not-know-about-lincoln-slavery-and-emancipation

Racist ideas | Black and white in Britain | The wider world | After Slavery | Bristol and Transatlantic Slavery PortCities Bristol. (n.d.). Retrieved from http://discoveringbristol.org.uk/slavery/after-slavery/wider-world/black-white-in-britain/racist-ideas/

Reeves, T. N. F., Sarah Reber, and Richard V. (2020, June 16). Race gaps in COVID-19 deaths are even bigger than they appear [Educational]. Retrieved November 5, 2020, from Brookings website: https://www.brookings.edu/blog/up-front/2020/06/16/race-gaps-in-covid-19-deaths-are-even-bigger-than-they-appear/

Rendel, M. (1975). Law as an instrument of oppression or reform. *The Sociological Review*, 23(1_suppl), 143–171. https://doi.org/10.1111/j.1467-954X.1975.tb00036.x

Russell, A., & Rocca, R. (2017, July 6). Canadians are concerned refugees pose a terror threat. Should they be worried? *Global News*. Retrieved from https://globalnews.ca/news/3568629/canadians-are-concerned-refugees-pose-a-terror-threat-should-they-be-worried/

Saunt, C. (2020). *Unworthy Republic: The Dispossession of Native Americans and the Road to Indian Territory* (First). New York, NY: W. W. Norton & Company.

Schneider, M.-J., & Schneider, H. S. (2017). *Introduction to Public Health* (Fifth). Burlington, MA: Jones & Bartlett Learning.

Skretteberg, R., & Skjeflo, T. (2020). *79.5 million people displaced in the age of Covid-19* [NGO]. Oslo, Norway: Norwegian Refugee Council. Retrieved from Norwegian Refugee Council website: https://www.nrc.no/shorthand/fr/79.5-million-people-displaced-in-the-age-of-covid-19/index.html

Smith, D. L. (2011). *Less Than Human: Why We Demean, Enslave, and Exterminate Others* (1st ed.). New York, NY: St. Martin's Press.

Soucheray, S. & 2020. (2020, August 14). US blacks 3 times more likely than whites to get COVID-19 [University]. Retrieved November 7, 2020, from Center for Infectious Disease Research and Policy website: https://www.cidrap.umn.edu/news-perspective/2020/08/us-blacks-3-times-more-likely-whites-get-covid-19

Southern Poverty Law Center. (2020). Stephen Miller [Private Advocacy]. Retrieved November 7, 2020, from Southern Poverty Law Center website: https://www.splcenter.org/fighting-hate/extremist-files/individual/stephen-miller

Special Broadcasting Service. (2016). First Contact [Television]. Retrieved November 7, 2020, from SBS | Documentary website: https://www.sbs.com.au/programs/first-contact

Special Broadcasting Service. (2020). Go Back To Where You Came From Live [Television]. Retrieved November 7, 2020, from Go Back website: https://www.sbs.com.au/programs/go-back-to-where-you-came-from

Spence, M. D. (2000). *Dispossessing the Wilderness: Indian Removal and the Making of the National parks.* New York, NY: Oxford University Press.

Statistics Canada. (2016, June 29). 150 years of immigration in Canada [Government]. Retrieved November 1, 2020, from Canadian Megatrends website: https://www150.statcan.gc.ca/n1/pub/11-630-x/11-630-x2016006-eng.htm#def4

Sweet, J. H. (2003). Spanish and Portuguese Influences on Racial Slavery in British North America, 1492-1619. *Proceedings of the Fifth Annual Gilder Lehrman Center International Conference*, 1–33. New Haven, CT: Yale University. Retrieved from https://glc.yale.edu/sites/default/files/files/events/race/Sweet.pdf

Szoke, H. (2012, December 14). Racism exists in Australia – are we doing enough to address it? [Government]. Retrieved January 14, 2016, from Australian Human Rights Commission website: https://www.humanrights.gov.au/news/speeches/racism-exists-australia-are-we-doing-enough-address-it

Taggart, K., Aleaziz, H., & Leopold, J. (2020, October 29). More Than 40 Immigrants Have Died In ICE Custody In The Past Four Years. Here Are Thousands Of Records About What Happened. *BuzzFeed News*, Online.

The Staff Reporter. (2002, November 28). The Churchill you didn't know. *The Guardian*. PPToV-a1846. Retrieved from http://www.theguardian.com/theguardian/2002/nov/28/features11.g21

The United Nations High Commissioner for Refugees. (2019). *Global Trends: Forced Displacement in 2018* (p. 76) [UN]. Geneva, Switzerland: United Nations High Commissioner for Refugees. Retrieved from United Nations High Commissioner for Refugees website: https://www.unhcr.org/5d08d7ee7.pdf

The United Nations High Commissioner for Refugees. (2020). *Global Trends: Forced Displacement in 2019* (p. 84) [UN]. Geneva, Switzerland: United Nations High Commissioner for Refugees. Retrieved from United Nations High Commissioner for Refugees website: https://www.unhcr.org/5d08d7ee7.pdf

Thompson, N. (2016). *Great Human Odyssey* [Video Recording]. Boston, MA: PBS. Retrieved from https://www.pbs.org/wgbh/nova/video/great-human-odyssey/

Tolts, M. (2010). Population and Migration: Migration Since World War I. In *The Yivo Encyclopaedia of Jews in Eastern Europe.* Retrieved from https://yivoencyclopedia.org/article.aspx/Population_and_Migration/Migration_since_World_War_I

Torjesen, I. (2020). Covid-19: Pre-purchasing vaccine—sensible or selfish? *BMJ, 320*, m3226. https://doi.org/10.1136/bmj.m3226

Trudeau, J. (2017, January 28). Justin Trudeau on Twitter [Social Media]. Retrieved November 7, 2020, from Twitter website: https://twitter.com/JustinTrudeau/status/825438460265762816

Trump, D. J. (2020, May 18). *The United States Suspends Contributions to the World Health Organization* [Official Letter]. Retrieved from https://twitter.com/realDonaldTrump/status/1262577580718395393

Tsiolkas, C. (2013, September). Why Australia hates asylum seekers: Our governments and press have demonised boat people for 15 years. Organisations like the Asylum Seeker Resource Centre worry they're fighting a losing battle [News]. Retrieved November 7, 2020, from Essays website: https://webcache.googleusercontent.com/search?q=cache:1oXnvHv3JykJ:https://www.themonthly.com.au/issue/2013/september/1377957600/christos-tsiolkas/why-australia-hates-asylum-seekers+&cd=2&hl=en&ct=clnk&gl=us#mtr

UN News. (2020, June 19). Human Rights Council calls on top UN rights official to take action on racist violence. *UN News.* Retrieved from https://news.un.org/en/story/2020/06/1066722

United Nations High Commissioner for Refugees. (2018, October 12). UNHCR urges Australia to evacuate off-shore facilities as health situation deteriorates [UN]. Retrieved November 7, 2020, from UNHCR website: https://www.unhcr.org/news/briefing/2018/10/5bc059d24/unhcr-urges-australia-evacuate-off-shore-facilities-health-situation-deteriorates.html

United Nations High commissioner for Refugees. (2019). *Europe Resettlement* (p. 3) [UN]. Geneva, Switzerland: United Nations High Commissioner for Refugees.

Ware, H. (2012, July 24). Who are Australia's "boat people", and why don't they get on planes? *The Conversation*. Retrieved from http://theconversation.com/who-are-australias-boat-people-and-why-dont-they-get-on-planes-8361

Weinberg, G. L. (1995). *A Global History of World War II*. Cambridge, UK: Cambridge University Press.

Weinberg, G. L. (2014). *World War II: A Very Short Introduction*. Oxford, UK: Oxford University Press. Retrieved from http://public.ebookcentral.proquest.com/choice/publicfullrecord.aspx?p=1802470

Wells, S. (2002). *The Journey of Man: A Genetic Odyssey* (Random House Trade Paperback). New York, NY: Random House Trade Paperbacks.

WHO EMRO. (2020). Public health priorities in emergencies [Information resources]. Retrieved January 13, 2021, from WHO Health Emergencies website: http://www.emro.who.int/eha/information-resources/public-health-priorities-in-emergencies.html

World Health Organization. (2020a). COVAX: Working for global equitable access to COVID-19 vaccines [UN]. Retrieved January 15, 2021, from With a fast-moving pandemic, no one is safe, unless everyone is safe website: https://www.who.int/initiatives/act-accelerator/covax

World Health Organization. (2020b). WHO called to return to the Declaration of Alma-Ata [UN Website]. Retrieved November 6, 2020, from WHO website: http://www.who.int/social_determinants/tools/multimedia/alma_ata/en/

World Health Organization. (2021, January 8). WHO Director-General's opening remarks at the media briefing on COVID-19 – 8 January 2021 [UN]. Retrieved January 15, 2021, from Director General Speeches website: https://www.who.int/director-general/speeches/detail/who-director-general-s-opening-remarks-at-the-media-briefing-on-covid-19-8-january-2021

Yuko, E. (2020, June 12). Racism kills: Why many are declaring it a public health crisis. *Rolling Stone*, Online.

Zabludovsky, K. (2020, December 22). There Is anger and resignation in the developing world as rich countries buy up all the COVID vaccines. *BuzzFeed News*. Retrieved from https://www.buzzfeednews.com/article/karlazabludovsky/mexico-vaccine-inequality-developing-world

zhou, N. (2018, October 13). UN: "health crisis" demands closure of Australia's offshore detention centres [News]. Retrieved November 7, 2020, from The Guardian website: http://www.theguardian.com/australia-news/2018/oct/13/un-health-crisis-demands-closure-of-australias-offshore-detention-centres

About the Author

Veronica Fynn Bruey is a multi-award winner, an author, a passionate academic-advocate, and an innovator with an extensive interdisciplinary background, holding six academic degrees from world-class institutions across four continents. She is the founder and editor-in-chief of the Journal of Internal Displacement; the co-founder and Executive Director of Tuki-Tumarankeh; the founder of the Law and Society's Collaborative Research Network (CRN) 11: 'Displaced Peoples' and project lead of the International Research Collaborative: Disrupting Patriarchy and Masculinity in Africa; and the founder of the Voice of West African Refugees (VOWAR), located at the Buduburam Refugee settlement in Ghana. She has authored four books, several book chapters and peer review articles in reputable academic journals. Veronica is a born and bred Liberian war survivor.

Internally Displaced People and Mental Health Issues

Lucy Njarui Njiru[2]

Abstract

Reports from many parts of the world have shown an increase in mental health burden across all ages. The impacts of mental health on global development goals have led to mental health inclusion in the Sustainable Development Goals. Despite the high number of individuals needing mental health care services, access to these services remain a challenge in many low and middle-income countries. Evidence has shown that the situation is worse among internally displaced people (IDPs) in comparison to their counterparts. Effective treatment for mental, psychological, and emotional problems is minimally costed. Despite this, treatment coverage for these illnesses remains low across all populations. This chapter provides a brief overview of mental health concerns among IDPs. Clinical presentation of common psychiatric conditions among IDPs is examined to provide readers with an enhanced foundation for understanding these conditions. Assessment in mental health is a crucial component since it lays a basis for treatment and intervention planning. Hence, assessment in mental health has also been discussed in this chapter. In addition, main risk and protective factors for post-traumatic stress disorder (PTSD) have been examined to help plan for effective prevention programmes. Finally, we will present some of the most effective treatment modalities for post-traumatic stress disorder that can be used in managing PTSD among IDPs.

Key Words: Mental Health, Internal Displaced People, Risk and Protective Factors, Posttraumatic Stress Disorder (PTSD)

---

2   Lecturer & Head of Psychology Department, Amref International University, Kenya. Email: lucynjiru8@gmail.com

1. Mental Health Concerns among Internally Displaced People

With an estimated 41.3 million internally displaced people (IDPs) globally at the end of 2018 (Internal Displacement Monitoring Center, 2019), IDPs' mental health needs cannot be ignored if Health for All is to be realised. The IDPs are viewed as one of the highest risk groups for mental illnesses worldwide (Salami, Iwuagwu, Amodu, Tulli, Ndikom, et al., 2020). Several studies have indicated that IDPs may suffer from mental health concerns, including anxiety, post-traumatic stress disorders (PTSD), depression, somatisation, and existential dilemmas. For instance, reports in the United States have shown that IDPs are more likely to experience trauma and its aftermath, including PTSD (López-Zerón & Parra-Cardona, 2015). A study conducted in some camps around towns of Fasher and Nyala in Darfur seeking to establish mental health issues among IDPs showed that PTSD was rampant at 54% while general distress was at 70% (Abdalla, Hamid et al., 2010). The study also demonstrated that about 72% of the IDPs were generally discontented with the living conditions citing reasons such as unemployment, insecurity, and insufficient food items. In a related study, high prevalence of PTSD and suicidal thoughts were reported among internally displaced populations in Nakuru County, Kenya (Getandu, Papadopoulos, & Evans, 2015). Also, Getandu et al. revealed that Kenya's internally displaced individuals scored poorly in quality of life and life satisfaction scales. Disgruntlement with government and fear for their lives and their children were other mental health challenges experienced by these individuals. Besides, being older, widowed, lacking social support systems, and limited government support were conspicuously linked to poor mental health.

Similarly, Mels, Derluyn, Broekaert, & Rosseel (2010) study on the psychological impact of forced displacement and related risk factors on Eastern Congolese adolescents affected by war revealed that the mean scores for the Impact of Event Scale-Revised and the Hopkins Symptoms Checklist – 37 for adolescents were higher in IDPs in comparison to non-displaced adolescents. Mels et al. noted that PTSD among the participants was associated with traumatic exposure and daily stressors. Moreover, another study comparing Iranians who had been settled in the Netherlands and those who were internally displaced demonstrated that externally displaced Iranians rates of depression (77.6%), and anxiety (58.5%) were higher in comparison to the non-displaced Iranians at 21% depression rate, and 20% anxiety rate (Gerritsen, Bramsen, Deville, Willigen, Hovens et al., 2006). Mels et al. and Gerritsen et al. studies seem to assert that externally displaced are at a higher risk for mental health illnesses than their counterparts.

Reports from many parts of the world indicate that displaced children are particularly vulnerable to mental health difficulties. For example, Salami et al. (2020) conducted a scoping review of literature in 2019 examining the health of externally displaced children in Sub-Sahara Africa. The study concluded that internally displaced children experienced higher degrees of mental health difficulties, including internalising symptoms and PTSD compared to non-displaced children. These difficulties were associated with generalised anxiety, worry, grief, obsessive-compulsive thinking, and negative outlook towards life.

2. Clinical Presentation of Post-Traumatic Stress Disorder in IDPs

Although IDPs are likely to present with many mental illnesses following traumatic exposure, this chapter will emphasise PTSD. Globally, one of the most predominant mental disorder associated with internally displaced populations is PTSD (Kessler et al., 2017). PTSD is a psychiatric condition that develops in some people exposed to or witnessed a life-threatening or traumatic event (Iribarren, Prolo, Neagos, & Chiappelli, 2005). Biologically, humans experience a wide range of reactions after exposure to a traumatic event. However, some people naturally recover from initial symptoms, while others maintain the symptoms (Atwoli, Stein, Koenen, & McLaughlin, 2015). Severe symptoms may lead to social, occupational, and cognitive dysfunction.

Additionally, undertaking daily activities such as cooking, bathing, and tidying the house may become challenging. Individuals who maintain severe symptoms for more than one month may be diagnosed with PTSD, while those who present with symptoms for less than one month are diagnosed with acute stress disorder (APA., 2013). The course of PTSD varies from one individual to another. Some people symptoms significantly reduce within six months; other symptoms last longer, while other symptoms become chronic.

According to DSM-5, to be diagnosed with PTSD, an adult must have all of the following for at least one month: at least one re-experiencing symptom, at least one avoidance symptom, at least two arousal and reactivity symptoms, and at least two cognition and mood symptoms (APA., 2013). Further, APA asserts that indicators for re-experiencing symptoms are flashbacks, or in other words reliving the trauma over and over, accompanied by physical symptoms – bad dreams, or a racing heart or terrifying thoughts. It is worthwhile noting that re-experiencing symptoms may be a source of difficulties in a person's everyday routine.

Avoidance symptoms that have been well-defined by DSM-5 include: staying away from places, events, or items that are aides-mémoires of the traumatic experience, and circumventing thoughts or feelings interrelated to the traumatic event (Iribarren et al., 2005). Often, avoidance symptoms may necessitate a change of an individual's personal routine, which interferes with one's life. Another critical category of PTSD symptoms is those linked to arousal and reactivity including being easily startled, feeling tensed or "on edge", having trouble with sleep, and angry eruptions. Arousal symptoms may make it challenging to undertake daily activities like eating, sleeping, or concentrating because they occur frequently, and make one feel mad and stressed.

A wide range of cognition and mood symptoms have been pointed out by APA, (2013), including being unable to recall the traumatic event's main parts and undesirable thoughts about oneself or the world. Besides, a person may report inaccurate feelings of blame or guilt and disinterest in activities previously enjoyed. These symptoms can start or get worse after the traumatic experience. They may also make one keep away from significant others like family and friends. Worse still, one's ability to function in all spheres of life may become a challenge. Unfortunately, research has demonstrated that PTSD is closely associated with clinical depression, substance use issues, and anxiety-related problems (Ayazi, Lien, Eide, Swartz, & Hauff, 2014; Kaysen, et al., 2008; Flory & Yehuda, 2015). Hence, the need for mental health professionals to routinely assess for these disorders among internally displaced individuals. Table 1 provides warning signs of trauma in adults. If trauma is not resolved, it can lead to PTSD.

Table 1: Common Warning Signs of Trauma in Adults

Behavioural Symptoms	Physical Symptoms	Emotional Symptoms
Isolation	Night terrors	Anger
Numbness or insensitivity	Lack of energy	Depression
General disorientation	Physical illness	Panic attacks
Compulsion	Sleep disturbance	Unresponsive
Eating disorders	Poor concertation	Anxiety
Impulsiveness	Shakiness	Emotional outbursts

It is significant for professionals working with IDPs to be cognizant of how PTSD manifests in children and teens because some of their symptoms are dissimilar to those of adults. According to APA (2013), some PTSD extreme symptoms observed in children below six years old are bed-wetting even after learning to use the toilet, losing ability to talk, and acting out the traumatising event during playtime. Some children may develop behaviours deemed as destructive, disruptive, or disrespectful. Feelings of guilt for not taking measures to avert the traumatic event from occurring may engulf older children. Also, these children may struggle with thoughts of revenge.

3. Risk and Protective Factors for Development of PTSD in IDPs

As discussed earlier, not every internally displaced person who witnesses, or is exposed to a traumatic event develops PTSD. Indeed, most people will not develop the disorder. Factors that make some people develop PTSD may be perceived as risk factors, whereas those factors that reduce a person's risks are deemed protective factors. Both protective and risk factors are discussed below.

Ryan, Chaudieu, Ancelin, & Saffery (2016) indicate that biological and physiological factors account for increased susceptibility or resilience to negative physical and mental health consequences such as PTSD after exposure to stress and trauma. Furthermore, Ryan et al. claim that this divergent susceptibility is influenced by hereditary factors and the nature, intensity, and duration of the stress. They postulate that epigenetic mechanisms may play a vital role in the biological response to traumatic events. Adults exposed to trauma during younger age and females are more likely to develop PTSD (APA., 2013). Specific genotypes may either reduce or increase the risk of PTSD following exposure to traumatic situations. Studies investigating important diseases linked to hereditary factors have provided evidence pointing on genetics's role in PTSD. For instance, an inquiry on the relationship of parental trauma exposure and PTSD to PTSD, depressive and anxiety disorders in adult offspring of Holocaust survivors shown a strong association between parental PTSD and higher risk to PTSD in offspring (Yehuda, Halligan, & Bierer, 2001). The study also reported that the offspring were more likely to present with depressive and anxiety issues in their lifetime. Elsewhere, Leen-Feldner and others (2013) provided evidence on offspring psychological and biological associates of parental post-traumatic stress. In particular, parental PTSD is closely linked to offspring mental health concerns, including behavioural and internalising problems and malfunctioning of the hypothalamic-pituitary-adrenal axis.

Intertwined environmental, societal, family and economic factors account for vulnerability to PTSD among IDPs. A war between the Ugandan government and the Lord's Resistance Army in Uganda led to internally displaced populations. Roberts, Ocaka, Browne, Oyok, & Sondoro (2008) conducted a cross-sectional study to examine the risk factors associated with PTSD and clinical depression in this population. More than one trauma experience, lack of basic needs such as water and food, being a female, marital status, sexual abuse or rape, and loss of a close relative were recorded as crucial risk factors for PTSD and psychiatric depression. Other risk factors for PTSD reported among IDPs include getting hurt, living through dangerous traumas and events, witnessing a person being hurt, seeing a corpse, limited social support, feeling hopeless and helpless, and dealing with extra stress resulting from a loss of income, or home, or loved one (Auxéméry, 2012). Poverty, lower education, childhood adversity particularly exposure to trauma, parental separation, and/or death, and dysfunctional families also play a critical role in PTSD. Notably, other factors that predispose the general population to PTSD may also surface among IDPs. These include: having a prior history of mental illness such as childhood emotional problems by age six years, panic disorder, depressive disorder, obsessive-compulsive disorder, negative appraisals, and inappropriate coping mechanisms (APA., 2013; Auxéméry, 2012).

Even though a controversial matter, individual factors may increase vulnerability to PTSD. Jakšic, Brajkovic, Ivezic, Topic, & Jakovljevic (2012) carried out a systematic search of the literature on the role of personality traits in the vulnerability and resilience to PTSD. They found out that most studies suggested an association between PTSD and personality issues, including negative emotionality, hostility, anger, nervousness, neuroticism, novelty-seeking, harm avoidance, and self-transcendence. On the other hand, personality traits such as optimism, low negative emotionality, extraversion, self-directedness, hardiness, and conscientiousness were reported as protective factors in most revisited studies.

4. Assessing the Mental Health Problems of IDPs

Assessing IDPs' mental health problems remains a challenge because of factors associated with a time delay (identifying newly displaced persons, being able to pool resources, and being able to avail appropriate treatment interventions). Despite this, it can be argued that there are known indicators of mental health problems among IDPs, and therefore, predictions of likely psychological and emotional concerns are possible. Subsequently, mobilising health care resources, and planning to avail psychological assessment tests and offering early prevention, and/or early treatment to avert further development and complication of mental health symptoms is a practical possibility. Such early planning would advance positive health outcomes for the IDPs. It must be recognised that all these measures require effective collaborations and networking among all mental health stakeholders.

Therefore, it is appropriate to propose screening phases in displaced populations to reduce the mental health burden and associated healthcare costs. Towards this end, community-based outreach services may form an effective initial screening phase to minimise the number of inappropriate self-referrals often observed in healthcare settings. Second, a common standard of mental healthcare screening should be developed and adhered to at this level. Moreover, cultural variations in expression and presentation of mental health symptoms must be considered in all screening phases. Furthermore, the importance of mental health promotion and education are highlighted. Building the capacities of locally respected professionals, including elders, traditional healers, community health workers, and midwives, is vital for more effective communication of the basic knowledge regarding mental health problems and the need to seek appropriate help to avert complications. Individual responsibility should be underlined and encouraged in health promotion and education messages.

Besides, effective screening and assessment of mental health problems at healthcare settings require that health professionals possess an implicit understanding of local health beliefs and concepts of mental health, illness, and disease. Mental health professionals must have information on how these displaced individuals and families access healthcare services. This information is critical in ascertaining the prevalence rate of mental disorders, and any hidden sickness or death associated with cultural health beliefs and concepts. Professionals working with displaced populations need to keep in mind that screening and assessment for mental health problems among IDPs must be monitored throughout all phases of displacement, and that community outreach services must be maintained over long periods. These efforts will ensure that IDPs' mental health needs are adequately addressed, leading to better health outcomes.

We recommend that mental health professionals screen for PTSD and associated commodities in internally displaced populations. Valid and reliable measures to screen for PTSD include Trauma Life Events Questionnaire (Kubany et al., 2000); Primary Care – PTSD Screen (Prins et al., 2003), Trauma Screening Questionnaire (Brewin et al., 2002), Short Posttraumatic Stress Disorder Rating Interview (Connor & Davidson, 2001) among others. Critical co-occurring mental disorders associated with PTSD are alcohol use disorder, substance use disorder, and tobacco use disorder. Screening tools for these disorders include the CAGE (Cooney et al., 1995), Alcohol, Smoking, and Substance Involvement Screening Test (Saunders et al., 1993), Alcohol, Smoking, and Substance Involvement

Screening Test (Humeniuk et al., 2008), Drug Abuse Screening Test (Gavin et al., 1989), Drug Use Disorders Identification Test (Berman et al., 2005), and so forth.

In terms of PTSD diagnostic purposes, mental health professionals may consider measures like the Clinician-Administered PTSD Scale (Blake et al., 1995) and the Posttraumatic Stress Disorder Checklist for DSM-5. As regards diagnosis of other PTSD related comorbidities, measures such as the Alcohol Use Disorders and Associated Disabilities Interview Schedule (Grant & Hasin, 1990), Composite International Diagnostic Interview, version 2 (DiNardo et al., 1994), and Mini International Neuropsychiatric Interview (Sheehan et al., 1998) may be important.

As noted earlier, other common PTSD associated mental problems among IDPs are major depressive disorder and anxiety disorders. Mental health providers need to use screening and diagnostic measures with sound psychometric properties continually. For instance, Patient Health Questionaire-9 (Nandakumar et al., 2019), Beck Depression Inventory (Beck, Steer, & Brown, 1996), Zunk Depression Scale, Child Depression Inventory (Figueras Masip, Amador-Campos, Gómez-Benito, & del Barrio Gándara, 2010), Hamilton Depression Rating Scale are recommendable measures for depressive symptoms screening purposes (Raimo, Trojano, Spitaleri, Petretta, Grossi, & Santangelo, 2015). Beck Anxiety Inventory and Pen State Worry Questionnaire (Meyers, Miller, Metzger, & Borkovec, 1990) are important tools for screening anxiety. Apart from using standardised tools, thorough clinical intake interview is vital in understanding underlying issues, identifying co-occurring illnesses, and informing treatment planning (Leahy, Holland, & McGinn, 2012). Use of assessment tests with limited training in their administration, scoring, interpretation, report writing, and communication of results to patients is unethical and discouraged (APA., 2018a; KCPA, 2015).

5. Evidence-based Treatment for PTSD in IDPs

Evidenced-based treatment modalities for PTSD can be divided into two broad categories: trauma-focused and non-trauma focused modalities. We discuss concisely trauma-focused modalities such cognitive behavioural therapy (CBT), prolonged exposure therapy (PE), cognitive processing therapy (CPT), and eye movement desensitisation processing (EMDR). Trauma-focused modalities concentrate on memories associated with the traumatic event and thoughts and feelings that engulf an individual after experiencing a traumatic event. Even though non-trauma focused modalities do not focus on feelings, thoughts, and memories linked to the traumatic event, they aim to minimise symptoms of PTSD. Examples of non-trauma focused modalities discussed are stress inoculation therapy (SIT), and interpersonal therapy (IP).

Foremost, cognitive behavioural therapy is a form of psychological treatment that focuses on the interconnection between thoughts, feelings, and behaviours and their impact on an individual's mental and physical functioning (Leahy et al., 2012). The proponents of this treatment argue that functioning can be reinstated by altering a person's unhelpful thinking (Corey, 2012). CBT sessions are given weekly over 12 to16 weeks (Jacobs, Mason, Harvil, & Schimmel, 2012). Individual or group session formats are recommended. We can speculate that when a displaced person witnesses a traumatic event, he/she may interpret the event in unhealthy ways. For example, he/she can think that this world is a dangerous place.

Further, an individual's thought pattern may contain negative over generalisations and catastrophic outcomes. This way of unhealthy thinking will lead to feelings of numbness and fearfulness. These unhealthy ways of thinking need to be replaced with positive ways of thinking to regain positive feelings. The therapist's role is to encourage the client to identify distorted thoughts and replace them with new healthy thoughts.

The efficacy of CBT in minimising PTSD symptoms among IDPs has been proven in numerous studies across the globe. For instance, a narrative review and a meta-analysis of psychological interventions studies focusing on treating PTSD and related mental illnesses among refugees and internally displaced were carried out in 2017 (Nocon, Eberle-Sejari, Unterhitzenberger, & Rosner, 2017). This study documented that CBT was an effective psychological intervention for treating PTSD among IDPs and refugees. In a related study, Murray, Cohen, Ellis, & Mannarino (2008) reviewed the literature on CBT as a treatment of trauma and traumatic grief among refugee youth. They established that CBT emphasises psychoeducation and parenting skills, relaxation, affective modulation, trauma narrative, in vivo desensitisation, conjoint child/parent sessions, and improving safety and coping skills efficacious PTSD symptoms reduction.

Second, prolonged exposure therapy is a form of cognitive-behavioural therapy for treating PTSD using two main procedures: imaginal and in vivo exposure. Both imaginal exposure and in vivo exposures target the trauma memory, internal and external reminders that generate anxiety and re-experiencing of the traumatic event, and the situation that is avoided (Leahy et al., 2012). Further, Leahy et al. indicate that imaginal exposure comprises narrating the story (traumatic event) aloud, recording, and listening to it over and over again, preferably in the therapist clinic. It can also involve virtual-reality recreation, watching videos/images/pictures related to the trauma, painting/drawing images from the trauma, and/or writing about the trauma. The client will continue to practice imaginal exposure at home on their own, that is, without the therapist's presence. In-vivo exposure focuses on exposure to the actual trauma scene or similar life events (Foa, Keane, Friedman, & Cohen, 2009). Prolonged exposure helps the client to understand and rationalise the traumatic event. PE sessions can last 8 to 12 weeks or more until the client no more prolonged experiences anxiety (Sones, Thorp, & Raskind, 2011). 60 to 90 minutes sessions are recommended. Apart from imaginal and in vivo exposures, other essential components of P.E. are breathing retraining and psychoeducation about common responses to trauma and PTSD symptoms (Walkins et al., 2018). A review of PTSD assessment and treatment carried out by Lancaster, Teeters, Gros, & Back (2016) demonstrated that prolonged exposure therapy is an excellent psychological intervention for PTSD management. Watkins, Sprang and Rothbaum (2018) review on available evidence-based psychotherapy interventions for PTSD reported that P.E. has strong evidence addressing memories, thoughts, and feelings associated with a traumatic situation.

Cognitive processing therapy is another form of cognitive-behavioural therapy that is relevant to the management of PTSD. It is known for helping clients learn how to revise and confront irrational beliefs related to the trauma. Twelve sessions of CPT would be good enough to allow new thoughtfulness and conceptualisation of the traumatic situation leading to normal functioning. Main components of CPT include psychoeducation regarding PTSD, thoughts, and emotions, identifying and writing automatic thoughts that sustain PTSD related symptoms, and Socratic questioning to help the patient understand his/her unhelpful thoughts in order to modify them. Walkins et al. (2018) found that CPT is an effective treatment for PTSD because it focuses on thoughts, memories, and feelings that follow traumatic experience. Several meta-analyses have demonstrated that CPT is efficacious in PTSD symptoms reduction (Cusack et al., 2016; Watts, Schnurr, Mayo, Young-Xu, Weeks, & Friedman, 2013).

Eye movement desensitisation and reprocessing therapy is a form of psychological intervention that was fashioned to eliminate the distress caused by a traumatic event, reformulate negative beliefs and reduce physiological arousal linked to the trauma (Shapiro, 2007). An EMDR therapist will provide an individual with an opportunity to recall and talk about traumatic memories while being guided to move their eyes from side to side in a cadenced manner. Shapiro (2017) indicates that EMDR entails eight treatment phases including history taking, preparing the client, assessing target memory, processing the memory to adaptive resolution, installation, body scan, and evaluating the results. These stages are executed in about 6 to 12 sessions. Meta-analysis conducted by Moreno-Alcázar et al. (2017) established that EMDR therapy is good in reducing PTSD symptoms in young people. Moreover, the clinical guidelines for treating PTSD developed by American Psychological Association commends EMDR therapy (APA., 2018b).

Stress inoculation training is a form of cognitive-behavioural therapy that has been one of the most effective interventions for managing PTSD (Hourani et al., 2016). According to Leahy et al. (2012), SIT aims to reduce anxiety and stress by training individuals on coping skills such as deep muscle relaxation and breathing exercises. Individuals are also taught how to manage stress by using assertiveness skills, cognitive restructuring, thought stopping, role-playing, and guided self-dialogue. SIT is often used concurrently with other cognitive behavioural therapy techniques.

Jackson, Baity, Bobb, Swick, & Giorgio (2019) provided strong evidence on the efficacy of SIT as a non-trauma focused treatment intervention for PTSD among war veterans.

Interpersonal therapy is a time-bound psychological treatment for depression and PTSD Graf, E.P., & Markowitz, J. C. (2012). IPT focuses on an individual and her/his relationships with other people. It focuses on interpersonal difficulties because they influence psychological problems. The therapist's role is to help an individual see how the past trauma and PTSD symptoms have impaired his/her interpersonal functioning. Hence, the goal of IPT is to increase interpersonal functioning. Bleiberg & Markowitz (2019) revealed that IPT has benefits in both clinical depression and PTSD symptoms reduction. Campini, Schoedl, Pupo, Costa, Krupnick, & Mello, (2010) examined the efficacy of group interpersonal psychotherapy for post-traumatic stress disorder, depression and anxiety, and found that treatment gains were realised during the study period. Similarly, Jiang, Tong, Delucchi, Neylan, Shi, & Meffert, (2014) randomised clinical trial among Sichuan earthquake survivors revealed that both interpersonal psychotherapy and treatment as usual for PTSD and depression were valuable.

Summary

In this chapter, we discussed the prevalence of mental illnesses found among IDPs. These include PTSD, depression, anxiety, and substances abuse problems, among others. One of the most important mental illness (PTSD) warning signs and symptoms in IDPs was highlighted. Insights about the importance of conducting assessment in mental health were provided. To help educate IDPs in preventing PTSD, risk and protective factors for PTSD were briefly examined. Finally, since the management of mental disorders is important in achieving global developmental goals, various effective evidence-based modalities were examined in this chapter.

References

Abdalla, Hamid et al., (2020). Mental health problems among internally displaced persons in Darfur, *International Journal of Psychology* , 45(4), 278-85.DOI: 10.1080/002075910003692620

American Psychological Association. (2018a). *Ethical principles of psychologists and code of conduct,* Washington, DC: Author.

American Psychological Association. (2018b). Clinical practice guidelines for the treatment of PTSD. https://www.apa.org/ptsd-guideline/ptsd.pdf

American Psychiatric Association. (2013). Diagnostic and statistical manual of mental disorders, 5th ed. Washington, DC: Author.

Atwoli L., Stein D. J., Koenen K. C., & McLaughlin K. A. (2015). Epidemiology of post-traumatic stress disorder: Prevalence, correlates and consequences. *Current Opinion in Psychiatry*, 28(4), 307–311. doi:10.1097/yco.0000000000000167

Ayazi, T., Lien, L., Eide, A. Swartz, L., & Hauff, E. (2014). Association between exposure to traumatic events and anxiety disorders in a post-conflict setting: a cross-sectional community study in South Sudan. *BMC Psychiatry* 14, 6, https://doi.org/10.1186/1471-244X-14-6

Auxéméry, Y. (2012). Post-traumatic stress disorder (PTSD) as a consequence of the interaction between an individual genetic susceptibility, a traumatogenic event and a social context, *Encephale*, 38(5), 373-80. DOI: 10.1016/j.encep.2011.12.003. 24.*PMID:* 23062450 Review. French.

Beck, A.T., Steer, R. A., & Brown, G. K. (1996). *Manual for the Beck depression inventory-11.* San Antonio, TX: Psychological Corporation.

Bleiberg, K. L., & Markowitz, J. C. (2019). Interpersonal Psychotherapy for PTSD: Treating Trauma without Exposure. *Journal of psychotherapy integration,* 29(1), 15–22. https://doi.org/10.1037/int0000113

Corey, G. (2012). *Theory and practice of group counselling, 8*[th] *ed.* Belmont: C.A. Brooks/Cole pp. 70-118.

Campini, R. F., Schoedl, A. F., Pupo, M.C., Costa, A. C., Krupnick, J. L., & Mello, M.F. (2010). Efficacy of interpersonal psychotherapy-group format adapted for post-traumatic stress disorder: an open-label add-on trial. Depression and anxiety, 27:72–7.

Cusack, K., Jonas, D. E., Forneris, C. A., Wines, C., Sonis, J., Middleton J. C., et al.... (2016). Psychological treatments for adults with post-traumatic stress disorder: a systematic review and meta-analysis, *Clin. Psychol.* 43, 128–141.

Figueras Masip, A., Amador-Campos, J. A., Gómez-Benito, J., & del Barrio Gándara, V. (2010). Psychometric properties of the Children's Depression Inventory in community and clinical sample. *The Spanish journal of psychology, 13*(2), 990–999.

Flory, J. D., & Yehuda, R. (2015). Comorbidity between post-traumatic stress disorder and major depressive disorder: alternative explanations and treatment considerations. *Dialogues in clinical neuroscience, 17*(2), 141–150. https://doi.org/10.31887/DCNS.2015.17.2/jflory

Foa, E.B., Keane, T. M., Friedman, M. J., & Cohen, J. (Eds.) ed (2009). Effective treatments for PTSD: Practice Guidelines from the International Society for Traumatic Stress Studies, 2nd ed. New York: Guilford Press.

Graf, E.P., & Markowitz, J. C. (2012). *Interpersonal psychotherapy for post-traumatic stress disorder (PTSD)* In Markowitz, J. C, Weissman, M.M, editors. Casebook of interpersonal psychotherapy. New York: Oxford University Press.

Hourani, L., Tueller, S., Kizakevich, P., Lewis, G., Strange, L., Spira, J. et al. (2016). Toward preventing post-traumatic stress disorder: Development and testing of a pilot predeployment stress inoculation training program, *Military Medicine,* 181(9), 1151–1160, https://doi.org/10.7205/MILMED-D-15-00192

Jacobs, E., Mason, R. L., Harvil, R. L. & Schimmel, C. J., (2012). *Group counselling: Strategies and skills* 7th *ed.* Belmont: C.A. Brooks/Cole. Pp 69-90; 91-127.

Jackson, S., Baity, M. R., Bobb, K., Swick, D., & Giorgio, J. (2019). Stress inoculation training outcomes among veterans with PTSD and T.B.I. *Psychological trauma: theory, research, practice and policy, 11*(8), 842–850. https://doi.org/10.1037/tra0000432

Jiang, R. F., Tong, H. Q., Delucchi, K. L., Neylan, T.C., Shi, O., & Meffert, S.M.(2014). Interpersonal psychotherapy versus treatment as usual for PTSD and depression among Sichuan earthquake survivors: a randomised clinical trial. *Confl Health* 8, 14 (2014). https://doi.org/10.1186/1752-1505-8-14

Gerritsen, A. A., Bramsen, I., Devillé, W., van Willigen., L. H., Hovens. J. E., & van der Ploeg H. M. (2006). Physical and mental health of Afghan, Iranian and Somali asylum seekers and refugees living in the Netherlands. *Social Psychiatry and Psychiatric Epidemiology*, 41: 18-26

Getandu, E. M., Papadopoulos, C., & Evans, H. (2015). The mental health, quality of life and life Satisfaction of Internally Displaced Persons Living in Nakuru County, Kenya, *B.M.C. Public Health*, 15, 755.

Internal Displacement Monitoring Center. Internal displacement. Geneva; 2019.

Iribarren, J., Prolo, P., Neagos, N., & Chiappelli, F. (2005). Post-traumatic stress disorder: evidence-based research for the third millennium. *Evidence-based complementary and alternative medicine: eCAM, 2*(4), 503–512. https://doi.org/10.1093/ecam/neh127

Jakšic N, Brajkovic L, Ivezic E, Topic R, Jakovljevic M. (2012).The role of personality traits in post-traumatic stress disorder (PTSD). *Psychiatr Danub*, 24(3), 256-66. PMID: 23013628

Kanel, K. (2012). *A guide to crisis intervention*, 4th ed. Belmont, CA: Brooks/ Cole Cengage Learning.

Kaysen, D., Pantalone, D. W., Chawla, N., Lindgren, K. P., Clum, G. A., Lee, C., & Resick, P.A. (2008). Post-traumatic stress disorder, alcohol use, and physical health concerns. *Journal of behavioral medicine, 31*(2), 115–125. https://doi.org/10.1007/s10865-007-9140-5

Kenya Counsellors and Psychologists Association (2015). Code of ethics. Nairobi, Ken: Author.

Kessler, R. C., Aguilar-Gaxiola, S., Alonso, J., Benjet, C., Bromet, E. J., Cardoso, G., Degenhardt,

Koenen, K. C. (2017). Trauma and PTSD in the WHO World Mental Health Surveys. *European journal of psychotraumatology, 8*(sup5), 1353383. https://doi.org/10.1080/20008198.2017.1353383

Lancaster, C. L., Teeters, J. B., Gros, D. F., & Back, S. E. (2016). Post-traumatic Stress Disorder: Overview of Evidence-Based Assessment and Treatment. *Journal of clinical medicine, 5*(11), 105. https://doi.org/10.3390/jcm5110105

Leahy, R.L., Holland, S.J.F., & Lata, K. (2012).*Treatment Plans and Interventions for Depression and Anxiety Disorders,*2nd ed. McGinn New York: The Guilford Press.

Leen-Feldner EW, Feldner MT, Knapp A, Bunaciu L, Blumenthal H, Amstadter AB.(2013). Offspring psychological and biological correlates of parental posttraumatic stress: a review of the literature and research agenda. *Clin Psychol Rev, 33*(8),1106-33. DOI: 10.1016/j.cpr.2013.09.001. PMID: 24100080.

López-Zerón, G., & Parra-Cardona, J. (2015). Elements of change across community-based trauma interventions, *Journal of Systemic Therapies, 34*(3), 2015,60-76.

Meyer, T. J., Miller, M. L., Metzger, R. L., & Borkovec, T.D. (1990). Development and validation of the Penn State Worry Questionnaire. *Beh Research and Therapy, 28,* 487-495.

Mels, C., Derluyn, I., Broekaert, E., & Rosseel, Y. (2010). The psychological impact of forced displacement and related risk factors on Eastern Congolese adolescents affected by war

Moreno-Alcázar, A., Treen, D., Valiente-Gómez, A., Sio-Eroles, A., Pérez, V., Amann, B. L., & Radua, J. (2017). Efficacy of Eye Movement Desensitization and Reprocessing in Children and Adolescent with

Post-traumatic Stress Disorder: A Meta-Analysis of Randomized Controlled Trials. *Frontiers in psychology,* 8, 1750. https://doi.org/10.3389/

Murray, L. K., Cohen, J. A., Ellis, B. H., & Mannarino, A. (2008). Cognitive Behavioural therapy for symptoms of trauma and traumatic grief in refugee youth. *Child and adolescent psychiatric clinics of North America, 17*(3), 585–ix. https://doi.org/10.1016/j.chc.2008.02.003

Nandakumar, A. L., Vande Voort, J. L., Nakonezny, P. A., Orth, S. S., Romanowicz, M., Sonmez, A. I., Ward... Croarkin, P. E. (2019). Psychometric Properties of the Patient Health

Questionnaire-9 Modified for Major Depressive Disorder in Adolescents. *Journal of child and adolescent psychopharmacology, 29*(1), 34-40. https://doi.org/10.1089/cap.2018.0112

Nocon, A., Eberle-Sejari, R., Unterhitzenberger, J., & Rosner, R. (2017). The effectiveness of psychosocial interventions in war-traumatised refugee and internally displaced minors: systematic review and meta analysis. European journal of psychotraumatology, 8(sup2), 1388709. https://doi.org R10.1080/20008198.2017.1388709

Nosè M, Ballette F, Bighelli I, Turrini G, Purgato M, Tol W, et al. (2017). Psychosocial interventions for post-traumatic stress disorder in refugees and asylum seekers resettled in high-income countries: Systematic review and meta-analysis. *PLoS ONE* 12(2): e0171030. https://doi.org/10.1371/journal.pone.0171030

Raimo, S., Trojano, L., Spitaleri, D., Petretta, V., Grossi, D., & Santangelo, G. (2015). Psychometric properties of the Hamilton Depression Rating Scale in multiple sclerosis. *Quality of life research: an international journal of quality of life aspects of treatment, care and rehabilitation, 24*(8), 1973–1980. https://doi.org/10.1007/s11136-015-0940-8

Roberts, B., Ocaka, K.F.., Browne, J., Oyok, T., & Sondoro, E. (2008) Factors associated with post-traumatic stress disorder and depression amongst internally displaced persons in northern Uganda. *B.M.C. Psychiatry* **8**, 38 (2008). https://doi.org/10.1186/1471-244X-8-38

Salami, B., Iwuagwu, S., Amodu, O., Tulli, M., Ndikom, C., et al. (2020). The health of internally displaced children in sub-Saharan Africa: a scoping review. BMJ Global Health,5: e002584. doi:10.1136/bmjgh-2020-002584

Shapiro, F. (2007). EMDR, adaptive information processing, and case conceptualisation. Journal of EMDR Practice and Research, 1, 68–87.

Shapiro, F. (2017). *Eye movement desensitisation and reprocessing (EMDR) therapy: Basic principles, protocols and procedures, (3rd ed.)* New York, NY: Guilford Press.

Sones H.M., Thorp, S.R., Raskind, M. (2011). Prevention of post-traumatic stress disorder. *Psychiatr Clin North,* 34(1), 79-94. PMID: 21333841.

Watkins, L. E., Sprang, K. R., & Rothbaum, B. O. (2018). Treating PTSD: A Review of Evidence-Based Psychotherapy Interventions. Frontiers in behavioral neuroscience,12, 258. https://doi.org/10.3389/fnbeh.2018.00258

Watts B. V., Schnurr P. P., Mayo L., Young-Xu Y., Weeks W. B., Friedman M. J. (2013). Meta-analysis of the efficacy of treatments for post-traumatic stress disorder. J.Clin. Psychiatry 74, e541–e550. 10.4088/J.C.P.12r08225

Yehuda R, Halligan SL, Bierer LM. (2001). Relationship of parental trauma exposure and PTSD to PTSD, depressive and anxiety disorders in offspring. J. Psychiatr. Res.35(5), 261–270.

About the Author

Lucy Njarui Njiru is the Head Psychology Department at Amref International University, Kenya. She completed her PhD at Daystar University, Kenya. She received her Master's Degree at Eastern Michigan University. Dr Lucy is one of the founders of the Academy of Mental

Health Practice, Kenya. She is the executive director and founder of Copeline Counseling and Assessment Center. As a licensed and certified clinical psychologist, she has worked as a private practitioner and serves as a consultant, researcher, trainer, and curriculum developer with various corporate institutions. Also, Dr Lucy has extensive experience in programs design and administration. She is an alumnus of the prestigious Ford Foundation International Fellowship Program. Her research interests include the efficacy of treatment modalities in individual and group psychotherapy in African settings, trauma, substance abuse, mood disorders, and violence/victimisation issues.

Sustainable Development Goals and Refugees, Poverty and Health Issues

Puranjoy Ghosh[3]

Abstract

The strength of public health policy, public health care services, combined efforts of the health institutions and its professions that pledged for the care, preservation and protection of the valuable resources (read human) of the state, have been well-experimented with the outbreak of infectious covid-19. Even being matured and convinced in realizing the uncertainty and unpredictability of this infectious zoonotic virus the initiatives in implementing the protective measures in the light of disaster management by the enforcement agencies along with its coordinating-contributory agencies have evoked incertitude, inter alia: 1) the accuracy of the information, being aired and its trustworthiness; 2) the trustworthiness upon the governance machinery about the public health emergencies. The survival instinct of the living creature, irrefutably, predominates the behavioural pattern and while in a predicament it becomes violent even. In an ordered society like human being where the behavioural pattern has been conditioned adaptively by the normative frameworks prioritizing thereof the humanity as an integral part of formal living – any maladaptive responses in the society like ill and misleading medical ordinances by the endorsed health care agencies, the defiance by small social groups in complying preventive norms of the pandemic, hoarding and stockpiling of essential resources, marriage ceremony of the son of peoples' representative in Karnataka during the nation-wide lockdown, transportation of migrants, etc. Are healthy response of lack of social responsibility, social cohesion or solidarity and integrity. However, those indications measure the strength of democracy but bespeak the scapegoating conditions orchestrated to pursue 'the

---

3   Assistant Professor, School of Law, KIIT (Deemed to be University), Bhubaneswar, Odisha. Email: puranjoyghosh@kls.ac.in

rule of law' and 'equality' for the mass myriad. What is more, painstaking is a preferential and discriminatory approach to implementing agencies in a nation warranted by cooperative federalism principles. In the present discourse, an endeavour is undertaken to critically analyse the country's public health policy and its impact upon the psycho-social relationships and mental health of the citizens in such social emergency when the free movement for the greater interest of the society has been suspended.

Keywords: Mental Health, Public Health Policy, Social Emergency

Introduction

Humankind prefers the preservation of life and health to death and sickness hence, on that account every individual gets down to better conditions of living and livelihood, be it within one's community or society, and that is the ordaining of nature, in default, the survival instinct leads to bargain the conditions of living and livelihood to harness the resources surrounded thereby. Over the centuries congregated political responses across the globe, in order to remove the disparities and discrimination of minimal social conditions of human beings, and also viewing at achieving good governance and civil societies, ultimately, have worked out the Rehabilitation and/or Resettlement programmes for the Displaced Persons, to provide conditions to those displacees to eke out a dignified living. Political sovereigns under territorial demarcations though, categorized such displacees into '*migrants*' and '*refugees*' and often discriminatory approach also perceived, however, to ensure the possibility of resettlement in a true spirit of international cooperation and to ensure social security have become obligations of the Contracting States given U N. Refugee Convention 1951[Article 24(1)(b)]. Though access to Public Health services has not explicitly been categorised in such a Convention, the common determinants and implications of social, economic, cultural, and environmental aspects within such resettlement programmes, irrespective of geographical boundaries, are reminiscent of preservation of good health as well. The fusion of various policy-propositions actuated (Millennium Development Goals, Sustainable Development Goals) and involved through various global summits to endorse every humankind as a global citizen, however, disparate and discriminatory treatments to the migrants and refugees have become a settled and usual practice by almost all political sovereign across the globe. Global summits since post World War – II to promote Human Rights have urged to the nations across the globe to customize their respective formal institutions in congruence with Rule of Law, and attenuate the governance machinery, prioritizing thereof the legacies of human rights and, catena of international instruments are being concluded on that behalf to survive the universal challenges, i.e., humanity (socio-economic justice) and sustainability (environmental).

1. Pandemic Governance and Sustainability

Increasing homogenization of the ideas on liberal trade has redefined the marketplace of goods, services, capital, people, and ideas in India. It may have created many economic growth opportunities, but to accommodate the same within the governance-framework and partisanship in the distribution of opportunities thereof have caused serious inequity to the health and health system which has shown its face quite soon the outbreak of COVID 19. The gradual expansion of trade permeates most developing nations to transpose the policy frameworks focus towards; a) de-regulation; b) privatization; and c) cost-reduction in social services for sustaining economic growth, perceiving thereof the expansion of opportunities of development in the mainstream society. Moreover, privatization with the constitution of Regulatory Bodies to monitor the balance between free-market principles and strong democratic governance has caused privation of thoughtful public policies, social protection mechanisms, and inequities in access to the health care. The causal relevance of increasing population as well as economic reforms, annexed through the ratiocinative approach of government to homogenize and ensure the necessary rights to the citizens in the context of a progressive process of the decentralized-developmental model has evolved a significant correlation between increasing income inequality and market capitalization because most of the private-owners predominantly reflect their acquisitive behaviours respecting the rational choices. As a result, imparting of the upturn of GDP curve and the arithmetical scorecard of equivalence, though, exhibits economic prosperity but such economic prosperity of the nation fails to provide equal opportunities to each level of the society, in particular, forced migrants and refugees, who are to move away from their nativity for mere sustenance (called economic migrants) in social exclusion. The expedition of human civilization with the scientific advancement to the extent of Robotics and Artificial Intelligence in the context of post-outbreak of COVID 19 pandemic scenario, has already changed the outlook of the capitalists to belittle the significance of ordinary human beings and has put forward to redefine the existential question of the illiterate, semi-literate, unskilled or semi-skilled working forces that overcrowded the labour market in particular to the developing nations. Over the centuries, the Mercantile world has substantiated the incremental productive role of *capital* (one of the critical resources of total valued outputs) and that managerial efficiency fosters productivity and marginal utility. Efficient use of resources and accountabilities for the stewardship of those resources under credible leadership evince valued economic outcomes and growth.

Moreover, such a leader(s)' credibility lies in trust-building, commitment, honesty, integrity, accountability, and even when carried through the contentious *agency theory*. Thus, with the innovation of scientific alternatives, liberalization has characterized the quantitative relations in human society where labour has been considered as means and limited services. Thus, the global challenges are zeroed in on the health services, health systems rather opportunities of livelihood, while the issues of *migrants* and *refugees* are but tailpieces.

The diachronic narratives of globalization in governance in pursuit of development get on towards markets and networks and not concomitant to the cross-sectional perspective of the substantive constitutional focus of '*democratic socialism*' and '*social welfare*'. The concepts of economic rationality and utility-maximization have changed the policy formulation relating to the State's allocation and distribution of resources. Hence, in the current layout of developmental reforms, the desired outcomes of equity, social welfare, structured relationship by trust, social participation, voluntary associations for the common good, in particular in the sectors like public health, education, etc. lose out to the values and ideals of democracy, social welfare, empowerment and social cohesion.

The raison d'être of good-governance and normative framework of social welfare, singularly, in a socialist democratic country are a) increment in the well-being of the subjects, and b) prevention of impairment of well-being, 3) to ensure the social solidarity and common good, 4) distribution and allocation of state resources to secure equitable social-conditions that is intensively desired for the attainment of satisfaction to lead a dignified livelihood and not *ad libitum*. To promote such structured social relationships amongst the communities in a country of multiculturalism like India, even when being determined based on the variances of outcomes; proportional, differential, different treatments sneak into the intermediate stages and processes within the governance framework to strengthen and evolve our social cohesion, solidarity and the social order of associational-togetherness in the society. It is the gradual progression in the practice of governance through the allocations and distributions of State resources to private agencies in pursuit of development, in no way changes the acquisitive behaviours of those private agencies, instead, turns aside in fostering social equity, trust and social solidarity. Such move denotes: i) that increasing reduction of stocks of State's resources through privatization cannot render all services and risk-mitigation or loss prevention that a State with greater stock could undertake; ii) shift of liability unto the private agencies and gradual dependence upon the private agencies; and iii) failure in ensuring optimum and effective performances for the well-being of the subjects of the State in sudden non-proportional changes without providing any incentive, either near or in future.

2. Pandemic Health Administration, Capital and Refugees/Migrants

Survival instinct is not contingent on alternative-choice or exchange ratios in the market. Proclamation of lock-down in the outbreak of pandemic COVID has put on view that; a) deficiency of infrastructure in the health sector due to careful negligence of the State over decades; b) questionable compliance of precautionary health norms by the subjects; c) absence of national spirit in the political menu; d) lack of trust upon the State health-care institutions and authorities. Mostly unorganized associations voluntarily came forward to relieve the sufferance of the economic migrants that reflected the disposition to parcel out humanity with the State agencies but hardly any trust upon the health care system, health institutions, and authorities. Since independence, India has failed in gaining the public-trust in public health strategies, which is important and significant (Phelan, et al., 2020) in particular in an emergency period like pandemic COVID. Sustainability of socio-economic developmental goals in the backdrop of new public management mechanism exhorts focus towards equitable social benefits of subjects irrespective of social layers, and perchance. The driving forces of market rationale influence the incrementalism approach then punctuated equilibrium, least budgetary allocations for the socio-economic sustainability of the subjects would be couched in. Erosion of public trust espoused with demeaning cooperation of public-health service institutions' authorities has also made the efficacy of the governance questionable. One of the objectives on the other side of not protecting the right to health services in the chapter of Fundamental Rights in the legal framework of the country may be, perhaps, the cost of the assertion of such right by any subject would vary much lesser in comparison to the cost of liabilities of the State. Equity (Patient Protection and Affordable Care Act, 2010) and other legal principles relating to human rights and the causal relations between the State and its subject might have justified the true spirit of Rule of Law.

James Coleman (1988) has advocated that *trust* within the *network of relations* in human society facilitates to accumulate *social capital* which would be gainful in particular to achieve common goals. The reciprocity of cooperative and productive behaviours could be had in the web of relationships of individual of diverse institutions of the human society who invest their attitude of *selflessness* or to say non-pecuniary expectations in their interpersonal interactions aiming at cooperating each-other to deal the realities collectively. Thus, social capital is the valued output of collective predispositions of members of multiple institutions, fosters optimistic expectations of cooperative behaviours of other agents of such institutions while mitigating the common harsh realities. The aforesaid productive behaviours have sometimes direct, sometimes indirect, or at times induced economic impact in accompanying society's development at various levels. However, such efficiency-exchange effectiveness through valued-cooperative behaviours has hardly been quantified in terms of monetary value. The interrelationships of diverse institutions/ organizations of a nation in different social contexts positively influence the nation's economic dynamics irrespective of their structural and functional presence in society. Francis Fukuyama has also viewed social capital from the economic perspectives, and concluded that it reduces transaction costs, underpins the associational life, which is *sine quo non* of stable liberal democracy (Fukuyama 1995). Therefore, the incremental benefit of social capital reduces the risks of hostilities (means in the vocabulary of economics – the externalities and the social costs) (Darcy, Chris, Sinclair and Jason, April 26, 2020) amongst the members of such institutions, even though one hangs on in the non-native territory. The significance of *social capital* in the background of COVID 19 pandemic is that India's constitutional and institutional design since independence concerning the country's administration has been orchestrated en route precautionary at the earlier, en route precautionary gradually reformatory. However, each episode of assembling peoples' mandate at any level of the society, be it micro, messo or macro, *poverty, literacy (education), malnutrition, minimum wages,* etc. are some common agendas up to now equally relevant. Today, in India, the felt-want for even the economic development journey is primarily twofold: a) deficiency of required infrastructure; and b) capacity building. Impact of progressive-reforms engineered in pursuant to liberalization has given rise to common perception in India on the subject of nexus between political power and business interests to the deeper informal structure of various regional and local authorities that have been bringing into being various socio-economic profiles and significant inverse relationship between common good, social solidarity and top-line growth of private sectors. Increasing numbers of private hospitals implicate minimum compliance of those conditions that require renewal of licence from regulatory bodies while the obligation of the State unto subjects remain misheed. The intrinsic flaw of non-enforceability of Directive Principles (Article 47) against the State has kept in check many a taxpayer to seek for the accountability and non-performance of primary obligations unto the subjects – i.e., homogeneous health care services for the subjects. Asset monetisation and foreign investments are two prime considerations in the neo-liberal official opinion, has been pushing the governance dynamics as a Minimalist State. The expedition of social welfare predominantly banks upon the Tax Revenue, mostly collected from the salaried individual. Simultaneously, the focus of 'Make in India' initiatives hold on to the images of scales of economic growth through the progress of the non-salaried communities and the aberrant tax base in the country's legal framework low-yielding revenue collection and tax compliance as well. A comparative report asset side by side between two booming economies in Asia would delineate the indolent attitude of the State regarding its primary duty. India is in the sixth position as global manufacturing output (only 3% of the global manufacturing outputs) with second-order in highest global population whereas China leads with 28.4% of global manufacturing outputs and tops the list (www.weforum. org). Both China and India rely upon the planned economy; however, the difference in the approach to dealing with human resources made the difference in economic growth scales. China is having an aggressive compulsory education policy with state capitalism, plays a more aggressive role in resource allocation and mobilization for innovation. Thus, the economic development moved from factor-driven to efficiency-driven and then to innovation-driven. Simultaneously, in India, the primary education lies with the State government while higher education with the Union (Wenjuan, 2019), Thus skilled or efficient labour for the large scale manufacturing units in India, resulting in the agricultural labourers as incapable for it. Therefore, the contemplated projection of privatization for nation's economic growth and enlargement of the provisions to enjoy the marginal benefits of economic growth by the mass myriad is directed to create the space of "economic rent" for the private agencies and the vulnerable citizens are to choose amongst the various layers of health services from the market. To put it more simple words, the benefits of health care services – the legacy of the fundamental right as provided under Article 21[4] of the Constitution is thereby undermined. Even the statutory duty of performing Corporate Social Responsibility (Sec 135, Companies Act, 2013) considering the socio-demographic characteristics

---

4   Article 21 is protection of life and personal liberty No person shall be deprived of his life or personal liberty except according to procedure established by law. The Article prohibits the deprivation of the above rights except according to a procedure established by law.

of the country, has not been designed effectively to arrange funds from the private agencies in providing the sufficient opportunities for the vulnerable section of the society to avail of standard health care services at State specified fixed price. Mutual *trust* in the backdrop of *rational interests* appears to be antithetical to the integrant of social capital, for, in social capital, it must be the perpetuation of *selflessness* (may be called social obligations) to deal with harsh realities. *Trust* and *allocation of resources* are common factors in both the contexts, i.e., in the *capital* and *social capital*. However, the difference is that in the former case, the actors are chiefly finite economic agents of the society and quantifiable within the fold of annual GDP while in the latter case it is complex subjective networks.

3. COVID and Sustainable Development Goal

In today's Anthropocene age, human beings' living conditions have transformed the human ecosystem and been shaping the planet's environment (Baum, 2019). The outbreak of present pandemic has reminded the increasing frequency of zoonotic diseases within such short span of time, for example, from SARS2 to COVID 19, and brings to mind about the extant equation between sustainable development and public health for, the ecological transition appears to be riskier to the health of poor people owing to their "likelihood of living in hazardous locations prone to flooding or landslides, or close to waste sites, with inadequate housing and inadequate access to health care, clean water, sanitation, and other essential services" and "also more likely to be living with an existing infectious disease burden and are more susceptible to under-nutrition due to increases in food prices than people who are not in poverty" (Cornelsen, Dangour, Honorary, Shankar, Mazzocchi & R.D, 2013). In the year 2015 Lancet Commission On Planetary Health (Whitmee, et.al, 2015) considering the trend of extant scale of development has recommended that "over-reliance on GDP as a measure of human progress, the failure to account for future health and environmental harms alongside present-day gains, and the disproportionate effect of those harms on the poor and people in developing nations—ironically the groups who often have least say about policy matters" and that might in near future emerge as global challenge of nature's life support system. The commensurability of the extant ecosystem of governance has mortgaged "the health of future generations to realize economic and development gains in the present" and the social-behaviours of today's progressive human civilizations on the championship of *consumerism* gradual depreciation of natural Capital; nature's subsidies to human livelihood have become highly inequitable, inefficient due to unsustainable patterns of resource consumption – in turn, adversely affecting the health of the vulnerable and marginalized section of the society. Hanging back between timely action and effect in the policy framework has been contributing the inefficient implementation, impeded the governmental institutions to ensure minimal common conditions to every member of the human societies to avail of equitable opportunities and sharing to natural resources, and social benefits, particularly, the forced migrants and refugees. For a healthy, sustainable and equitable society coordinated and cooperative actions of Individuals, Communities and organizations besides State Institutions are quintessential to ensure sufficient resources to maximize the public health care services. Lack of coalescence in espousing the *nature's capital* and *social capital* in governance mechanism; absence of strategized approach and judicious integration to confine multi-sectoral collaborative and coordination approaches through the regulatory framework in designing and implementing Public Health Service Programmes, Policies, and Legislations contrive compounding risks to public health care services and thereby diluting *human capital* of the nation (Smith, H.C., Nohrstedt, Weible, et al., 2014). Even in the backdrop of 'liberal trade' regime, the relational and participatory model of governance mechanism could make financial provisions for the sustainable improvement in public health care service system by reforming the 'tax-base' of non-salaried individuals of the country.

The experience of *social distancing* frame of reference during the outbreak of COVID – 19 pandemic has contemplated lack of relational governance and lack of trust upon the government during such emergent period, caused many adverse selections and moral hazards amongst the migrants and refugees due to a) asymmetrical as well as imperfect information in the market from various institutions; propaganda of misleading and unauthorized information in social media; b) lack of cohesion and social solidarity amongst various public authorities in streamlining discreet and uniform preventive and curative measures; c) declining public trust in governance in particular in implementation that resulted in the decline of social capital (Putnam,1995).

Enlargement of social benefits to the reaches of marginalized and vulnerable sections of the society by adopting the trickle-down economic model of floating wealth appears to have progressed segregation of solicitude and warmth of humanity and equality in today's progressive world due to acculturation of consumerism and the acquisitive behaviours of the rich members of the society. The graphical representation portrayed below exhibits the eventuality of the aforesaid economic model of governance.

Conclusion

Much prominence upon deregulation and privatization in governance framework in pursuit of 'free-trade' regime without arranging the equitable and sustainable resources to the marginalized and vulnerable sections of the society in line has been debilitating the stronghold of constitutional aspirations of social welfare in a *socialist, democratic* country like India. What should be prioritized at this hour and even the *sustainability* principles, irrespective of geographical limits also require the integration of *formal* and *informal powers* of the society to ensure social-equity which in turn would not only uphold the standardized quality of fundamental provisions of healthy lives rather would create sustainable markets across the globe? People-Profit-Planet equations with the aspirations to get hold of sustaining the growth of the society quintessentially require, considering as being the need of ecosystem perspective, to prioritize the common standard *lifestyles* in the society amongst all through regulatory distribution mechanism (like *anti-trust legislation* for market regulations) which would not only appraise the use of natural resources rather would enervate the proclivity of profit accumulation, global warming(by addressing the high-carbon consumerist lifestyles), human-health for all – one alternate to dispose of the economic and health inequalities in the society.

Reference

Alexandra L. Phelan *et al.*, The Novel Coronavirus Originating in Wuhan, China Challenges for Global Health Governance, (2020) Available at https://jamanetwork.com/journals/jama/article-abstract/2760500 (last visited on June 20, 2020 at 21:05 IST)

Allen, Darcy and Berg, Chris and Davidson, Sinclair and Potts, Jason, On Coase and COVID-19 (April 26, 2020). Available at SSRN: https://ssrn.com/abstract=3585509 or http://dx.doi.org/10.2139/ssrn.3585509

Article 47 of India's Constitution directs the State to raise the level of nutrition and the standard of living and improve *public health* as among its primary duties.

Coleman, J.S. (1988), "Social capital in the creation of human capital", *American Journal of Sociology,* Vol. 94, pp. 595-S120: Coleman, J.S. (1990), *Foundations of Social Theory,* The Belknap Press, Cambridge, MA.

Fran Baum, Governing for Health – Advancing Health and Equity through Policy and Advocacy, (2019), Oxford University Press.

Fukuyama, Francis. (1995), "Social capital, civil society and development", *Third World Quarterly,* Vol 22, No 1, pp 7– 20, 2001

Green R., Cornelsen L., Dangour A.D., Honorary R.T., Shankar B., Mazzocchi M., Smith R.D. (2013) BMJ *(Online),* 347 (7915).

https://cdn.statcdn.com/Infographic/images/normal/21059.jpeg (last visited on July 30, 2020 at 20:15 IST)

https://www.weforum.org/agenda/2020/02/countries-manufacturing-trade-exports-economics/(last visited on June 6, 2020, at 21:53 IST)

Jenkins-Smith, H.C., Nohrstedt, D., Weible, C.M., et al. (2014) "Advocacy coalition framework: Foundations, evolution, and ongoing research." In P.A. Sabatier and C.M. Weible (eds.), *Theories of Policy Process* (3rd ed.). Boulder, CO: Westview Press

Patient Protection and Affordable Care Act, 2010, otherwise known as Obamacare.

Putnam, R. D. (1995). Bowling Alone: America's Declining Social Capital. Journal of Democracy 6 (1), 65-78.

Sarah Whitmee, *et al.,* Safeguarding Human Health In The Anthropocene Epoch: Report Of The Rockefeller Foundation – Lancet Commission on Planetary Health, (2015) 386 (10007), at 1973-2028.

Zhang, Wenjuan. (2019), Constitutional Governance in India and China and Its Impact on National Innovation, Liu KC., Racherla U. (eds) Innovation, Economic Development, and Intellectual Property in India and China. ARCIALA Series on Intellectual Assets and Law in Asia. Springer, Singapore.

About the Author

Puranjoy Ghosh completed his LL.B. & LL.M. from the University of Burdwan, W.B. Dr Puranjoy Ghosh started his Advocacy career in Civil Laws for seven years, and since 2002 he is teaching profession in various Law Institutes. He has completed his Doctoral Degree in Law from the University of Burdwan in 2013. He joined in School of Law, KIIT in 2012. His area of interests are Corporate Law, Private Laws, Procedural Laws and Jurisprudence.

Right to Fair Compensation and Transparency in Land Acquisition, Rehabilitation and Resettlement Act 2013 and Marginalisation of Oustees in India

Norvy Paul[5]

Abstract

Right to Fair Compensation and Transparency in Land Acquisition, Rehabilitation and Resettlement Act 2013 of India needs to be read from sustainable challenges put forward by SDGs that aim at leaving no one behind. The Act primarily enlists areas that vent to land acquisition for development under the precept of primaeval hegemony of public purpose and eminent domain understanding prescriptive norms of compensation and devoid of the context of decision making of economic and non-economic asset loss, especially of natural and social capitals compelling them to be willing sellers. The requiring body often applies the sub silent doctrine of Social Impact Assessment forgetting social, psychological and physical aspects of life, under the pretext of the public hearing that force free consent obtained by an abusive process of the majority led by political regime though offered solatium of market value but not equal to the social value which often produces frustration against strive of welfare state due to the deprivation at heights and advantages at an abyss. Since the law attempts to follow proportional equality with a hollow heart, the SIA assured in the law concentrate social returns and not social costs that lead to the marginalisation of oustees of displacement at economic, social, psychological and political life. This could have been avoided if the acquisition had not taken place, and if it happened with social licensing, that opens space for dialogue and participation in decision making. This

---

5   Senior Lecturer in Social Work, The Catholic University of Eastern Africa, Nairobi. Email: frnorbypaul@gmail.com

marginalisation can never overcome if space-time-place continuum has not reckoned adequately while designing resettlement action plans facilitated by social licensing that include reintegration via intervention and reclaim of social and individual identity. The paper is an attempt to understand marginalisation of oustees in India on the background of Right to Fair Compensation and Transparency in Land Acquisition, Rehabilitation and Resettlement Act 2013 and recent displacement occurred in the country considering its provision of land acquisition, Social Impact Assessment, compensation provisions offered to Internally Displaced People of the country.

Key Words: RFCTLARR Act 2013, Marginalisation, Pubic Purpose, Displacement

Introduction

Displacement causes multiple havoc in the lives of the displacees at individual and community levels and their environment. Development projects though presume to be landmarks of better living standard and quality of life of people of the country or geographical area it is implemented need not be always bringing the expected results. It negatively impacts on the life of displacees often and generate divergent risks to their life. These projects have also provided the best available resettlement packages, as the authorities claim, though not sufficient to mitigate the pain and loss they underwent from time to time. Various scholars have studied displacement and its effects on oustees and proposed various models to address them: Entitlement Theory and Capability Approach (Sen, A), Impoverishment Risk and Reconstruction Framework (Cernea, M), Sustainable Livelihood Approach (Chambers and Conway), Asset Based Community Development (DFID) and Social Framework for Projects (Vanclay). Each model proposed a better side for the project development and implementation without negatively affecting the displacees' lives.

While displacing people for development projects, each country follows policies, acts and guidelines issued, enacted and promulgated from time to time considering the type of administration they follow. In India, the Land Acquisition Act of 1894 was in place till the amendments in the act made in 1984. In 1993, 1997 and 2003, 2007 various policies were issued to guide the land acquisition for development projects apart from various laws like the Forest Protection Act, Railway Act etc. In 2011 a land acquisition policy was being promulgated by India's government, which gradually paved way to enactment of Right to Fair Compensation and Transparency in Land Acquisition, Rehabilitation and Resettlement Act 2013 (RFCTLARR 2013) and then gradually issue Rules and Regulations to supplement the Act in 2015. The law considered different dimensions of development needs of the country in the wake of new economic reforms and its requirements paying due diligence to the demands or requirements of people who are displaced for such development projects. As per the development paradigms, those displacees for development projects are supposed to be development partners and shareholders or people sharing the benefit of the project or improve the quality of life after displacement and not marginalised or disposed of. Looking into various provisions in the acts and proposed displacees of different projects en masse is due to understanding whether the act provides provisions for enhancement of displacees or become benefit sharers or marginalised displacees of development projects.

1. Right to Fair Compensation and Transparency in Land Acquisition, Rehabilitation and Resettlement Act 2013 (RFCTLARR 2013)

The law has four objectives which remained as ideal though practicality is being questioned as impacts of LARFCRR 2013:

1. To ensure, in consultation with institutions of local self-government and Gram Sabhas established under the Constitution of India, a humane, participative, informed and transparent process for land acquisition for industrialisation, development of essential infrastructural facilities and urbanisation with the least disturbance to the owners of the land and other affected families

2. Provide just and fair compensation to the affected families whose land has been acquired or proposed to be acquired or are affected by such acquisition.

3. Make adequate provisions for such affected persons for their rehabilitation and resettlement.

4. Ensure that the cumulative outcome of compulsory acquisition should be that affected persons become development partners, leading to improved post-acquisition social and economic status and matters connected with or incidentally thereto (www Indiacode.nic.in).

The Act specifically categorised five dimensions for acquisition: 1. defence, 2. rural infrastructure, 3. affordable housing, 4. industrial corridors, and 5. infrastructure projects including Public-Private Partnership (PPP) projects central government owns the land (acquisition for private entities). The Act provides 16 exemptions and tried to define public purpose in Section 2(1) of the Act but opened venues to Private initiatives under public purpose. The Act theoretically put forward that the consent of at least 80% of the project affected families shall be obtained through a prior informed process before government uses its power under the Act to acquire the land for private companies. To acquire the remaining land for the public good and a public-private project, at least 70% of the affected families invited criticism towards marginality in political life, leading to bypassing the social licencing process. The law is credible in defining landowner but disguised implication to marginalise oustees socially and economically. The urgency clause in the Act for expedited land acquisition keeps triggering citizens' lean individual rights to public right and political right and leads to elite purchase that does not abide with constitutional rights. The terms of market value Section 27 Schedule I keeping Indian Stamp Act reinstated rural households' common property resources and social capital building institutions – both landowners and livelihood losers.

Responding to the criticism raised against the RFCTLARR 2013 on 18th December 2015 issued the rules and regulations to pacifying the opposition though law remained the same.

1. Classification and project approval shall be consistent with provisions of the Act. The correctness of the need shall be enquired by the District collector and ensure minimum land is acquired.

2. Notice shall be posted in conspicuous places and hearing objections provision need to be assured.

3. Prepare rehabilitation and publish a rehabilitation plan which requires verification individually.

4. Post-implementation social audit along with SIA compliances.

Provisions 2 & 4 are always implemented, but elite purchase always rules unilaterally and administrative capacity. Issue notice to the affected person by the authority. Thus the Act and rules and regulations opened chances to:

1. Provide an opportunity to be heard

2. Furnish note on reasons for eviction to evictees

3. Just, fear and reasonable compensation and rehabilitation package

4. Appeal or review of eviction before higher courts

As part of the state-wide implementation, five States of the country amended the provisions such as consent, Social Impact Assessment, the objection of the affected citizens, and local bodies' participation. However, they were challenged in supreme court saying as a violation of article 21 of the constitution, arguing that the right to live with Dignity also implies the right not to be displaced unless there is overwhelming public interest.

2. Understanding Marginalisation (Economic, Social, Psychological and Political) in Displacement

Marginalisation poses the question "to what" defined by categorisation and defining marginalisation means go beyond categorisation (Kanbur, 2007). Messiou (2012) states that marginalisation has multiple conceptualisations, its experience and recognition in society. Often marginalisation is subjective as experience, but objective as others recognise and legitimacy is questionable (Mowat, 2015). Marginals lack inclusion and one of the dangerous forms of oppression that prevent people from participating in social life. So "understanding (conceptual and experiential) of marginalisation must, therefore, also be part of our sense of place; our construction of our metaphorical location as participants in social transformation" (Howit, 2016 p.7).

As a slippery and multi-layered concept, marginalisation has aspects in sociological, economic, and political debates. It is a status where a person is living in the outskirts of the society with the feel of being isolated compared to others (economic, cultural political and social) and the thinking that they accord the mainstream philosophy. It means a person or community is made to feel like they are different and treated differently experiencing the effect of being discriminated to be alone while being surrounded by everyone and creates a feeling of being alone. To be marginalised is to have a sense one does not belong and, in so doing, to feel that one is neither a valued member of a community and able to make a valuable contribution within that community nor able to access the range of services and/ or opportunities open to others. In effect, is to feel, and be excluded" (Mowat, 2015 p.7). Individuals' marginalisation looks into isolation or exclusion experienced mainly in two terms societal and spatial (Chaskar, 2015). Socio-space attached to boundaries does not look into the process of exclusion but how it is processed to contribute exclusion (Sibely D., 2004). It points to marginality, reduced opportunity to initiate actions or resources to sustain life (Burton & Kagan, 1996) attaching the concept of Us versus They framework of social inclusion (Hansen, 2012) evident in the life of the millions who are with poverty, unemployment, disability, socially, economically, and politically discriminated and displaced (Chaskar, 2015) recognised as social exclusion arising out of inequality and barriers of social injustice and inequality, vulnerability, identity and poverty both structural and cultural.

Marginalisation operationally and methodologically measuring would be challenging in distinguishing and articulating it from the other risks. Considering marginalisation in displacement, it moves them to the margins and gradually triggered by the vulnerability due to social anomaly and absence of social control. This puts pressure on adopting and adapting new coping mechanisms to survive (IDMC, Global Report on Internal Displacement, 2017). Marginalisation is a multidimensional concept in displacement which is socially built on space and place and influenced by economic and political (powerlessness generated by the application of *elite purchase* and application of eminent domain) factors which affect the mental health (psychologically) of the oustees. Identification of marginalisation in displacement is to distinguish between slippery of the terms that bring dichotomy of core and periphery, mainstream and outskirts, visible and invisible, formal and informal. Thus marginalisation experience of an individual always accompanied by societal experience. It commences at an individual's economic dimensions and later spreads to social, psychological and political aspects of oustees life.

Economic marginalisation is an outcome, and is a process, in inequality. It also speaks of inequality due to rapid growth in the globalised economy of neo-liberalism accompanied by inequality both pan and within the country. In every development project prior to land acquisition compensation needs to be paid and the untimely or delayed distribution of compensation packages especially finance generates stress and challenge livelihood and requires displacees to acquire the skill to manage project compensation. Interestingly these projects displace people leading to being vulnerable and marginalised, often economically and then social, political, cultural etc. Studies of W.Fernandes (2000) and Cernea (1995) confirm the economic marginalization that leads to Ardener's concept on Muted Group and they are otherwise called as either physically displaced or economically displaced (livelihood loss direct or indirect). It leads to displacement-poverty-inequality-violence nexus. Most of the displacees, as economic resources lose, lead to a decrease in quality of life or income level that spend for daily living as the resources often accessed in pre-displaced areas are becoming nil or depleting to generate poverty low economic profile. Thus, economic marginalisation is a situation that displacees undergo as a result of reduced income, reduced employability, an economic liability, health issues, poor amenities, and economic indebtedness. Economic deprivation of displacees is evident in obscene of human capital and quality of living as a resultant of inventory approach looking forward to the profitability of project which forces oustees to struggle to generate new geography in the absence of economics of recovery (DeWet, 2011; Paul, 2013; George & Irudaya, 2017).

Social marginalisation is much attached to social order. It is a changing, multi-pronged, layered terminology connected with the people's social living, which varies in its experience at society, at global and community level that speaks of 'oppression, exclusion, vulnerability and discrimination' (Burton & Kagan, 2015). Space is a significant contributor to the social marginalisation that entails the material and discursive relationship between space and society where marginalisation is becoming the process of peripheral. Space is formed by individuals in their place and home, landscape. (Mitchell, 2008; Trudeau & McMorran, 2011). In displacement, people who are resettled need to reinvent places amidst and against unsettled changes that create imagined boundaries build on the authenticity of power to delineate. Thus social marginalisation of the displacees which is exclusion through injustice needs to understand from social identity and participation based on cultural capital, activities performed in and through landscape concept or socio-space which is "powerfully real and powerful" (Soott, 2009) which is not single reality because exclusion experience varied in groups but needs to position it as required of explanations. Positioning exclusion depends on valuing of 'undesirable (Sibley, 1995). Marginalisation, therefore, consists of the separation of people, stigma, gender and stratification that speak of the rule of power over powerless by which dominant groups contribute to socio-spatial builds of marginalisation of individuals or group who are alienated by judging as outsiders of mainstream (Sibely, 2004). Marginalisation thus created a person different in society and treated differently (Paul, 2013; Mohanty, 2009) which generates a new definition in the family relationship, space and distance in identifying of individual belonging to marginal with loneliness, helplessness and homelessness leading to alienation and deprivation generated out of social dichotomy of Us v/s They or public v/s private or landscapes of exclusion; core or periphery; haves and have-nots. Displacees thus becomes have-nots and socially excluded of the community losing social status as they experience inequality a modern derivative of social stratification. This gradually leads to a spectrum of dispossession and transforming life as life misspent evident in social vulnerability, disempowerment, family and social ties loses or hiatus due to poor social support, loss of personal and social identity defined in time, space and place triggered by social and political apathy, alienation and exclusion (Shills, 1954; Sibely, 2004; RFCTLARR 2013; Tradeu & McMokes, 2018; Burton & Kagen, 2015; Vanclay,2017).

Understanding an individual within the framework his living experience helps to depict subjective and emotional dimensions of marginalisation in its full sense (Mowat, 2015). The displacees face psychological disturbance by rooting out from familiar situations to a new situation where displacees lived from the time of ancestors, their worshipping places, religious affiliation to church/temple, their burial grounds and relocate a new place which is strange to him/her (Mathur, 1998). The terminological ascription and stigma attaching them as outsiders creating group identity mean non-accepted in the community and newcomers to host community results in poor self-esteem and self-confidence generated out of the experience of injustice, vulnerability and social marginalisation. Place and personal memories are an integral part of human beings as they make meaning to their lives, and their loss creates a vacuum in daily living and their existence (Vanclay, 2017). This can be more psychological boundaries than an apparent social order in society (Sibely, 2004). The evictees, many of them are emotionally disturbed lowering of mental health status since they have to fight with government or powerful agency/system, people or institutions who have the wrong kind of mindset and setting them in unfamiliar place bring social stereotyping as outsiders and unfamiliarity breeding by social isolation and social exclusion implied with alienation (Brunila, 2011). They were often demotivated and compromised their life to be victims than victorious (Colson, 2003). As the displacees are evicted by loss space and time structures, a process of alienation of self-causes stress and anxiety generating poor self-esteem and self-image due to or added with the stigma of public and subjective experience stereotyping, loss of public security and wellbeing reflected in the loss of trust and confidence in themselves and society. This forces them to be helpless and lonely, producing psychosomatic disorders, mental illness for individuals that can be defined as psychological marginalisation (Colson, 1983; Fernades, 2000; MoWat, 2015; Walicki, 2017; IDRC, 2017).

Development and Displacement is a political process in which power asymmetry imbalances risks in displaced life (IDMC, Global Report on Internal Displacement, 2017). The guiding principle 'greater good for the larger numbers' is applied in forced displacement that glorifies the paradigm of progress and modernity (Baviskar, 1995; Drydyk &

Atiya, 2006). There are several legal frameworks in countries like India. Unfortunately, governments use constitutional or legal or administrative provisions like public purpose or eminent domain to acquire or expropriate land compensating people through consultation and negotiation built up by enlisted support and co-operation accommodating potential evictees partners (Vanclay, 2017). It results in making poor poorer and creating poorer outcomes by 'created consent' instead of genuine consent making displacees willing seller. Thus diminishes the favourable chance of sustainable livelihood (Verma, 2004; Paul, 2013) by the imposing State's power (Nadani & Swain, 2016) or marginalising them politically to become burial grounds instead of temples negating as an equal partnership of reciprocal respect, faith, openness and better information sharing (Jain, 2006). Thus political marginalisation of displacees stems from the denial of rights as citizens, and human beings that include the political right in the capacity to be not dispossessed resulted from the impersonal and dehumanising application of laws that make displacees to a status of powerlessness. The application of informed consent leads to double alienation buy-in participation and the creation of proletariat for capitalist build a rift between the haves and have-nots due to the power asymmetry that poises the option between ethical and human rights. Ignoring both pave the way to the elite purchase of land constructing gap between ideal value sharing and actual which observed in state-sponsored exclusion and buy-in of people's participation avoiding social licensing that spare no ground than powerlessness evident in violation of individual rights and discrimination commencing from poor land valuing for compensation and rehabilitation package awarding to the displacees (Paul, 2013; RFCTLARR 2013; Vanclay, 2017).

3. Understanding RFCTLARR 2013 and Marginalisation

Analysing the RFCTLARR 2013 with a reading on marginalisation discloses that the Act ignores the needs of poor Indians who must have affordable housing and attaches an arbitrary mark-up to the historical market price that neither looked into social justice nor the efficient use of resources. Incongruous to other laws of India Section101 of RFCTLARR 2013 provides the provision to return the acquired land within three years if the same is not implemented or unused, but it does not speak about what then if consent is not obtained and negative social impact assessment. It does not define the word acquisition which provides space for real estate and building industry giving no choice of participation to economically marginalised and politically muted. The Land Acquisition Act removes the need for social impact assessment for PPP projects. Presuming 'property right is not as a fundamental right as some other rights are' the acquisition of land creates the market of *have nots* and as mostly acquired space are of invariably poor and uneducated. They are the 'have-nots' who have hardly any channels available to say 'no' to letting go of the resources vital to their survival. To achieve the public good by being concerned in listening to them, capacity building of the stakeholders and make avail of a credible platform for negotiations could have initiated to balance the benefits of liberalization against the risks and costs to the displaced people, in particular the vulnerable segments of the population who become a mere sanctioning authority and watchdog of development projects. Even if they express their descent and willingness to negotiate, they often fall to be vulnerable to organised parties' pressure. This calls for consideration of the top-down approach and policy implications as equal before the law, the right to be heard and participation in decision making. Providing consent of 80% contradicts local self-government empowerment as political authority for the difficult nature of assessing social change which requires innovation and creativity in development-oriented resettlement and practising social equity and social justice. Greater common good or national interest in preference to communities forms a perfectly moral and legal justification for land acquisition law but does not acknowledge displacement and its traumatic overtone, and is unwilling to take the responsibility of rehabilitation. The post-displacement period has been a matter of lowest concern for the project planners, especially legal provision to create rehabilitation sites and rehabilitate in groups as far as possible.

Indian legal systems are individualistic, and therefore a challenge in the court is problematic as it is frequent in displacement, throwing people with the inferior right, out of the land. Marginalisation thus even-sided by the rule of law and justice system as it provided exceptions in linear industry corridor and expressway though it is illegal the supreme court says they cannot deny. The oustees find themselves in a position of helplessness, powerlessness, landlessness, placelessness, alienated and most importantly joblessness which diminishes the chance of sustainable livelihood as found in many cases of India like ICTT, Vizhinjam Harbour, CIAL, Singur, Narmada River, Koodamkulam where social welfare risks especially homelessness and social disarticulation is apparent. In RFCTLARR 2013, individuals are eligible for compensation and resettlement. Act speaks of the reestablishment of common property resources or replacing them through socio-cultural and other community support systems but often failed to provide horizontal network by applying PPP and emergency clause. To implement such provisions, it requires to accept a shift of probable liability to acknowledged liabilities that is to implement 'use right' not 'acquiring right' to the development project implementers.

Resettlement of group or society is preferred in the Act as an entity but mostly unrealised leading to resettlement in a host community where equality and mutual understanding, consistent with each group's desire to preserve its own identity and culture is ignored. This will automatically disempower and dispossess both host and resettled community though seeks not to disturb the socio-cultural relations (social harmony). Considers dislocation of communities and the benefits in the policy are out of charity and on the assumption that people should adjust themselves to the situation once a decision to displace them is taken to prioritise the welfare of a few; superseding the minority over majority creating marginality. The right to live is provided in most resettled packages in terms of compensation; mostly replacing land for land that is non-fertile, non-arable and without proper infrastructure ignoring social isolation and alienation of oustees packages are provided (resettlement is given in CIAL, ICTTI, Highways etc.). Even in these projects, marginalisation has grown up to extreme via violation human rights violation as seen in Narmada, Singoor when mass population transfer is taken place against people's will. It is a development cleansing which is also called development nationalism. People's collective rights and protests have won a race earlier in few cases but marginalization still continued as the land acquired never returned to people if not used profitably for public interest which is against the Act's provision.

The act attempts to use public purpose acquisition to sell or lease land to private person/projects in a welfare state knowing it may not be possible if the Act follows bottom approach as proposed in the act of having 80%/70% people consent. The buy-in process is evident as the provision of informed consent application is necessary for projects but often applied prior informed consent of 80/70% of proposed evictees, at short notice of the urgency. Because of provisions for acquiring, the private negotiation exceptions in the Act overrule the required consent of 70% public and 80% private project implying majority consent but often challenged of intention public purpose. The proposed project may not pass the test of reasonableness if it follows the law's stringent provisions. The act provides provision for the adequate notice period, but the Act's urgency clause is not explicit, pointing to the threat of act towards marginalisation. This invoked protest against Tehri dam, Narmada, Singur, Nandigram, Koodamkulam, ICTT, CIAL, Highway projects. However, the application of public purpose and eminent domain provides provisions to challenge people's consent and bypass the social license of people's consent. The principles of transparency and accountability, especially in reintegration or at least rehabilitation, are thus challenged. Rehabilitation and resettlement package never realised, but praxis is a mirage in the desert. Because once evicted, it becomes evictees' burden to obtain rehabilitation package through efforts that demean their lives and increase stress and anxiety of the future.

Provisions of compensation up to four times more than market value and lease in the case of renewable energy acquisition are yet another debatable issue. Nevertheless, the question is it enough or not, four times or 20 times, when often implemented project affects air/water/environment? The answer is never can compensate what is lost, and it can only trigger marginalisation. The rules and regulations direct compensation for housing and displacees without having land for up to 5Lakhs or Rs.20000/for 20 years' subsistence amount. The land title is given to women to empower, but empowerment is not realised when land is provided in distance or marshy or rocky area. But the question of non-transferability and non-employability of the skill of artisans and unskilled workers is not addressed adequately, leading to economic marginalisation.

But poor empowerment made of the decision on RFCTLARR 2013 shows the grim picture of evictee's life where dispossession becomes their right and not a restoration. Evictees consent detailed as a sign of people's participation which is taken for granted because law ensures people's participation confirming the development paradigm as normative and makes the framework of acquisition as lawful meaning to say compensation policy. Land acquisition in history is always on top-down approach with authoritarianism clubbed with an unfair deal and prejudiced either of capitalist mind or socialist mind to institutionalise where property right is no fundamental right to generate income for an administration that trickle down the development to rural poor. Therefore, the law is mercantile capitalism that predisposed to expropriate individual right via a repressive mode that leads to political and economic marginalisation. A transition from centralised economy/state key player in the liberalised economy in 1990 triggered large land and developmental diversity requirements where FDI is the focussed with investment incentives. Liberalisation is 'reorganised and reintegrated' into state policy gradually. The summit of this progress reached in the enactment of RFCTLARR 2013 where pre-eminence is given to eminent domain where prescriptive normative compensation has not addressed the practical decision making while displacing landowners. Though the law confines 70/80% consent of landowners, a created consent is mutually and voluntarily accepted by sellers and buyers and sellers become disadvantaged sellers (buy-in) so that no person has the power to make way above public purpose.

Public purpose often predicates elites' intervention and limits localising's interests on socio-economic, cultural conditions even unable to access SIA and become sub-silent land ouster but ignored or forgone by land buyers. Marginal members of land ouster – lowball perspectives – depends on the relationship to political actors because free consent mostly induced by political actors and when belonging to opposite political ideology, it is dicey. The public hearing process is an abusive process to assemble politically motivated majority voice to procure development model and piecemeal attention. SIA communication on acquisition is focussed on better use, under the relation of public purpose. Compensation paid after SIA is expected to compensate to restore socio-cultural dimensions but socio-cultural values not often quantified where the question of not rehabilitation but reintegration is raised. The incidental net benefit and enumeration due to displacement ignore the deprivation of socio-economic-cultural values intertwined with IDPs' social, psychological and physical lives. Public purpose mostly disguised with public interest mooted by political transactions designed in the legal framework where land ouster sometimes is not included in payroll due to poor education. Whereas consent cannot be blocked due to public purpose and political mooting which is "perennial spring of all prodigality and all disorders to the inmost fibre of the legal framework".

The economic and political systems, until recent years, kept the culture of silence against the socio-cultural implications of the development. On the one hand, nothing is said about the prior informed consent, and on the other hand, Act takes PAPs and their problems for granted of culture, religion, social organization and community life. Policy accepts the fundamental principle *eminent domain* to acquire private property. The desirability and justifiability of each project set its objective as the active participation of affected people but becomes an oasis in the desert in the Indian context where the contradictory principle *eminent domain* is active. The Act has the power to supersede all the enactments to displace whole communities in the name of 'public purpose'. The court cannot decide but only can direct the district collector to hear their petition and submit a report to build the 'temples of development'. The overall control and superintendence of the formulation, execution and monitoring of the rehabilitation and resettlement plan shall vest in the Administrator for Rehabilitation and Resettlement which is always coloured with development paradigms that displacement is inevitable and eminent domain stands above individual rights.

Solatium, a market price approach where value for money is offered as compensation and not for values – value for life and culture – demands an evaluation of value integration as a result of SIA in the displacement process. Reintegration is not part of the law at any stage but depends on the decision of political powers. i.e., integration of deprivation of individual interests and incidental benefit in the public interest that orient towards welfare paradigms (deprivation of socio-cultural values) is absent in RFCTLARR 2013 and orients towards social returns of social investment costs borne by IDPs. It will bring among displacees triple foundations of unequal society; denying access to mainstream to poor clubbed with lawful inequality, without the provision in the system a few people are given preferences that exclude the majority and the creation of keeping alienated people who struggled to survive till last (Gaventa,1999). Thus fair compensation law for acquiring land for development contradicts its proclaimed mission development and welfare of all.

Conclusion

RFCTLARR 2013 has been enacted to provide fair compensation to those evicted for development projects categorised into five aiming primarily to follow distributive justice, and then development be people-oriented and citizen endorsed. The act provides provisions such as evictees consent, social impact assessment, fair compensation, resettlement packages, but a primacy is given to public purpose than individual rights. This can ipso facto lead to marginalisation at different levels and different dimensions. As evident from studies, laws, and its provisions to compensate people for each project induce a decrease in income and hike in the family and personal expenses. This is added with reduced employability of the oustees as they were unskilled in other jobs triggered by their option for poor amenities and facilities including home types and new economic liabilities (Paul, 2013) causing downward movement of oustees in economic, livelihood and quality of life (Cernea, 2011). Though the law accommodates people to be resettled in groups or communities as far as possible often the social living of oustees has been broken and forced to adapt to new situations where social and individual identity and personal and social framework of space, place and time (Tradeu & McMokes, 2011) built on reciprocity and trust was at breach (Burton & Kagen, 2015). Stress and anxiety of acquisition and loss of self of oustees under the law are expressed as severe concerns of displacees but not reckoned adequately, and this commences before acquisition or displacement as the participants presumed loss of space, place, the experience of personhood that results from social isolation to poor self-image and blank future ahead of them (MoWat, 2015). The political marginalisation is often identified among the oustees as they experienced the denial of rights and discrimination or improper application of laws or manipulation of laws in its application by bureaucracy invoking the term like public purpose or eminent domain (Paul, 2013). This is even tacitly accepted as marginalisation as the government considered it 'matter of cause' (RFCTLARR 2013). The discrimination and manipulation of laws or rules often led to political marginalisation.

References

Adams, P. (1980, October 11). CRA and Aboriginals. *The Age*, p. 24.

Baviskar, A. (2011, December 10). What the Eyes Does not See: The Yamuna in the Imagination of Delhi. *Economic & Political Weekly*.

Belcher J R, D. F. (1990). *The Needs of Depressed Homeless persons: Designing Appropriate Services.* Retrieved October 05, 2017, from Community Mental Health: https://doi.org/10.107/bf00752776

Bourdieu, P. (1984). *Distinction: A Social Critique of the Judgement of Taste.* Cambridge, MA: Harvard University Press.

Bruinila, K. (2011). The Projectisation, Marketisation and Therapisation of Education. *European Education Research Journal, 10*(3), 421-432.

Burton, M., & Kagan, C. (1996). Rethinking Empowerment: Shared Action against Powerlessness. In M. &. Burton, & I. R.Spears (Ed.), *Psychology and Society: Radical Theory and Practice* (pp. 197-208). London: Pluto Press.

Burton, M., & Kagan, C. (2015, March). *Marginalisation.* Retrieved September 21, 2017, from http://www.compsy.org.uk/Chapter13all. PDF: http://www.compsy.org.uk/Chapter13all.PDF

Caro, D. H., & Mirazchiyski, P. (2011). Socioeconomic Gradients in Eastern European Countries: Evidence from PIRL 2006. *European Educational Research Journal, 11*(1), 96-110.

Chancer, L. S. (2013, September 04). *Sociology, Psychoanalysis, and Marginalisation: Unconscious Defense and Disciplinary Interests,* Sociological Forum, 28:3. Retrieved September 2017, from http://www.jstor.org/stable/43653892

Chaskar, A. G. (2015, October). *A Study of Female Marginalization Reflected in the Selected Five Indian Post Colonial Novels.* Retrieved December 8, 2017, from http://hdl.handle.net/10603/97291

Colson, E. (2003). Forced Migration and Anthropological Responses. *Journal of Refugee Studies, 16*(1), 1-18.

Cook, I., Bhatta, R., & Dinkar, V. (2013). The Multiple Displacements of Mangalore Special Economic Zone. *Economic & Political Weekly, XLVIII*(1).

Cresswell, T. (1996). *In Place/Out of Plae: Geography, Ideology and Transgression.* Minneapolis: University of Minnesota Press.

Development and Human Rights Protection. (2009, June). *Rajagiri Journal of Social Sciences, 5*(1), 25-44.

Doyal, L., & Gough, I. (1991). *The Theory of Human Need.* Newyork: Guilford.

Duncan, J., & Duncan, N. (2006). Aesthetic, Abjection, and White Privilege in Suburban New York. In R. Schein, *Race and Landscape in America* (p. 157076). New York: Routledge.

Fagan, B. (1993). Western Sydney as Outer Suburbia Marginalisation in Practice. In R. Howitt, *Marginalisation in Theory and Practice* (pp. 11-28). The University of Sydney.

Freire, P. &. (1994). *Learning to Question: A Pedagogy of Liberation.* Geneva: World Council of Churches.

George, A., & Irudaya, R. (2015, July). *Changing Cities and Changing Lives: Development Induced Displacement in Kochi, Kerala.* Retrieved September 21, 2017, from file:///C:/Users/norvy%20paul/Downloads/5-9-1-SM%20(1).pdf: file:///C:/Users/norvy%20paul/Downloads/5-9-1-SM%20(1).pdf

George, A., & Irudaya, R. (2017, August 21). *IDRC.* Retrieved September 21, 2017, from https://idl-bnc-idrc.dspacedirect.org: https://idl-bnc-idrc.dspacedirect.org/bitstream/handle/10625/56520/IDL-56520.pdf?sequence=2&isAllowed=y

Gropper, R. C. (1983). *Outsider in Urban Society by David Sibley*, Urban Anthropology, 12:1, Pp.79-81. (The Institute Inc) Retrieved 09 12, 2017, from http://jstor.org/stable/40552989

Hanson, J. (2012). Limits to Inclusion. *International Journal of Inclusive Education, 16*(1), 89-98.

Harvey, D. (1989). Class Structure and Residential Differentiation. In B. Blackwell, *The Urban Experience* (pp. 109-124). London: Oxford.

Harvey, D. (1992). Social Justice, Postmodernism and the City. *internatinational Journal of Urban and Regional Rsearch, 16*(4), 1-11.

Housing and Land Rights Network, Housing and Land Rights in India: Report for Habitat III P.54. (2017). Retrieved September 21, 2017, from http://goo.gl/gd3xpb.

Howitt, R. (1993). Marginalisation in Theory and Practice: A brief Conceptual Introduction. In R. Howitt, & R. Howitt (Ed.), *Marginalisation in Theory and Practice* (pp. 1-10). Sydney: university of Sydney.

Howitt, R. (1993). People Without Geography? Marginalisation and Indigenous Popele's in Geogrpahy Theory and Practice. In R. Howitt, *Marginalisatio in Theory and Practice.* 37-44: University of Sydney.

Howitt, R. (2016, January 4). *Marginalisation in Theory and Practice.* Retrieved Septemper 21, 2017, from file:///C:/Users/norvy%20paul/Downloads/Howitt,R_1993-ERRRUWP12-full.pdf

IDMC. (2015). *International Accountability Poject, Back to Development: A Call for What Development Could Be.* Retrieved September 17, 2017, from http://www.bit.ly/backtodevelopment.

IDMC. (2016, May). *Global Report on Internal Displacement.* Retrieved May 21, 2017, from goo.gl/CNtOG4

IDMC. (2016, May 11). *http:goo.gle/ZreJy1.* Retrieved September 21, 2017, from IDMC.

IDMC. (2017, May). *Global Report on Internal Displacement.* Retrieved from goo.gl.NbZPZa

Indiapedia. (2017, August). Retrieved October 05, 2017, from htttp://indipaedia.com/ind/index.php#homeless_people-_India

Introduction. (2014). In N. Paul (Ed.), *Development, Displacement and Marginalisation* (pp. 1-15). Cochin: VSS Publication.

Introduction. (2016). In N. Paul (Ed.), *Development, Displacement and Capitals* (pp. 1-6). Cochin: DCRD Publications.

Jenson, J. (2000). Backgrounder: Thinking about Marginalisation: What, Who and Why. Ottawa: Canadian Policy Research Networks Inc. http:www.cprn.org.

Kamalamma, K. (2010). *Kerb Publishers.* Retrieved October 05, 2017, from homelessness: http://www.krubpublishers.com/02#journal/T#Antc h#Antch#12#0#000#10#Web#Anth#12#2#000#abstract#PDF

Kanbur, R. (2007, April). *Conceptualising Economic Marginalisation.* Retrieved Sept 21, 2017, from www.people.cornell.edu: www.people. cornell.edu/pages/sk145

Kaushal, N. (2009, March). *Displacement: An Undesirable and Unwanted Consequence of Development,* The Indian Journal of Political Science. 70:1. Retrieved September 4, 2017, from http://www.jstor.org/ stable/41856497

Kolar, K. (2011). Resilience: Revisiting the Concept and its Utility for Social Research. *International Journal of Mental Health Addiction, 9,* 421-433.

Kothawale, S. R. (2015, October). *A Study of Female Marginalization Reflected in the Selected five Indian Post Colonial Novels.* Retrieved December 10, 2017, from http://hdl.handle.net/10603/97291

Kristiva, J. (1982). *Powers of Horror: An Essay on Abjection.* Newyork: Columbia University Press.

Kroll, J. (1986). A Survey of Homeless Adult in Urban Emergency. *Hospital and Community Psychiatry, 37*(3), 283-286.

La Gory, M. R. (1990, March 31). *Depression Among the Homeless.* Retrieved October 05, 2017, from Depression: https://www.ncbi.nlm.nih.gov/pubmed/2313079

Lemos, G. (2000). *Homelessness and Loneliness – the vant of conviviality.* London: Crisis.

Leonard, P. (1984). *Personality and Ideology: Towards a Materialistic Understanding of the Individual.* London: McMillion.

Measuring Social Capital and Displacement. (2011). In P. Jones, A. Francis, & R. S P (Eds.), *Eco-Social Justice: Issues and Challenges and Ways Forward* (pp. 45-64). Bangalore: Books for Change.

Messiou, K. (2012). Collaborating with Children in Exploring Marginalisation: An Approach to Inclusive Education. *International Journal of Inclusive Education, 16*(12), 1311-1322.

Messiou, K. (2012). Collaborating with Children in Exploring Marginalisation; An Approach to Inclusive Education. *International Journal of Inclusive Education, 16*(12), 1311-1322.

Michel, D. (2008). New Axioms for Reading the Landscape: paying attention to Political Economy and Social Justice. In J. Wescoat, & D. Johnson, *Political Economies of Landscape Change* (pp. 20-50). Dorrech, The Netherlands: Springer.

Mitchell, D. (2008). New Axioms for Reading for landscapes: Paying Attention to Political economy and Social Justice. In J. &. Wescot (Ed.), *Political Economics of Landscape Change* (pp. 20-50). Dordrecht, Netherlands: Springer.

Mohanty, M. (2009, April-June). *Development and Tribal Displacement: Reflections on Core Issues,* The Indian Journal of Political Science, 70:2, pp.345-350. Retrieved September 04, 2017, from http://www.jstor.org/stable/42743900

Mowat, J. G. (2015). Toward a New Conceptualisation of Marginalisation. *European Educational Research Journal, 14*(5), 454-76.

Munn, P., & Llloyd, G. (2005). Exclusion and Excluded People. *British Educational Research Journal, 31*(2), 205-55.

Nadani, W., & Swain, M. (2016). *Pushed Aside: Displaced for Development in India.* IDMC & Norwegian Refugee Council.

Patkar, M. (1998, September). *The People's Policy on Development, Displacement and Resettlement: Need to Link Displacement and Development,* Economic and Political Weekly, 33:38, pp.2432-2433. Retrieved September 19-25, 2017, from http://www.jstor.org/stable/4407178

Paul, Norvy (2013). In C. F. Kerala, & S. T (Ed.), *Community Food Security and Social Transformation* (Ed.) (pp. 5-11). New Delhi: Excellent Publishing House.

Land Acquisition Act (2013, September). *Ministry of Law and Justice.* Retrieved November 20, 2017, from http://indiacode.nic.in/acts-in-pdf/302013.pdf

Paul Norvy (2014). In Understanding Social Capital Kerala, & N. Paul (Ed.). Cochin: VSS Publications.

Paul, Norvy (2016). A Case Study of Airport and Climate Change in Kerala. (2016). In N. Paul, & P. Jones (Eds.), *Social Work and Health: Inclusive practice, Research and Education* (pp. 178-192). Cochin: DCRD Publications.

Paul, Norvy (2012). A Social Work Students Identification of Critical Pathways in Relating Social Work Theorum with Practicum. (2012). *Indian Journal of Social Sciences, 1*(2), 6-14.

Paul, Norvy (2013) Commercial Sex Workers and Awareness about HIV/AIDS. (2013). *Health Action, 40*(10), 17-20.

Paul, Norvy (2012) Community Agricultural Literacy and Community Empowerment: A Case Study on Kadakkarappally Coastal Panchayath in Kerala. (2012, June). *Indian Journal of Social Sciences, 1,* 32-41.

Paul, Norvy (2009) Development, Displacement and Human Rights. (2009). *Rajagiri Journal of Social Sciences, 10*(1), 15-20.

Paul, Norvy (2014) Displacement and Marginalisation: A Case Study on Vallarpadam International Tranship Container Terminal in Kerala. (2014). In N. Paul (Ed.), *Development, Displacement and Marginalisation* (pp. 273-289). Cochin: VSS Publications.

Paul, Norvy (2015) Domestic Migration in Kerala: Issues, Challenges and Responses: An Analytical Reading. (2015, December). *EPRA International Journal of Economic and Business Review, 3*(12), 71-74.

Paul, N. (2013). *Development, Displacement and Marginalization.* Cochin: VSS Publications.

Paul, N. (Ed.). (2016). *Development, Displacement and Capitals.* Cochin: DCRD Publications.

Petras, J. &. (2001). *Globalisation Unmasked: Imperialism in the 21*[st] *Century.* London: Zen Books.

Petrou, A., Angelides, P., & Leigh, J. (2009). Beyond the Difference: From Margins to Inclusion. *International Journal of Inclusive Education, 13*(5), 439-448.

Paul, Norvy & P X, Francina (2013) Psychological Empowerment in the Women Empowerment Programmes of Neighbourhood Groups: A Study on Kudumbasree Mission of Kerala. (2013). In P. Tarumar (Ed.), *Global Vision of Women Empowerment* (pp. 49-54). New Delhi: Victorious Publication.

Razar, M., Friedman, V. J., & Warshofky, B. (2013). Schools as Agents of Social Exclusion and Inclusion. *International Journal of Inclusive Education, 17*(11), 1152-1170.

Reddy, R. K. (2008, July-September). Rehabilitation or Re-exclusion. *Indian Journal of Political Science,* 505-518.

Reporter, S. (2017, September 15). *www.thehindu.com.* Retrieved October 05, 2017, from http://www.thehindu.com/todays-paper/tp-national/tp-karnataka/there-are-746-homeless-people-here-survey/article3622305.ece

Paul, N. and Meena Karimi (2013). Resilience a Way Towards Social Inclusion: A Comparative Study on Vulnerability and Invulnerability among Persons with Disability. (2013). In V. D. Rajath, & R. G. Clive (Eds.), *Socially Vulnerable: Inclusion and Strategies* (pp. 197-210). Udupi, Mangalore: Dept of Sociology, Crossland College.

Paul, N. (2016). Understanding the Health of Transgender Women in India. (2016). *De Paul Journal of Scientific Research, 3*(2), 211-225.

Paul, N. (2016). Understanding the Land Acquisition Act and R & R Policy of India. (2016). In N. Paul (Ed.), *Development, Displacement and Capitals* (pp. 23-49). Cochin: DCRD Publications.

Rose, M. (2002). The Landscape and Labyrinths. *Geoforum, 33*, 455-67.

Samling, C. L., Ghosh, A. K., & Hazra, S. (2015). *Resettlement and Rehabilitation: Indian Scenario DECCMA Working Paper, Deltas, Vulnerability and Climate Change: Migration and Adaptation, IDRC Project Number 107642.* Retrieved September 21, 2017, from www.deccma.com: www.deccma.com

Shils, E. (1954). Authoritarianism: "right' and "left". In R. a. M.Jahoda, *Studies in the Scope and Method of the Authoritarian Personality* (pp. 119-220). Glencoe: Free Press.

Shodganga.(201708).*Shodganaga.*RetrievedSeptember21,2017,fromhttp:// shodhganga.inflibnet.ac.in/bitstream/10603/97291/8/08_chapter1. pdf: http://shodhganga.inflibnet.ac.in/bitstream/10603/97291/8/08_ chapter1.pdf

Sibely, D. (2004). Introduction-Borders and Boundaries. In D. Sibley, D. Jackson, M. Sibley, & N. Washbourne, *Cultural Geography: A Critical Dictionary of Key Ideas* (pp. 153-54). http://ebookcentral.proquest.com.

Sibely, D. (2004). Public/Private. In D. Sibley, D. Jackson, M. Sibley, & N. Washbourne, *Cultural Geography: A Critical Dictionary of Key Ideas* (pp. 155-159). http://ebookscentral.proquest.com.

Sibley, D. (1995). *An Introduction to Geographies of Exclusion.* Retrieved September 21, 2017, from http://ww.litstudies.org/: http:// ww.litstudies.org/SUPA/SIBLEY%20Intro%20to%20Geographies%20 of%20Exclusion%20Critical%20Encounters-%20Ch.%2046.pdf

Soott, H. V. (2009). Representation, Politics Of. In R. Kitchin, & N. Trift (Eds.), *International Encyclopedia of Human Geography* (Vol. 9, p. 457). Amsterdam: Elsevier.

Sullivan G, B. A. (2000, October). *Pathways to Homelessness Among the Mentally Ill.* Retrieved October 05, 2017, from Homelessness: http://homelesshub.ca/about-homelessness/mentalhealth/depression#and#suicide

Trudeau, D., & McMorran, C. (2011). The Geographies of Marginalisation. In V. J. Del Casino Jr, M. E. Thomas, P. Cloke, & R. Panelli, *A Companion to Social Geography* (pp. 437-453). London: Blackwell Publishing Ltd. Retrieved September 21, 2017, from http://profile.nus.edu.sg/fass/jpscmm/2011%20trudeau_mcmorran.pdf

UNDP. (2016, May 11). *DRAFT Guidance Note: UNDP Social and Environmental Standards.* Retrieved November 20, 2017, from Standard 5: Displacement and Resettlement: http://intranet.undp.org/unit/bpps/Dl/SES_Toolkit/default.aspx.

Vanclay, F. (2017). *Project-induced displacement and resettlement: from impoverishment risks to an opportunity for development?* Retrieved November 22, 2017, from Impact Assessment and Project Appraisal: https://doi.org/10.1080/14615517.2017.1278671

Walicki, N. (2017, July 17). *briefing-paper-2030-agenda.* Retrieved November 23, 2017, from internal-displacement.org: http://www.internal-displacement.org/assets/publications/2017/20170713-idmc-briefing-paper-2030-agenda.pdf

Washbourne, N. (2004). Globalisation/Globality. In D. Sibley, D. Jackson, M. Sibley, & N. Washbourne, *Cultural Geography: A Critical Dictionary of Key Ideas* (pp. 161-165). http:ebookscentral.proquest.com.

Wright, M. (2006). *Disposable Women and Other Myths of Global Capitalism.* New York: Routledge.

A Gender-Based Perspective on the Internal Migrants' Issue Associated with COVID-19 Pandemic

Anupama Haridas[6]

Abstract

Since the report of the first case in India on 30 January 2020, the COVID – 19 pandemic is the most disproportionately affected health crisis in recent times with more than Fifty thousand confirmed cases in the country by May 2020. The subsequent lockdown to curb the virus's spread has caused severe economic devastation and almost crushed informal workers' livelihood, small scale entrepreneurs and farmers. A significant chunk is the Internal Migrants or migrating people within the country, mainly for economic improvement. According to the World Bank, at least 40 million internal migrants have been impacted by lockdown, even losing their lives in the process of reaching their native. Under such a crisis, the women affected are either wives of migrant workers or low paid or informal sector workers like domestic workers, daily waged building workers. Wives of migrant workers don the hat of familial heads in their villages and depend on their husbands' remittance to run families. As a patriarchal society, the non-availability of these monthly income places them in a vulnerable position. As informal sector workers, women have to face the mental trauma of abandonment by their employers, coupled with their domestic responsibilities to make ends meet. This article tries to delve into women's crisis under such circumstances, like loss of livelihood, vulnerability to domestic violence, improper menstrual hygiene, and reproductive health, which lack widespread media attention.

Keywords: Internal migrants, Female Migrants, COVID-19, Gender

---

6   Assistant Professor, Department of Social Work, AJK Arts & Science College, Coimbatore, India. Email: anupamaharidas@gmail.com

Introduction

Till the COVID-19 pandemic hit the Indian subcontinent, the migrants were invisible workers toiling hard for their bleak future. The pandemic and subsequent lockdown were followed by news of the vast majority of migrant workers hurrying to reach their homes set in mostly rural villages in India. It was indeed a pathetic journey where migrants were seen in a seemingly endless voyage mostly on foot, forced by insecurity due to the unavailability of food, shelter and employment and the expectation that a home is waiting for them at the end of it, the news reported the unfortunate deaths of some of these migrant workers (Sen, 2020).

The exhaustion caused by long-distance travelling by foot and inadequate facilities enroute has resulted in many migrant workers' deaths. Much uproar is made over how they died, but their identities like names and other details about what they do for a living are often missed. Thus, disregarding and sidelining an entire population of basic service providers and workers. The workers lack an identity of their own. Their place of birth, family details and other personal details go unnoticed and come under one category that is 'Migrant Worker'. They were on the horns of a dilemma, between starvation and pandemic. Since the Partition between India and Pakistan, it was the first time India was facing such a kind of mass migration without food or accommodation for a night (Biswas, 2020). Women migrant workers belong to even lower strata when it comes to the visibility of their trauma.

From the demographic point of view, migration is one of the three basic components of population growth of any area, including fertility and mortality. But both fertility and mortality operate within the biological framework, and migration does not. It influences the size, composition and distribution of the population. More importantly, migration influences people's social, political, and economic lives (Lusome & Bhagat, 2006). Internal migration is the type of migration which involves a change of residence within national borders (Dang, 2005).

Since India's first case on 30 January 2020, the COVID – 19 pandemic is the most disproportionately affected health crisis in recent times with more than 10.2 million confirmed cases, 9.76 Million recoveries and 1,48,000 deaths in the country by 27 December 2020. To curb the spread of the novel virus and keep infections at bay. A nationwide 21-day lockdown was called for by the Government of India, to prevent the spread of COVID-19 infections in the short term, although its impact is yet to be known.

Almost half the world's workers are under the immediate threat of losing jobs, the International Labour Organization (ILO) said (Brownsell, 2020). The sobering disclosure will ring alarm bells in economies throughout the world, with every nation on the planet likely to be affected by the damaging fallout from the spread of coronavirus. Around 1.6 billion workers in the informal economy – nearly half of the global workforce, and those at the riskiest echelons of the employment ladder – are in danger of losing their livelihoods, said the ILO, the oldest agency of the United Nations, in its latest report according to Al-Jazeera on April 2020 (Brownsell, 2020). As COVID-19 measures paused international trade, shut down airports and left businesses bankrupt, tens of millions of people have lost their jobs. Moreover, for many, being unemployed in the middle of a pandemic means losing their income and losing healthcare access. According to the World Bank (PTI, April 2020), the lockdown in India has impacted the livelihoods of a large proportion of the country's nearly 40 million internal migrants. Around 50,000–60,000 moved from urban centres to rural areas of origin in a few days.

Like many other crises, migrants may be specifically at risk to the direct and indirect impact of COVID19. Their capacity to prevent the infection, receive adequate healthcare and cope with the economic, social and psychological consequences of the pandemic depends on diverse factors, which includes; their living and working conditions, the dearth of understanding of their cultural and linguistic diversity in service provision, xenophobia, their limited local knowledge and networks, access to rights and extent of incorporation in post community often related to their migration status (Lorenzo, 2020).

Sex wise differences are very prominent in Indian Migration data. A majority of migrants are females (Lusome & Bhagat, 2006). The poorer amongst them work in brick kilns, as farm labour or on construction sites. The women who have a basic education work in the service industry in cities, as salesgirls, beauticians, or waitresses. Many young women are employed in several small-scale industries, such as the garment sector. Surprisingly, the face published to represent a migrant worker is almost always male (Ramya & Lakshmi, 2018). Women migrant workers or the wives of migrant workers who chose to stay back in their villages have to face similar trauma during this pandemic. While the former has the mental trauma of abandonment by employers coupled with their domestic responsibilities, the latter has to ensure there is fuel and water at home even though there is no monthly remittance this time from their husband. People from North-Eastern states of India, differ in their appearance with people from the rest of the country, owing to their Mongoloid facial features which resembles more with Chinese nationals. The young women migrants from the Northeast are especially targeted because of their different looks, which is a severe form of gender and racial prejudice.

This paper tries to delve deeper into the issues of internal migrant workers in India, with special reference to female migrants generally and especially during the COVID-19 pandemic and subsequent lockdown. The author also relies on secondary data to understand the government's measures to support issues of female migrants during the lockdown and afterwards. With the newly acquired visibility of migrant issues due to COVID-19 pandemic, will the government address their issues more inclusively, especially those of women migrant workers?

1. Living Conditions and Pattern of Migration

UN (1993) defines migration as a movement pertaining to crossing administrative boundaries during a given period. This article focuses on internal migration in India, which has been defined by Dang (2005), as a movement pertaining to change of residence in the confines of the national borders. Migration also includes the disturbance of work, interruption in schooling, social life, and other patterns of life (Adzei & Sakyi, 2014). Migration is a cyclic behaviour involving the regular, seasonal or annual journey from one place to another and back again. Internal migration is considered a vital livelihood strategy in India. India's labour market has mainly been identified by people's movement from rural and backward areas toward developed areas searching for livelihood (Turrey, 2016).

The internal migrant workers in almost all informal sectors live in unsatisfactory conditions in India. They often face inadequate provision of drinking water facilities, the sanitary conditions are unhygienic, and most live in open spaces or makeshift shelters (Rani & Shylendra, 2001). As most of them are not legally registered, they cannot avail the Public Distribution System (PDS) provided by the Government (Turrey, 2016). Internal migration is substantially greater in percentage than external or international migration in India. It is in response to a variety of economic, social, cultural and demographic factors. The World Economic Forum's report on migration and cities states, "interstate migration in India has increased twice in this millennium compared to the earlier decade of 1991-2001" (Ramya & Lakshmi, 2018). Sanitation is one of the important yardsticks to measure socio-economic development in a developing nation. Improved sanitation leads to improved health and improved environmental quality, thus supporting economic growth and sustainable development goals. Non-ending urban migration, crowding of urban poor in slums without safe water supply, inadequate sanitation facilities and increasing resource constraints have led to poor quality of life and community health in slums. In a study conducted on internal labour migrants across 13 Indian cities in India, about 38% migrants do not have access to sanitary latrines and practice open defecation. This situation is alarming. Only 36% of the households possessed their latrines. Hence, migrants are far behind the national scenario with respect to access to sanitation. The study also says that, concerning electricity connection, poor migrants are far behind the national scenario of slum dwellers with a relatively higher proportion of households either do not have a connection or draw electricity from street lights (Akoijam, Brogen & Kerketta, 2017).

2. COVID-19 Pandemic

The seventh virus known to attack the human respiratory system, SARS-COV-2 is a genus Beta coronavirus. It affects the respiratory tract mainly by binding to the ACE-2 receptors chiefly found in lungs and heart. Countries like the United States, Italy, France, and the United Kingdom suffered great losses during the COVID-19 pandemic, and large numbers of deaths were reported (David, Dabire and Ljzab, 2020). Coronavirus continues its spread globally, with nearly 40 million confirmed cases in 189 countries and more than one million deaths (BBC News, 2020). No other pandemic has had impact and implications in humanity's socio-economic areas in recent times, as COVID 19. Michael J. Buchmeier, professor of infectious diseases, explains that this virus, while deadly, is thought to be about as contagious as the seasonal flu, with one person infecting another two or three.

In contrast, with measles, where one person can infect 18, or chickenpox, one person can infect 12. However, these two highly contagious diseases are controlled by vaccination. But it is a virus that has never been seen in humans, so absolutely no one is immune to it. That added to the fact that it spreads as quickly from person to person as influenza, and infects the upper respiratory system, is what makes it so dangerous without a vaccine. Because the COVID-19 virus is found in the upper airway — including the mouth and nose — the infection can be spread through coughs, sneezes, huffing and puffing, and likely even loud talking.

Moreover, we learn that infected people are unknowingly spreading the virus days before they begin to experience symptoms. Some may not experience symptoms at all. Neither SARS nor MERS spread as quickly or widely and "is capable of causing very severe disease" (UCI Health, 2020). Indian Government has been trying to fight the spread of infections through methods like 41 days' lockdown, social distancing and self-quarantine. In India, the first case was identified in Kerala's southern state in a student who came back from Corona epicentre Wuhan. Maharashtra has till now came out with an alarmingly high rate of the pandemic. The authorities say the lockdown is key to saving lives, but the lack of planning has hit the country's poorest and most vulnerable citizens hard. In the absence of work, many migrant workers are now dependent on food handouts from governments or charities for survival – some reduced to begging. "There are two types of stranded, the visible and the invisible," Anindita Adhikari, of the Stranded Workers Action Network (SWAN), says. "Those who are in shelters are visible. But there are a large number of people who are not in shelters. They live under the flyovers and sleep on footpaths, or stuck in workplaces, labour camps or slums. Prashanth Bhushan, lawyer-activist, says the condition of the shelters is also uneven. "In some feeding centres, people have complained of 2km-long food queues, and there have been stampedes over food running out" (Pandey, April 2020).

Migrants may be particularly vulnerable to the direct and indirect impact of COVID19, as in many other cases. Their ability to avoid the infection, receive adequate healthcare and cope with the economic, social and psychological impact of the pandemic can be affected by a variety of factors, including their living and working conditions, lack of consideration of their cultural and linguistic diversity in service provision, xenophobia, their limited knowledge about the local community and lack of networks. Also, reduced access to rights and inclusion in the post community is often related to their migration status (Lorenzo, 2020). In 2017, the ILO stressed the necessity to respect human rights as a response to the crisis and outlined a strategic approach, including confirming basic income security for those losing jobs during this period, along with advanced social protection coverage. Also, the Migrant Workers (Supplementary Provisions) Convention, 1975, states that migrant workers who have resided legally in the territory for employment, shall not be regarded as being in an irregular situation for the mere fact that they have lost their employment (for instance as a result of the economic impact of the COVID-19). However, a question (Ellina, 2020) arises: how far nations can adopt these standards in the changing employment scenario caused due to the pandemic?

3. Gender and Migration

Recent statistics reveal that a big chunk of the migrants within India are female. The most impoverished work in brick kilns, as farm labour or on construction sites, and some working in an industry like garments and apparels sectors migrate and live in hostels close to their place of work (Shanthi, 2000). Female migration in India is reportedly almost three times that of male migration. Although most of it is said to be marriage induced, it may not be strictly true (Shanthi, 2000). Female migrations are classified into three types in the last decade by Ramya and Lakshmi (2018):

1. Autonomous female migration: Middle-class girls moving to cities to work at Export Processing Units, Textile factory, Food Industry, Assembling Units. for improving their livelihood opportunities

2. Relay Migration: In recent years, relay migration is seen when a rural family sends their daughters as a maid and cook at households in the urban area. Second daughter steps into the shoes of the elder one and then the third daughter replaces the second, and so on, as each one gets married.

3. Family Migration: In this case, the wife, instead of staying back in the village prefers to join her husband in the hope of getting some employment in the urban area.

Table 1: Internal Migrants by Sex, India 1981-2001 (in Million)

Years	Lifetim Migrants (in millions)			F-M ratio of migrants	Percentage of migrants to total Population		
	Persons	Male(M)	Female(F)	F/M	Persons	Male	Female
1981	201.6	59.2	142.4	2.41	30.3	17.6	43.9
1991	225.9	61.1	164.8	2.71	27.4	14.6	41.2
2001	309.4	90.7	218.7	2.41	30.6	17.5	44.6

Source: Census in India 1981, 1991& 2001(Cited in Singh, 2016).

4. The Pandemic and Its Impact on Female Migrants

The year 2020 is the 110th anniversary of International Women's Day celebration and slated to be a critical year, a new beginning for the centuries-long struggle. It is the 25th year of the Beijing Platform Action, formulated to bring about path-breaking outcomes for gender equality. Instead, Feminism has been locked-down, and the progress of achieving gender-equality seems to be retarding, arrested in the cuffs of the pandemic. In content appearing from across the world, the pandemic has been appearing a disaster for gender justice. It has exposed the existing inequalities and even to some extent, further deepened them (Kanksshi & Anjali, 2020).

COVID-19 pandemic, one of the worst happenings in humanity's history, has broken the health, the social and economic structure of the entire world. Government of every country is trying to control the pandemic by imposing several measures, including lockdown and discipline of social distancing. In India, because of the diversified population, different income groups, and people's social habits, the extended lockdown has severely impacted the lifestyle. Daily wage earners and migrant workers are severe sufferers. Extended lockdown leads the workers to exhaust their handful of savings forcing them to start their hometown journey. While struggling for daily bread and butter, the unavailability of transport facilities worsens their journey.

According to UN Women, the impacts and implications of the COVID-19 are different for men and women and may create greater inequalities for people who are in vulnerable positions, such as migrants. International Organisation of Migration (IOM) in its World Migration Report 2020 says, around 74% of the service industry is represented by women, which also includes domestic work, and in many cases experience job insecurity. During the COVID-19 outbreak, mobility and travel restrictions are threatening the income of migrant women. Furthermore, the impact of the employment crisis under COVID-19 may disproportionately affect less protected population groups, such as women and migrants. The pandemic has led to the loss of income and jobs for many of the 8.5 million women migrant domestic workers, with their health, safety and well-being often ignored. The economic downturn has left women migrant workers sending fewer remittances, a lifeline for families and communities in their countries of origin, especially during crisis times. Some of the significant implications on women migrant workers during lockdown areas listed below.

4.1 Loss of Jobs

Workers are reported to be losing their jobs in large numbers in some sectors, especially women workers (Pandit, September 2020) because they tend to work in the informal economy. In unstable conditions without formal employment contracts and limited coverage by labour laws, employers can more readily end their employment in response to the economic decline caused by the COVID-19 pandemic. Women migrant domestic workers are at particular risk of losing their jobs due to COVID-19 as they tend to be in informal employment, often unregistered and excluded from labour protections. The lack of assistance and protection mechanisms for women migrant domestic workers, their social isolation due to language and cultural differences, and the limited availability of accurate information heighten their vulnerabilities during the pandemic (UN Women).

4.2 Domestic Violence

Within confined spaces, there are issues related to security, money and health conditions. Therefore, gender-based violence exacerbates individual families, plus living conditions are not even healthy and can lead to violence against the household's susceptible members. Many women are shut in with their perpetrators in the imposed lockdown to contain the virus, and helpline numbers are limited in scope due to relocation or mobility restrictions. According to a recent report in India Today, all around the globe, but more particularly in India, the instances of domestic violence against women and young girls have increased by 100 % since the lockdown (Kanksshi & Anjali, 2020). Another report says, Domestic violence cases in India have increased since the March 24 lockdown with husbands venting their frustration on wives, who have no escape from their abusers (PTI, 2020).

Women migrant domestic workers are encountered by a significant risk of abuse, leaving them susceptible and unable to reach their homes due to heightened travel restrictions. Violations of the human rights of women migrant workers in domestic and care work – excessively long hours, no defined days off, lack of social guard (maternity leave, sick leave and employment injury benefit), sexual and gender-based violence and limitations on freedom of movement –are further skyrocketed during the pandemic (Laura, 2020). Domestic violence numbers have shot-up because of forced co-existence, cramped and restricted living conditions, economic insecurity, and worries about contracting the virus. This is exacerbated for migrant women who stumble with language barriers and lack of accessible information to essential services (health, justice and social services), which have, in turn, been severely truncated by COVID-19.

According to UN Women (2020), migrant women may be compelled to stay with potential perpetrators and may not leave abusive relationships because of travel constraints, quarantine measures or job loss. Migrant women and girls who undergo gender-based violence battle to access healthcare and essential support services due to constraints on movement closed clinics and scares of contracting coronavirus. This points to male psychological anguish due to loss of work and income for short-term and subsequent brutal behaviour and/or confinement at home with abusive partners. Psychological wellbeing of women will be more adversely affected than men's from financial and emotional stress, combined with physical violence (Laura, 2020).

4.3 Menstrual and Reproductive Health

Adolescent girls and women among migrant workers in India have been encountering enormous difficulties whilst living in lockdown. Since the lockdown extension, the supply of essentials, including sanitary items, has been affected, particularly because it was not previously counted among essential goods. A major cause of concern for many women migrant workers and their adolescent girls is menstrual hygiene, as they travel back to their hometowns either on foot or in packed trucks. With hardly any washrooms along highways and meagre money to buy sanitary napkins, they hope to get their next menses only after reaching home. Horrifying experience of Lakshmi, a single mother of three girls, hailing from Chattisgarh was reported in The New Express Daily (Jose, May 2020). They had started from Bengaluru and spent ten days already on the road, hitching rides with trucks. Lakshmi could not buy sanitary napkins for her daughter, since they have been mostly travelling on highways, where shops are closed due to the COVID lockdown. Similarly, many migrant women labourers, who use cotton pads during their menstrual cycle, are compelled to use un-sanitised cloth pieces. They have to walk much distance, and there is no privacy to change. The limited or, sometimes, no access to running water, makes matters worse. "We use one bottle of water to relieve ourselves behind the bushes. Washing the cloth is impossible as there is not enough water," Lakshmi's 16-year-old daughter said (Jose, May 2020).

4.4. Increased Risk of Contraction

It is an everyday norm that women are the chief caregivers in their homes, communities, and health facilities, which puts them at a greater risk of contracting COVID-19. Migrant women working as domestic helps in households caring for children, the ailing, and the aged, face an increased threat of contracting the virus as they are mostly in direct contact with people who may have COVID-19. Majority of women migrant domestic workers, cleaners and care workers in COVID-19 have had to deal with increased workloads to guarantee cleanliness and hygiene and give the indispensable care, often without personal protective paraphernalia or overtime reimbursement (Jose, 2020).

4.5 Socio-Economic Implications

As they do not have the necessary documentation to fulfil the Know Your Customer (KYC) details needed for banks, most migrants cannot access banking facilities. Hence, to send money to families left behind, they are forced to rely on informal methods. This primary economic issue is exacerbated for women migrants.

COVID-19 has exacerbated the weight of unpaid care work on most women, including migrant women, as an outcome of the closure of schools, kindergartens, creches and other public and social services. As part of a comprehensive response to the pandemic, this extra burden on women needs to be addressed (UN Women, 2020). Sushmita Dev states "Nobody is thinking of women in crisis as there is a lack of gendered approach in handling crises. Women make 65% of the unorganised sector. All of a sudden, they are rendered unemployed. The burden of unpaid care work is also shouldered by women alone in most households. It is a double whammy" (Cited in Kanksshi & Anjali, 2020).

Northeast India's situation has a much-worsened situation and from where thousands of young men, and women, travel a long way to work in our bigger cities. Many people in Northeast India have mongoloid eyes and facial features that resemble people from other East-Asian nations like China, Japan or Korea. During these times of COVID-19, the young women from the Northeast, are harassed because they look different, have been especially targeted. Since COVID-19 started in Wuhan, China, there have been several deplorable incidents of women being spat upon, even assaulted, and called 'Corona' because they resembled Chinese people in their looks. This represents the worst of racial and gender prejudice (Kalpana, 2020).

5. Women Migrant Issues and Media

1. [7]The pregnant wife of a migrant labourer, who walked over 100 km from Ludhiana in Punjab, delivered a girl baby shortly after reaching Ambala in Haryana but the baby died shortly after birth.

2. [8]A tenacious 15-year-old Jyoti asked her father to sit on the rear side carrier of her cycle, as they were stuck in Gurugram due to nation-wide lockdown, and covering 1200 km in seven days, took him to his native place.

3. Two women migrant worker delivered babies while travelling to Odisha in separate trains on Sunday.

4. In Uttarpradesh' Lalitpur district, a woman migrant was forced to give birth under a roadside tree, after covering 500 kilometres on foot.

5. In COVID-19, there have been several cases of rampant discrimination against the north-east Indian community who have distinct mongoloid features. As in any other case, women are easy targets here also (Kalpana, 2020).

6. A 12-year-old Adivasi girl was walking home to Chattisgarh from the chilli fields of Telangana. Jamlo Madkam walked 140 kilometres in three days and finally collapsed due to exhaustion, dehydration and muscle fatigue, 60 kilometres away from her home (Nisha, 2020).

7. Another migrant woman dragged a sizeable wheeled suitcase down the national highway with an exhausted toddler sleeping on top. On her way home in Madhya Pradesh (Nisha, 2020).

8. vreena Khatoon, a 35-year-old woman, collapses and dies while travelling from Ahmedabad to Katihar on a Shramik train via the Muzaffarpur ordeal without adequate food and water. Her infant

---

7   May 23, 2020, www.indiatoday.in
8   May 21, 2020, www.hindusthantimes.com

child was attempting to play with her covered corpse on the railway station (Nisha, 2020).

9. A 58-year-old woman, Virottama Surendranatha Shukla, collapses and dies under the blazing sun while she was standing in the long line to register for a Shramik train from the Vasai station. All we know is that she was in her late fifties and had a preexisting medical condition (Nisha, 2020).

6. Towards More Inclusiveness: Measures by Government

1. At Basani, Varanasi, Rural Women Technology Park (RWTP) supported by the Department of Science and Technology (DST) is making facemask as per WHO guidelines and joined India's fight against the COVID 19 pandemic by extending a helping hand to migrant workers by training and engaging women in distributing food as well as hand sanitisers. The RWTP staff provide online training to create digital designs and generate finished products to support the women beneficiaries to utilize their time at home during the lockdown period productively. Approximately, 250 women were trained to install 'ArogyaSetu App' and send the ArogyaSetu App's link to more than 4000 families digitally. The app is of tremendous help to rural women for getting the information related to COVID-19. The RWTP concentrates on Women Empowerment through Skill Enhancement, Entrepreneurship Development, and Providing Market Linkages.

2. Thirty-six hours after the lockdown announcement, a relief package worth $24.4 billion and accompanying measures to help alleviate the adverse impact on the most vulnerable segments of the population was declared by India's finance minister. Foremost among these aims to provide food security via the government's Public Distribution System (PDS), and social security benefits including cash-based aid via Direct Benefit Transfers (DBT) to provide relief to "800 million poor Indians" under Pradhan Mantri Gareeb Kalyan Yojana (PMGKY).

3. A slew of other relief measures have also been announced, such as home delivery of cash and pensions by India Post in some states, and further livelihood support. These measures constitute the first of potentially many relief packages announced by the government, focusing on widening a safety net for the poorest of the poor. For those migrants who are neither beneficiaries of the National Food Security Act (2013), or NFSA, nor possess State cards (Sreenivasan, 2020), the government has promised a free supply of 5 kg of food grain per person and 1 kg chana (Split chickpeas) per family per month for two months,

4. The Finance Minister acknowledged the importance of the MGNREGS in procuring jobs to returning workers in rural areas. The government noted that work off-take increased in May. This followed directions from the Centre to restart the scheme after work hours fell drastically in April. The Centre has presently advised States/ Union Territories to work through the scheme and extend this to the monsoon season and provide jobs in plantations, horticulture, and livestock-related work. The CMIE's latest unemployment survey report also found that while various segments (small traders, salaried employees, entrepreneurs) have faced tremendous job losses, the number of farmers in the survey had risen, indicating that farm work has been a source of livelihood during the lockdown (Sreenivasan, 2020).

5. To take care of the vast internal migrants during their travel during the lockdown, on March 28, the central government directed states to use the State Disaster Response Fund to provide accommodation to travelling migrants. States were asked to set up relief camps along highways with medical facilities to encourage people to stay in these camps during the lockdown. The Women Development and Child Welfare Department had set up a counter at the Medchal transit point, where it distributed travel kits to women and children. The kits comprised soaps and sanitary pads.

6. In an order issued on April 29, the Ministry of Home Affairs allowed states to co-ordinate individually to transport migrants

using buses. On May 1, the Indian Railways resumed passenger movement (for the first time since March 22) with Shramik Special trains to facilitate the movement of migrants stranded outside their home state. Between May 1 and June 3, Indian Railways operated 4,197 Shramik trains transporting more than 58 lakh migrants. Top states from where Shramik trains commenced are Gujarat and Maharashtra and states where the trains terminated are Uttar Pradesh and Bihar (Madhunika, 2020).

7. NGO's like Praveen Lata Sansthan, Jagriti Sewa Sansthan and Stonesoup Trust have identified migrants, slum-dwellers, daily wagers and tribal women, women working under the MNREGA scheme, women living in slums in and across semi-urban and remote villages of Ajmer, Bundi, Bhilwara, Kota, Alwar, Jaipur Rural, Mumbai and Bangalore and seven districts in Uttar Pradesh. The latter need help during their monthly cycle. Through Give India Online NGO, these organizations do fundraising to provide reusable sanitary pads to these identified women during the pandemic.

7. The Missing Links in Inclusive Service Requirements During COVID-19

1. Universal accessibility to gender-responsive social protection measures assures that every individual, irrespective of migration status, has social safety coverage in times of need. During the COVID-19 pandemic, such access would help ensure that women migrant workers who lose their jobs would have a basic income and those with caregiving responsibilities would receive the necessary family and child benefits (Shashaank & Jithin, 2020).

2. Migrant women workers in informal sectors who are left jobless should be given alternative employment through Public Works Programmes, supporting women by employment generation through mask-making or other protective equipment.

3. Women migrant workers should have complete access to comprehensive health care, including sexual and reproductive health services. All residents should have access to COVID-19 testing, irrespective of their migration status. This is not only a human right under international law but also a commendable practise from a public health perspective (UN WOMEN, 2020).

4. To ascertain menstrual and sanitary hygiene, the distribution of sanitary pads and providing clean temporary washroom facilities along the highways would relieve women migrants travelling to their hometown.

5. Gender-responsive transport policies will have far-fledged implications for migrant women. While working towards a larger goal of making public transport inclusive and safe, intermediate steps including designated 'women's-only' transport for migrant women willing to return may be considered (Ipsita, 2020).

6. Mass awareness is important for effective dissemination of relief measures. Communication of relief measures must be done clearly and widely, and central and state governments should ensure their easy accessibility. Availability of essentials such as income and nutrition and effectively distributing the means to access these benefits – are instrumental in controlling the pandemic.

7. Social security schemes run by state governments are often subject to domicile restrictions, excluding migrant workers from providing benefits. Besides, while federal schemes like the PMGKY are universal, migrant workers are more likely to be excluded due to the mobility associated with their livelihood, their participation in the informal sector, and their absence from associations' rosters, which work towards ensuring outreach to the migrants.

8. The works of various NGOs working towards enhancing migrant visibility should be supplemented by significant improvements in collecting and compiling reliable data on migrants from the

government. This will ascertain in making economic growth more inclusive for migrants.

9. Functioning of toll-free Helplines for female migrant workers during the pandemic and afterwards too.

10. They are to be guaranteed Human Rights of Migrant women, irrespective of their migration status during these testing times and beyond, in compliance with international law. This implies ensuring access to essential services, such as police, health and social services, for all migrant women and sexual and gender minorities, including victims and survivors of gender-based violence.

11. The government should bridge the digital gap to support women migrants in money transfer online as many families rely on these women's monthly remittance. Access to ATMs and [9]Bank Mitras is hindered by the pandemic and constraints due to mobility and location. According to the Reserve Bank of India (RBI), only 45,000 out of India's 230,000 (less than 20 percent) ATMs are in rural areas. Combined with a much lower than usual inflow of cash to rural branches (a source of cash for ATMs), rural India faces issues accessing benefits even when schemes are well-targeted. In addition, only 30 percent of the 1 million Bank Mitras in the country are currently operational, due to the travel restrictions accompanying the lockdown. Reports indicate that even though their services have been declared essential, local authorities have imposed restrictions on their movement. Many households in these rural areas are often migrant households, whose ability to access their benefits and remittances will be constrained by these logistical issues.

Center for Financial Inclusion (Shreedharan & Jose, 2020), in its article, suggests the following recommendations to curb the insecure plight of internal migrants during the pandemic;

---

9 Bank Mitra Customer Service Point provides Kiosk Banking services to agents across the country.

1. Firstly, the PMGKY has been announced as the first of multiple relief packages by the finance minister. While relief packages and social security systems must be strengthened, substantial efforts should be made to disseminate information about these schemes and utilizing service points such as Bank Mitras, community stores as cash in/out points, digital financial touchpoints, and PDS delivery agents to facilitate access for those individuals and households that are not formally included in the financial system, such as migrants.

2. Secondly, the government must coordinate and work with private sector entities such as FinTech companies and technology solution providers (TSPs) to facilitate the system's smooth functioning, enabling cash transfers and other forms of aid. For instance, AePS (Aadhaar enabled Payment System), the payment system used for state-run DBT, has a higher error rate than other payment systems and clocks a high rate of failure in DBT transfers, urging the need for better solutions.

3. Thirdly, migrant workers must be brought under the aegis of state-level social protection schemes by (temporarily) lifting domicile restrictions, and be assisted in availing benefits from central government schemes. In the short run, this requires a step up to identify migrants, by leveraging social networks and local organizations that work with migrant workers. On the systemic level, this calls for increased visibility of migrant labour through improved documentation as well as amendments to existing regulations.

4. Fourthly, the government response in the coming months must outline a stimulus package to rejuvenate enterprises and incentivize employers that typically employ migrant workers once economic recovery commences.

Conclusion

Any pandemic has an enhanced impact on the marginalized or displaced people—Even-more-so when its women. The COVID-19 pandemic and the subsequent lockdown has hit the socio-economic milieu of the world and India badly. The internal migrants of India witnessed trauma and insecurity as never before. The women as accompanists, independent domestic helpers, and small scale industries in the service industry are invisible to media gaze.

Slowly and steadily, the public gaze moves away from migrant workers on the road to Unlock 1.0 (the term used for first phase opening of public spaces after lockdown). There is now much less news about their life when they return home, other than the regular reports about illness and death in state quarantine centres. Implications of the pandemic are yet to unfold. Migrant women workers mostly remain in the shadows of the dominant official and popular discourse. Transnational professional migrant working women are not visible in official state reports about the *Pravasi Bharatiya* (overseas or non-resident Indian). Oishi (2005) found that hardly any official recognition or support for women migrants was there – professional (ICT, engineering, medicine, nursing) as well as 'low skilled' (domestic, service, or construction industries). The gender perspective was utterly absent in our labour laws (Mazumdar & Neetha, 2020). While there are some fundamental rights on paper for women workers in the organised sectors, female-intensive work in the unorganised sector remains unscrutinised by labour laws. For example, paid domestic work which does not come under labour laws, is performed mostly by migrant women (Mazumdar & Neetha, 2020).

Migration is mostly anticipated to positively influence women in improved labour force participation, improving economic independence, the decline in fertility, and building better self-esteem but does not always occur. Female rural to urban migrants continue to be susceptible to social discrimination in wages and labour market segmentation which reserve the most repetitive, unskilled, monotonous jobs for women. They tend to work in unorganized informal sectors and experience long working hours for a meagre wage, unhealthy or perilous working conditions, and psychological, physical and sexual aggression. While men usually work in groups, women go for individualized work environments (e.g. Domestic service) where there are much more isolation and less prospects of establishing networks of information and social support. So measures designed to 'protect' migrants must be augmented by steps that empower (Turrey, 2016).

The crisis has also come up with some thought-provoking questions about crisis-induced migration trends, and lessons to be learned therein that supports further exploration. The current crisis has raised pertinent questions on the impact of reverse migration on the rural economy, changes in remittance flows, and household finance dynamics. It also presents research opportunities to address the gaps in financial services targeted towards low-income households and workers engaged in the informal sector (Turrey, 2016).

Women migrant workers and their issues have got little limelight even during this pandemic. It is high time that our policies become more gender-responsive. Shelter, travel, wages, health, and hygiene need to be addressed separately concerning women workers. This pandemic has proven a turning point for migrant workers in gaining more visibility in media, the general public and even among lawmakers. A positive response to address the 'will the pandemic open doors for new governmental policies that address women migrant worker's specific needs?' will provide an inclusive crisis intervention irrespective of women's status in the country.

References

Agarwal, K., & G Sharma, A. (2020). COVID-19 Pandemic & The Socio-Economic & Political Impact on Women. *Feminism in India*

Akoijam, Brogen & Kerketta (2017). Living Conditions of Internal Labour Migrants: A Nationwide Study in 13 Indian Cities. International Journal of Migration and Border Studies.

Dang, N. A. (2005). Internal Migrants: Opportunities and Challenges for the Renovation and Development in Vietnam. *APEC*.

Guadagno, L. (2020). Migrants and the COVID-19 pandemic: An initial analyse IS.

Gyeke, M. (2020). Conceptualization of Female Migrants' Experiences Across the Lifespan. https://www.researchgate.net/publicConceptualization_of_Female_Migrants'_Experiences_across_the_Lifespan.

Iyer, M. (2020). Migration in India and the Impact of the Lockdown On Migrants. *https://www.prsindia.org/theprsblog/*.

Jose, D. (2020, MAY). Period-An-Added-Worry-For-Migrant-Women-On-The-Move *https://www.newindianexpress.com/states/telangana/2020/may/27*.

Manoj, P. K., & Vidya, V. (2015, NOVEMBER, 11). Socio Economic Conditions of Migrant Labourers. *Indian Journal of Applied Research*.

Mazumdar, I., & Pillai, N. (2020). Crossroads and Boundaries, Labour Migration, Trafficking and Gender. *ECONOMIC AND POLITICAL WEEKLY, 55* (20).

Migrant's Wife Delivers Baby; Child Dies, https://ndtv.com/india-new/ COVID-19 (May 2020).

Oishi, N. (2005). Women in Motion: Globalization, State Policies, and Labor Migration in Asia. Stanford University Press, Redwood City CA

Pullanoor, H. (2020, July 20). COVID-19-Lockdown-Exposes-Indias-Looming-Migrant-Refugee-Crisis. https://qz.com/india/1858209/ covid-19-lockdown-exposes-indias-looming-migrant-refugee-crisis/

Puri, I. (2020). Women in Varanasi Extended A Helping Hand To Migrant Workers, Villagers Affected By COVID 19 Pandemic. *Department of Science and Technology*.

Raman, L., & Bhagat, R. B. (2020). Trends and Patterns of Internal Migration in India, 1971-2001. https://www.researchgate.net/publication/265278165_ Trends_and_Patterns_of_Internal_Migration_in_India_1971-2001

Ramani, S. (2020, MAY 17). Coronavirus-package-will-migrant-workers-benefit-from-the-centres-measures/article31603590.ece. *https:// www.thehindu.com/news/national/*.

Ramya, B., & Lakshmi, R. (2018). The Place and Position of Migrant Women Workers in India. https://www.researchgate.net/ publication/332091945_THE_PLACE_AND_POSITION_OF_ MIGRANT_WOMEN_WORKERS_OF_INDIA#fullTextFileContent

Rani, U., & Shylendra, H. S. (2001). Seasonal Migration-An Rural-Urban Interface in Semi-arid Tropics of Gujarat: Study of Tribal Village. *Journal of Rural Urban Development* (20).

Roop, Sen (May 8, 2020). "The Crisis of Migrant Workers in India", The Times of India, April 12, 2020, available at https://timesofindia. indiatimes.com/blogs/voices/the-crisis-of-the-migrant-workers-in-india/

Roy, D. (2020, July 20). Can Labour Reforms Help Women Migrant Workers During COVID-19? *https://wwww.thequint.com.*

S, E. (2020). *COVID-19 In India: The Shunned & The Forgotten Migrant Workers.* Feminism India. https://feminisminindia.com/2020/04/13/covid-19-india-shunned-forgotten-migrant-workers/

Samanthroy, D. E. (2020). Can Labour Reforms Help Women Migrant Workers During COVID-19? *https://www.thequint.com/voices/women/labour-reforms-help-women-migrant-workers-during-covid-19*

SAPRA, I. (2020, MAY). Why don't we see the women? The untold story of COVID-19 migration. *http://indianexpress.com.*

Shanthi, K. (2006). Female labour migration in India: Insights from NSSO data. Working paper No. 4. *http://www.mse.ac.in.*

Sharma, K. (2020). Even in COVID – 19 Women Don't Count. *https://english.mathrubhumi.com.*

Shreedharan, S., & Jose, J. (2020). Support for India's Migrants During COVID-19: Navigating Potential Gaps in the System. *https://www.centerforfinancialinclusion.org/.*

Shreedharan, S., & Jose, J. (2020). Support for India's Migrants During COVID19: Navigating Potential Gaps in the System. *https://www.centerfor financialinclusion.org.*

Sili, L. (2020). COVID-19 and the impact on women. *International Growth Centre.* https://www.theigc.org/person/laura-sili/

Singh, Taranjeet. (2016). Female Migration In India. International Journal Of Multidisciplinary Research Centre (IJMRC) Vol II (4), pp54-62. https://www.researchgate.net/publication/322764657_FEMALE_MIGRATION_IN_INDIA

Thapliyal, N. (2020). Migrant Women Workers On the Road: Largely Invisible and Already Forgotten. *http://www.mcrg.ac.in/*.

Trial by the Cycling Federation. https://www.hindusthantimes.com (May 2020).

Turrey, A. A. (2016). *An Analysis of Internal Migration Types In India In Purview of its Social And Economic impacts.* Gandhinagar Turrey, A. A. (2016). EPRA International Journal of Economic and Business Review. Vol.4(1), pp.157-164. http://epratrust.com/articles/upload/22. Aijaz%20Ahmad%20Turrey.pdf

About the Author

Anupama K Haridas is a freelance Professional Social Worker, with over 7 years' experience in various social work fields as Psychiatric Social Worker, Family Counsellor, Consultant for special needs children, and an educator finest colleges in Kerala, India. Working parallel as well as under the guidance of some of the accomplished professionals in the Social Work arena has sharpened skills as a social worker. AIMS multi-speciality hospital, De Paul School of Social Work, Mercy College, FIRM (NGO for marginalised), Family Counselling Centre under Central Social Welfare Board are few organisations working as a team member and also as team head enhanced professional acumen She is actively involved in the activities of Kerala Association of Professional Social Workers (KAPS) and being professionally involved in the issues related to marginalised, differently-abled, gender and child-related issues has given a compassionate and more in-depth understanding in these areas.

Health Service Delivery for Internally Displaced People: Issues and Challenges in India

Pinki Kumari[10] & Pushpalatha N[11]

Abstract

Despite the increasing magnitude of internally displaced persons, there is still no universal legal definition to define them, and hence, it remains a contesting terminology. Nevertheless, unlike refugees, they do not cross the country borders. Internally displaced persons (IDPs) in any country can be categorised majorly into three groups: people displaced due to conflict, people displaced due to natural disasters and people displaced due to developmental projects. Worldwide there are over 40 million IDPs, out of which 80% are women and children, and in India, the number was 2.4 million in 2016. The displacees have to face multiple problems as they are ousted from their original places such as social exclusion, marginalisation, poverty, and unemployment. Along with all these, there is a significant impact on their health. Lack of access to proper food, shelter, clean drinking water and sanitation results in several health problems. The process of displacement has an impact on the physical, mental and reproductive health of displacees. People suffer from the disease, disability, injury, malnutrition, trauma, depression and anxiety. There is an upsurge in maternal and infant mortality rate. The United Nations has come up with Guiding Principles on Internal Displacement in which principle 19 focuses on IDPs' health care provisions. Providing health care facilities to the displaced population is a challenging issue in India as there is an acute shortage of health care facilities. Health care workers face complex challenges

---

10   PhD Scholar (SRF), Department of Social Work, University of Delhi, Email: pinki.hrc@gmail.com

11   PhD Research Scholar, Dept of Studies and Research in Social Work, Tumkur University, Karnataka. Email: pushpa.brijesh@gmail.com

in providing care to displaced people. Lack of access to health care facilities, services, and supplies, including medicines, increases the problem's gravity. Responding to the IDPs' health care needs a multi-pronged approach from the state, NGO sector, and civil society. They need to take proactive steps to make health services available and accessible to IDPs. They need to come up with intervention plans which are culturally appropriate and financially feasible. This paper will follow the systematic review method to focus on IDPs' health and deliberate on state and NGOs' roles for effective health service delivery.

Key Words: Internally displaced persons, Health care services, Physical health, Mental health, The role of the state

Introduction

Displacement of people from one place to another due to any reason deprives them of all their privileges right from their homes, livelihood to their economic security and social safety. Forced displacement has become a global problem, and the number of people being displaced is increasing every year. Among the 80 million displaced, 26 million people have crossed country borders and are termed refugees (UNHCR-2019). The 1951 United Nations Convention defines a refugee as someone who "owing to a well-founded fear of being persecuted for reasons of race, religion, nationality, membership of a particular social group or political opinion, is outside the country of his nationality and is unable or, owing to such fear, is unwilling to avail himself of the protection of that country; or who, not having a nationality and being outside the country of his former habitual residence as a result of such events, is unable or, owing to such fear, is unwilling to return to it".

The increasing global trends in forced displacement are quite disturbing and have become an international agenda for discussion. Forced displacement includes refugees, who face internal displacement, international migrants and people who seek asylum in other countries. The reasons for displacement are persecution, conflict, violence and human rights violation in their own countries. The United Nations High Commissioner for Refugees (2019) puts the global data of people who have been forcibly displaced at 79.5 million at the end of 2019. Out of this, there were 26 million refugees, 45.7 million internally displaced people, 4.2 million asylum seekers and 3.6 million Venezuelans displaced abroad. Forty percent of the total displaced population were children below the age of 18 years.

If country wise data is compared, Syria has been the worst affected country regarding its population's forced displacement. "At the end of 2019, Syrians continued to be by far the largest forcibly displaced population worldwide (13.2 million, including 6.6 million refugees and more than six million internally displaced people). When considering only international displacement situations, Syrians also topped the list with 6.7 million persons, followed by Venezuelans with 4.5 million. Afghanistan and South Sudan had 3.0 and 2.2 million, respectively" (UNHCR, Global Trends, 2019). Regarding internal displacements of people in 2019, India records the highest number of internal displacement resulting in 5037000, including 5018000 due to natural disaster and 19000 because of conflict and violence (IDMC-GRID 2020).

1. Internal Displacement

Unlike refugees, many displacees do not cross their country borders. They remain within their own country but get displaced from their original place of habitat. They are known as internally displaced people (IDP). Despite the increasing magnitude of internally displaced persons, there is still no universal legal definition to define them, and hence, it remains a contesting terminology. According to the United Nations Guiding Principles on Internal Displacement (1998), internally displaced persons are "persons or groups of persons who have been forced or obliged to flee or to leave their homes or places of habitual residence, in particular as a result of or in order to avoid the effects of armed conflict, situations of generalised violence, violations of human rights or natural or human-made disasters, and who have not crossed an internationally recognised state border". This definition does not provide the IDP's with a legal status because technically they remain the citizen of that country where they have been displaced. Their problem diversifies because they can neither claim to be the original resident of the place where they have been displaced nor seek refugees' status.

Internally displaced people in any country can be categorised majorly into three groups: people displaced due to conflict, people displaced due to natural disasters and people displaced due to developmental projects. The number of IDPs worldwide has increased significantly, with around 15 million in 2010 to 43.5 million in 2019 (UNHCR, 2019). The Internal Displacement Monitoring Centre (2020) in its Global Report on Internal Displacement, but the total global figure of IDPs in 2019 as 50.8 million. Out of this, 45.7 million have been displaced due to conflict and violence and 5.1 million as a result of the disaster. Reports show that among the people who have been displaced, 18.3 million IDPs are children under the age of 15 and 3.7 million come in the elderly group with age over 60 years. If we see the regional trends of internal displacement, the maximum number of displacements in 2019 due to conflict and violence has been in Sub-Saharan Africa (53.7% of global total).

On the other hand displacement due to natural disasters, South Asia and East Asia clubbed together account for 76.9 % of the global total of internal displacement in 2019 (East Asia and Pacific region accounts for 38.6% and South Asia for 38.3%). The Internal Displacement Monitoring Centre (IDMC) has given a model that shows how they calculate the number of displacees worldwide. The following figure is a diagrammatical representation which sums up the process of internal displacement and its triggers.

Figure 1: IDMC Data Model

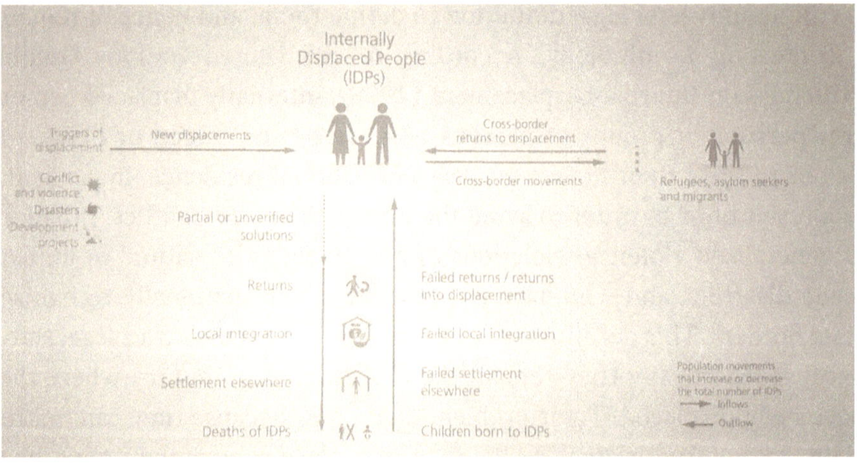

Source: IDMC Report, 2019

2. Internal Displacement in India

India has witnessed people's internal displacement due to all the three processes (Conflict, natural disasters and developmental projects) since a long time (IDMC, Norwegian Refugee Council Report, 2017). Internal conflicts in regions like Kashmir and North-East have led to the displacement of hundreds and thousands of people who never dared to return to their original place of habitat due to fear of violence. The armed conflict in the valley of Kashmir forced the Hindu population to flee from the valley. "More than 90 per cent of the Hindu population in the Kashmir Valley, the Kashmiri Pandits remain internally displaced due to this armed conflict. The government estimates that 250,000 fled from the valley during the 1990s, while Pandit groups believe at least 350,000 people were displaced, resulting in 100,000 living in the capital New Delhi and some 240,000 in Jammu" (The Observer Research Foundation, 2003). Conflict and violence have also triggered another 19000 new displacements in India in 2019 (IDMC GRID, 2020).

Every year natural disasters like flood and cyclone in places like Bihar, Bengal, Odisha, and Kerala take a toll on India's people and property. According to the latest data by IDMC (2019), a whopping 5018000 people were displaced in India in 2019 due to natural disasters. India stands second in the list only below Afghanistan in this case. The weather condition had been so in the last year that eight tropical storms struck India during 2019. The most dangerous of all of them was cyclone Fani which was equal to a category four hurricane. It had its significant impact on the states of Odisha, Andhra Pradesh and West Bengal. It led to a displacement of 1,0,000 people. Cyclone Vayu in Gujarat led to the evacuation of 2,89,000 people and similarly cyclone Maha (2019) which hit Kerala and Lakshadweep islands followed by cyclone Bulbul which struck Odisha, and West Bengal led to the displacement of another 1,86,000 people in India.

As India is becoming 'Shining India' and rising on the path of development, many people get displaced due to developmental projects such as hydroelectric projects, airports, roads, mining projects, and industries being put up mainly in tribal belts are rich in minerals. Acquiring land for

Special Economic Zones in India results in the displacement of many people who have no clue how they will be rehabilitated. In India, the Right to Fair Compensation and Transparency in Land Acquisition, Rehabilitation and Resettlement Act, 2013 deals with the rehabilitation of people who have been displaced due to developmental projects. This law (Chapter 1, section 3/c) defines an affected family under the following points, and all these people come under the displaced categories:

1. A family whose land or other immovable property has been acquired for a project;

2. A family which does not own any land but a member or members of such family may be agricultural labourers, tenants including any form of tenancy or holding of usufruct right, share-croppers or artisans or who may be working in the affected area for three years prior to the acquisition of the land, whose primary source of livelihood stand affected by the acquisition of land;

3. The Scheduled Tribes and other traditional forest dwellers who have lost any of their forest rights recognised under the Scheduled Tribes and Other Traditional Forest Dwellers (Recognition of Forest Right) Act, 2006 due to acquisition of land;

4. The family whose primary source of livelihood for three years prior to the acquisition of the land is dependent on forests or water bodies and includes gatherers of forest produce, hunters, fisherfolk and boatmen and such livelihood are affected due to acquisition of land;

5. A member of the family who has been assigned land by the State Government or the Central Government under any of its schemes and such land is under acquisition;

6. A family residing on any land in the urban areas for preceding three years or more prior to acquiring the land or whose primary source of livelihood for three years prior to acquiring the land is affected by the acquisition of such land.

3. Health Issues of Internally Displaced People

The displacees have to face multiple problems as they are ousted from their original places such as social exclusion, marginalisation, poverty, and unemployment. They face multiple crises all along from local to international levels. Along with all these, there is a massive impact on their health which all the stakeholders in this field usually ignore. According to the World Health Organisation (WHO), "Health is a state of complete physical, mental and social well-being and not merely the absence of disease or infirmity". The IDPs face such adverse situations during displacement and return and resettlement that their physical and mental health suffers a setback. The process of displacement has an impact on the physical, mental and reproductive health of displacees. People suffer from the disease, disability, injury, malnutrition, trauma, depression and anxiety (Stephen, 2017). The health problems suffered by the IDPs needs have been discussed in the section below.

Physical Health: Internal Displacement has significant effects on the affected population's physical health directly due to violence and injury or indirectly due to increased rates of infectious diseases and malnutrition (Zounoun et al., 2009). The displaced population is faced with multiple physical health problems due to their volatile nature. Lack of access to proper food, shelter, clean drinking water and sanitation results in several health problems. Lack of proper healthcare facilities leads to an upsurge in many diseases. Diseases that could be controlled otherwise in normal situations such as malaria, diarrhoea, etc., increased and become pandemic. Often people, especially children, can become prone to malnutrition in the absence of proper food availability. Multiple outbreaks of pandemics and spread of communicable diseases are also possible in crowded camp-like environments were these IDPs take refuge. The impact on health varies on different people. Children, elderly and female are more at risk of various physical health problems. Children do not get vaccinated in the process of displacement due to lack of health services. As a result of which they are exposed to many hazardous diseases. Many of them also die in the process of displacement and resettlement due to lack of proper facilities (Salami, Iwuagwu & Amodu, 2020).

Mental Health: The displacees suffer severe mental stress as the displacement and reintegration process is very emotionally draining. The loss of one's homes and livelihoods and separation from their family and loved ones leads to extreme stress and anxiety. Economic marginalisation is often accompanied by social and psychological marginalisation, expressed in a drop in social status, loss of confidence in society and themselves, a feeling of injustice and deepened vulnerability. Host communities often perceive them as a socially degrading stigma (Cernea, 2000b, p.7). Such a situation can give rise to a number of psycho-social related problems, such as post-traumatic stress disorders, psychosomatic illness, depression and anxiety. Living in such stressful conditions, exposure to violence, fear and trauma can lead to extreme human behaviour changes such as increased substance abuse, physical violence, domestic and sexual violence. The fact that no help and support is available to them during this phase makes the condition worse.

Reproductive Health: The displacement process and its impact on health are much worse in women and girls. Reproductive health care for IDP is recognised by the Inter-Agency Working Group on Reproductive Health in Refugee situation and the Reproductive Health Response in Conflict Consortium as a neglected area in Humanitarian Relief Operations. With limited or no access to resources and services, they increase maternal mortality rate, infant mortality rate, stillbirths, and low weight births (Nina, Paul & Matthias, 2008). Lack of immunisation facilities leads to higher infant mortality rates and increased risks of diseases in children. Women are at a higher risk of unintended and early pregnancy, unsafe abortion, and an increase in vaginal infection and sexually transmitted diseases. They are also heightened risk and exposure to violence, sexual abuse, and exploitation in transit and refugee camps. This can also severely impact their mental health as they go through a lot of stress and anxiety.

4. United Nations' Guiding Principles on Internal Displacement

Internal displacement has been seen as an international crisis, and international agencies have been working to mitigate this problem and its impact on the world. The United Nations has come up with Guiding

Principles on Internal Displacement. These guiding principles address the specific issues related to displacees and help in identifying their rights. They help the international community ensure that the IDPs who are forcefully ousted from their homes are given protection in this crisis. The scope of these guiding principles also includes providing protection and assistance during displacement and resettlement and rehabilitation. These guiding principles are divided into five sections (1-5) providing directions so that the displaced persons should enjoy all the rights and should not be discriminated (1, protected from displacement (2), protection during displacement if they are displaced (3), provisions to be made render humanitarian assistance (4) and action plans to draw concerning the return, resettlement and reintegration of the displaced (5).

Thirty principles deal with various facets related to displaced people in which principle 19 focuses on IDPs' health care provisions. It comes under section 3 in which principles related to the protection of IDPs during displacement are iterated. UN Guiding Principles, 19 (2004) states:

> All wounded and sick internally displaced persons, as well as those with disabilities, shall receive to the fullest extent practicable and with the least possible delay, the medical care and attention they require, without distinction on any grounds other than medical ones. When necessary, internally displaced persons shall have access to psychological and social services. Special attention should be paid to women's health needs, including access to female health care providers and services, such as reproductive health care, as well as appropriate counselling for victims of sexual and other abuses. Special attention should also be given to the prevention of contagious and infectious diseases, including AIDS, among internally displaced persons

It is very clear from the above principles that the health of the world's displaced population is an essential aspect that cannot be just ignored. Eighty million of people who are forcibly displaced, are in a state of refuge and providing health care facilities to them is one of the prime responsibilities of the state where they are taking refuge.

February 13, 2019, Supreme court order on the eviction of nearly one million Adivasis members and other forest communities throughout the country poses a serious threat to the sovereignty and self-possession of all those who are impacted. These communities have lived in forests for many years and are traditionally dependent on forest resources for their survival as identified by the Government of India itself are now persecuted by the same court.

Along with land rights, the tribes are also deprived of their rights to life and health. The dwindling of livelihoods of Adivasi communities is replicated in their fading capacity to bear the financial drain of seeking healthcare and also creating foreseeable cycles of indebtedness and impoverishment. With the lack of any functional health facility for primary healthcare and almost no government transport facility available in the areas, accessing a functioning health care facility is a serious encounter. This, impacts food consumption, healthcare, and other dimensions of the lives of women, children and families from these communities. Instances of pledging ration cards to local credit or securing money to meet healthcare expenses have appeared from these communities' narratives.

The Adivasi community lags behind the national average on several vital public health indicators. Women and children are the most vulnerable. Studies on maternal health show chronic malnutrition, higher morbidity and mortality, and lower provision of antenatal and postnatal services among Adivasis. Under-five mortality rates among rural Adivasi children remain startlingly high. The health indicators specific to scheduled tribes (STs) in each state indicate that more than 50% of the women are anaemic. More than 30% of the women have BMI less than 18.5 kg/m. More than 20% of the men have BMI less than 18.5 kg/m. This reflects a serious health concern that needs to be addressed by the health system. The nutritional status of children from tribal communities is extremely poor. The percentage of stunted children is above the national average, as is the percentage of severely stunted, where it is marginally lower than the national average (NFHS-4) (idronline.org).

5. Health Service Delivery for Internally Displaced People

Providing health care facilities to the displaced population is a challenging issue in India and elsewhere in the world due to many technical and political reasons. The nature and socio-economic characteristics of the host community plays a crucial role in this. In India, there is already an acute shortage of health care facilities and services. Under such circumstances, the displaced population is usually seen as a burden on the host community. This is true about both internal displacement and in the case of refugees. Health care workers face complex challenges in providing care and protection to displaced people. Lack of access to health care facilities, services, and supplies, including medicines, increases the problem's gravity (The Handbook for the Protection of the Internally Displaced People, 2007).

The image below describes the hindrances that are usually faced while trying to reach out to displaced people for providing them health care services. These have been shown in the image and also explained below.

Figure 2: Obstacles in health care service delivery mechanism

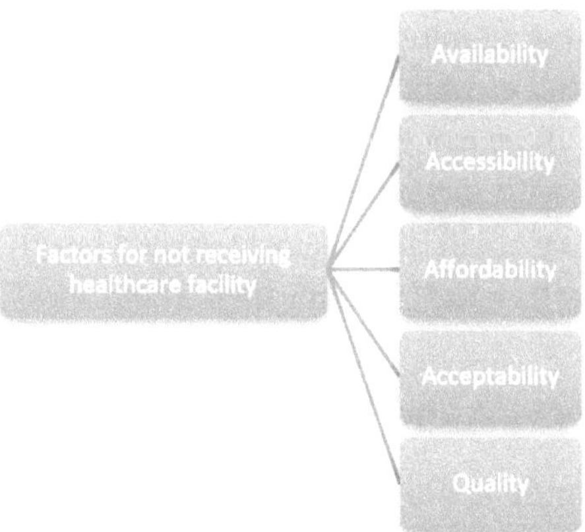

- **Availability:** Availability of health care facilities is a significant problem. Displaced persons often live in rural areas or on outskirts of urban areas. In such places, health care facilities may be absent, infrastructure may be damaged, and healthcare professionals might themselves be displaced or absent.

- **Accessibility:** Availability and accessibility are two different things. It might be possible that health services are present in some places, but the IDPs cannot access it for various reasons. These reasons may include caste-based discrimination, fear of host community, higher fees, long distance of the health care points, and lack of transport facilities.

- **Affordability:** Displaced people lose everything, including their source of livelihood and income. In such circumstances, they might be lacking the resources or financial ability to afford health care facilities when required. As India is a welfare state, the government's role becomes crucial in helping the IDPs get health care facilities through government machinery.

- **Acceptability:** Cultural and religious norms and practices play a critical role in India in every sphere. They can play the role of a supporter as well as become a hindrance many times. So, health care services must be provided in a culturally acceptable way, especially in tribal belts. Also, any information regarding this should be provided in the local language understood by the displaced persons and the host community.

- **Quality:** Ensuring minimum quality and standard in providing health care services is essential and challenging at the same time. In times of emergency, there can be a lack of qualified staff, people who are not well versed with the conditions of the displaced population, lack of understanding about displacement related health issues or sometime the staff may be biased towards their needs.

6. Role of Government and NGOs

It is the prime responsibility of the state of the highest healthcare facilities to all people in their jurisdiction. Internally displaced people also come under the state's jurisdiction. They might be displaced from one place to another, but until they cross the country's border, they are citizens of that country. The country's responsibility is to take every possible step to make health services available and accessible to IDPs. The national authorities need to develop intervention plans that are culturally appropriate and financially feasible, along with good quality services.

Responding to the IDPs' health care needs requires a multi-pronged approach from the state, NGO, and civil society. NGOs at local and international level have to team up and work together because it is an international issue. They need to take proactive steps to make health services available and accessible to IDPs. Civil society organisations need to raise awareness and advocate for policy changes, resource allocation and more effective programming. There needs to be an effective implementation of the schemes available for the displaced people. It is imperative that all the vulnerable groups are identified, and no one is left behind in the route of progress and development.

The role of the NGO sector in this area is very crucial. They can execute the following functions to act as influential players in providing quality health care services to IDPs:

» They are proficient of providing community-based outreach services which can be very operative in reaching out to every displaced person.

» They also accomplish the job of community mobilisation very effectively. They can also be very significant factors in negotiating with the host community as they have a good rapport building with the local host community.

» They can network with the government and work on analysing and assessing the displaced population's protection. They can be a vital inter-linkage between health care professionals, government authorities and the beneficiaries.

» They can also function as focal points to coordinate with other sectors such as water, sanitation, nutrition, etc., to provide good quality health care services to IDPs.

» Another vital function is to raise awareness and provide health-related information to relevant sectors such as displaced people and the host community. Such information can include information about the availability and location of health care facilities.

Conclusion

The WHO Constitution (1946) envisions "the highest attainable standard of health as a fundamental right of every human being". Right to health is not explicitly mentioned in India's constitution, but it is covered under article 21, which guarantees a fundamental right to life. Right to life has a much broader connotation: better livelihood, increased standard of living, and hygienic conditions at home and the workplace. Right to health becomes inherent to a life of dignity, and every citizen of India is entitled to a life of dignity. Violation of human rights can have serious implication on the health and well-being of the individuals. The state and NGOs' help should take every measure to ensure that health care services are provided to the IDPs and other services required for their reintegration in mainstream society.

The health challenges faced by internal displacees of all nature either conflict-induced or development-induced or calamity induced have been detailed by Cernea (1990) in his IRR model which proposed all displacees are faced with Risks and Impoverishment challenges. Health is one of the significant challenges that stem to other risks. The displacement leads people to lose current living situations and comforts that psychologically affect them and lead to mental health issues. Apart from mental health issues, physical health deteriorates due to the non-availability of health service delivery in the current living situations. Often the resettlement areas are devoid of civic amenities including water, sanitation, primary health service deliveries. The challenge is to address the risks proactively and deterring them without creating havoc in the daily living of the displacees. This demands a revisit to the paradigms of development and development approaches. The argument, displacement is inevitable as often validated by current development proponents, but the approach to displacement and the rights of the displacees are without objective humanistic approach. It is argued that while displacement is based on Need-based approach (public purpose), the right of the displacees (the right based approach that speaks not to displace) is ignored. The pertinent argument for raising is following a blend of Right and Need-Based approaches based on Humanistic theory (Maslow) that leads to the Right Rehabilitation Action Plan derived from Social Licensing (Vanclay, 2017) and its implementation lead to Economics of Recovery. The focus should be made to resolve IDPs' health challenges because an internally displaced person today can become a refugee tomorrow if not provided with the right kind of support and protection.

References

American Public Health Association (1992). *The Health of Refugees and Displaced Persons: A Public Health Priority.* Policy statement.

Cernea, M. (2000c). Risks, Safeguards, and Reconstruction: A Model for Population Displacement and Resettlement. In M. Cernea, & C. McDowell (Eds.), *Risks and Reconstruction: Experience of Resettlers and Refugees.* Washington, DC: The World Bank.

Cernea, M. M. (1990a). *From Unused Social Knowledge to Policy Creation: The Cost of Population Resettlement.* Cambridge Institute for International Development, Harward University.

Ekezie, W., Adaji, E. E., & Murray, R. L. (2020). Essential healthcare services provided to conflict-affected internally displaced populations in low and middle-income countries: A systematic review. *Health Promotion Perspectives,* Vol.10 (1), pp24-37.

Government of India (2013). *The Right to Fair Compensation and Transparency in Land Acquisition, Rehabilitation and Resettlement Act.*

Guerrier G, Zounoun M, Delarosa O, Defourny I, Lacharite M, Brown V, *et al.* (2009). *Malnutrition and mortality patterns among internally displaced and non-displaced population living in a camp, a village or a town in Eastern Chad.* PLoS One.

Hakamies, N, Geissles P. W. and Borchest, M (2008). Providing Reproductive Health Care to Internal Displaced People; Barriers Experienced by Humanitarian Agencies. Reproductive Health Matters. Pubmed.

IDMC – Norwegian Refugee Council Report 2017

Internal Displacement Monitoring Centre (2019). *Global Report on Internal Displacement.*

Internal Displacement Monitoring Centre (2020). *Global Report on Internal Displacement*.

Mixed Migration Centre (2019). *Rohingya Migration to India: Patterns, Drivers and Experiences*. Briefing paper.

Nadimpally, s., Venkatachalam, D., and Fatima, A. (2020). Eviction of Tribals: Forced Displacement and Its Links With Poor Health (idronline.org)

Observer Research Foundation (2003). Two-Day Conference on Kashmiri Pandits: Problems and Prospects.

Salami, B., Iwuagwu, S. and Amodu, O. (2020). The Health of Internal Displaced Children in Sub Saharan Africa; A Scoping Review. British Medical Journal of Global Health.

Stephen Ojo (2017). Challenges of Internally Displaced Persons. Human Security. www.researchgate.net

United Nations (2004). *Guiding Principles on Internal Displacement*.

United Nations High Commissioner for Refugees (2006). *The Handbook for the Protection of the Internally Displaced*.

United Nations High Commissioner for Refugees (2019). *Global Trends in Forced Displacement*.

About Authors

Pinki Kumari: Pinki is currently serving as a Human Resource Professional at Coal India Limited, a public sector undertaking of Govt. of India. She has completed her MSW, M.Phil and PhD in Social Work from Dept. of Social Work, University of Delhi. She has presented a number of papers in national level seminars/conferences and has published four papers in journal and edited books. Her interest areas include Labour issues (both in organised and unorganised sectors), Corporate Social Responsibility, Development and Displacement, and Environment.

Pushpalatha N is a Research Scholar in Social Work, Tumkur University, Karnataka and function as a faculty member in Department of Social Work, Bangalore University Karnataka. Having a handful years of experience in the field of social work she focuses to be expertise in marginalised and vulnerable groups in the society, especially Dalit Women, Girl Children, Rights Based Approach to Social Work, Displaced communities. She authored a number of articles and presented papers in the national and international forum.

Creating Harmony Among the Internally Displacees Through Narrative Performance: A Case of Gulu Uganda

Lucy Nabukonde[12]

Abstract

Displacees are earth-born who tend to tell they are natural events to their companions in asylums. This is because every human being is synonymous with the human narrative. Therefore, an oral narrative is senescent through which displacees express their fears, aspirations, hopes and dreams. When displacees reckon their personal experiences, they create personal stamina and some upshots in their mental representation to sustain life. Narrative performance enables the displacees to become aware of their feelings and thoughts experienced in the expatriate camp. The study sought the narratives of the internally displacees in Gulu Uganda by exploring their total experiences in displacement focusing on: the harmony created through narratives existing among the internally displacees in Gulu; the relationship between the harmony and the human emotions expressed in narratives of displacees in Gulu and the perception of displacement in the narrative among the internally displacees in Gulu. The hypothesis informed the study that narrative activity is a leading approach through which displacees express their new environment's comprehension. The findings revealed that the configuring of narratives by the internally displacees reunites, regenerates and harmonies their experiences.

Key Words: Displacees, Harmony, Narrative Performance, Gulu-Uganda

---

12 HoD & Senior Lecturer in Literature, Linguistics and Communication, The Catholic University of Eastern Africa, Nairobi, Email: sisterlucy2004@yahoo.com

Introduction

Uganda has been labelled as a home of notorious internal wars and conflicts since the 1970s. For instance, Northern Uganda has continued to face insecurity from Lord's resistance army (LRA) by Kony rebels for over thirty years. This major internal conflict between the government and the party mentioned above (LRA) has seriously confounded Gulu, Kitgum, Lira, Adjuman, Apac, Arua, Pader, and Moyo districts. The current conflicts in Acholi and Lango regions between the LRA and the Uganda government have roots in the history of ethnic violence and the contested nature of the Ugandan state. The internal conflict started with the north's marginalisation during the colonial period coupled with institutional weaknesses, troubled politics of post-independence Uganda where military units of different ethnic compositions aspired to regain power from a succession of Uganda governments under the influence of various external factors.

Unfortunately, this so-called well-known interior conflict has disrupted the country's socio-economic and socio-political activities, culminating in many killings of the northern Ugandan people and the massive displacement of many into camps following the destruction of their homesteads. According to the Acholi Religious Leaders Peace Initiative Report (1999), more than half of Gulu district people dwell in protected villages camps in shocking and appalling ailments. This means that over 1.2 million people have been forced into internal displacement in northern Uganda (World vision, 2004). Of the 750,000 people in Gulu and its inter – districts, about 450,000 have been living in a state of chronic internal displacement clustered in protected villages (Weeks, 2002). In Pabo camp, one of the largest protected villages in Gulu, about 42,000 people live within a fundamental quantity of two kilometres in crowded grass – thatched huts (traditional camps). There seems to be no hope nor a forum of voice from within or without regarding their story in displacement and enslavement at home.

Despite displacees being earth-born who tend to tell they are natural events to their companions in asylums, there is no doubt that every human being is synonymous with every human narrative. Peter Brooks argues that without repeating narratives, human life ceaselessly ends. He concludes that given the stories humans tell and hear, those dreamed of or imagined or wished are reworked in the narratives people narrate to them ourselves.

This study focused on oral narratives of internally displaced Acholis in Gulu Uganda. Oral narratives have been selected because orality is a primary mode of human expression. Structuralists such as Vladimir Propp, Milman Parry and Albert Lord studied oral creations and ignited scholarly interest in the study of orality. On the other hand, there are scholars who view orality as secondary to literacy. One such scholar is Jack Gooday, who argues that literacy is reflective consciousness while orality is incapable of handling logical processes and manipulating the world (Goody as quoted in Irele 2001, 24). Walter Ong also holds that orality is characterized by "paratactic and noncumulative narrativity" while literacy is characterized by "syntactic and cumulative narrativity and introspective analysis" (Miyashi, 1989). In analyzing harmony among the internally displacees narratives, we focused on structure and capacity to create connotation.

This study is situated against the broad backdrop of worldwide forced displacement. The problem of forced displacement is almost as old as humanity its self. Over generations, people have been forced to move from one place to another by varied natural and man-made factors, including war, social-political instability, and famine. Displacement leads to the creation of groups of people referred to as displaced populations. This study deals with internally displaced people, as a special category of displaced persons. The standard definition of internally displaced people according to United Nations High Commission for Refugee (UNHCR) is the one drafted by 1951 United Nations Geneva convention namely that: a displacee is a person who, owing to a well-founded fear of being persecuted for reasons of race, religion, nationality or membership of a particular social group or political opinion, is outside to country of his nationality or owing to such fear, unwilling to avail himself of the protection of that country (UNHCR, 1994)

The OAU definition also includes the following: any person who is owing to external aggression, occupation, foreign domination or events seriously disturbing public order in either part or the whole of his country of origin or nationality is compelled to leave his people's habitual residence in order to seek refugee with the internally displaced people (OAU convention Art. 1).

1. Understanding the Problem

The internal displacees in Gulu Uganda continue to suffer and harbour painful experiences even in their own country due to conflict by Kony rebels' aftermaths of the crisis despite the agreement of the great alliance between People's Movement (PNU) and former Rebels (LRA). Efforts and interventions by the non-governments and its international partners have tried to offer transport, food, medical care and other reconnaissance mission assistance to the victims without sufficiency. However, proper understanding, construction and interpretation of the stories of the internally displaced people (IDP) remain relatively low. According to Steele (1999), the world has not spared humanity hunger, cold, sorrow, pain, fear, loneliness, diseases, death, war, famine, or madness. Therefore, scholars should not hesitate to use available knowledge when writing about them and for them.

The state of affairs of forced displacement and the attendant humanitarian problems is critical in its wake and the danger of filtering displacees' experiences and perception through narrative an urgent need to listen to expressive soothing. Therefore, this study is situated against the background of forced displacement and the attendant humanitarian problems produced in the millennia's wake. Forced displacement refers to the involuntary mass movement of people due to unfavourable conditions in their natural homes. The problem of forced displacement continues to be a matter of concern for scholars of varied fields. Literature dealing with the whole of life can help enlighten the understanding of internally displacees. Literature, therefore, enables our understanding of the world by naming and defining experiences. This means that an understanding of how literature names the world through assigning images to phenomena is crucial in understanding ourselves and the world in which we live. Consequently, the study focuses on the narratives of the internally displaced people in Gulu, Uganda, assuming that these artistic creations demonstrate, the peoples' way of renaming their world through narrative.

Harmony and displacement are vital issues globally and in Africa, particularly where internal conflicts have torn the whole countries apart. The narrative has the value of storytelling in the representation of reality. This is based on the assumption that storytelling is a natural human activity through which human nature features are revealed. It is also based on the assumption that storytelling is a pleasurable activity and most humans, especially displaces relish to tell stories or to listen to them. Therefore, this study's focus enables collecting data from displacees through a natural and pleasurable means. There is a large body of knowledge produced by the internally displaced people studies; however, these have tended to be in social sciences, hardly any in the humanities. Available literature from NGO's working among internally displaced people in Uganda has scant information regarding the subject. Displaced peoples' study is a relatively new phenomenon, and many issues have not yet been systematically studied. Therefore, the study finds its niche in this glaring gap.

2. Understanding the Subject Theoretically

Our study is schematically informed by structuralist literary theory. Structuralism is one of the theories that advocate art for man's sake while stressing human freedom. According to Piaget, a literary structure embodies three fundamental dimensions. The first one is the wholeness or a sense of the internal coherence. The second one is the transformation. This is the capacity for structure or transforming material to hold substance; for instance, language can transform a sentence into many varieties without changing the basal form. The third dimension is the self-regulation quality which means that a structure does not appeal to factors outside of itself to make sense. For instance, Hawkes, (1989) observes that to make sense a narrative relies on its inner nature and not on some kind of external beingness.

Structuralism being a stable formulation to the study of idea corresponds to the basic premise that humans cannot interpret things in isolation; rather, they comprehend ideas by recognizing or creating structures. Therefore, humans do not just observe an absolute universe to understand, and they create their own. Structuralism has been described as a way of looking for reality, not individual things but their relationships.

Structuralist criticism holds that just as there are two levels (language and parole), literature has two levels: poetics and individual creative works. The poetics are the basic literary structure that enables the institution of individual works, and the individual works (in langue) are the underlying language that enables the generation of intelligible discourse. Moreover, the individual creative works are compared to parole, the specific utterances produced by the speaker of a specific language.

In this study, we applied a structuralist model adopted from ideas presented by A.J. Greimas. This model was adapted to the study for its advantage of concentrating on the relationship that helps generate meaning in literary works (Hawkes, 1989). With the intent of understanding the study more deeply, the researcher formulated a framework grounded on three cardinal concepts propounded by Geremia: firstly, all narratives are narrated within their its structure; secondly the fictional personae within the narrative (characters) operate on the level of function rather than content. This is to say that characters are not so crucial as individuals; rather, they are agents of a particular function. As agents of a given function, these translate into actants. Accordingly, an actant in a narrative may execute more than one function if she or he is more than one actant. Theretofore, having been transposed into two or more characters, they may be utilised to articulate one function making them one actant. Thirdly and finally, the function's value is binary opposition based on the view that the world takes shape because of the human ability to perceive the difference. The world is comprised of mighty opposites which give it order and meaning. This structuralist being theorized into literature implies that a displacee's narrative contains two actants whose relationship must either be oppositional or reverse. Therefore, this tends to generate fundamental oppositional actions such as disjunction and conjunction; separate and union; conflict and peace to mention but a few.

Structuralism rejects the view that there is an objective and absolute centre through which reality is viewed. This basic structuralism supposition facilitates our study in that various perceptions of the internal displacees in Gulu regarding their status will be ascertained through their narratives performance. These are often perceived as others from without in a relationship that assigns power to the host citizens. The binary opposition that is likely to affect their lives' perception was investigated through structuralism because it was extremely relevant to the entire research process's comprehension. The three tenets of structuralist informed the analysis of the internally displacees narratives in line with the set objectives. One of this study's curiosities was investigating how the internally displacees perceive themselves and their world by focusing on how they configure their experiences through the narratives gained.

3. Understanding the Internal Displacees through Narrative Approach

The concepts of harmony and displacement through review of narrative studies on internally displacees ought to be vividly sketched to comprehend the study thoroughly. Harmony and displacement experiences may shape the process of healing in the lives of the internally displacees. Customary, people live in their villages in a state of harmony or comparative concord. When noteworthy altitudes of battle arise, the harmony is disturbed, and the conflicts developed may eventually break into violence. When life is threatened by conflict and violence, people are often forced to leave their villages/homes, leading to displacement. Perhaps peace is always better at home.

Human beings usually struggle for a healthier state of life. Although there may not be a wholly agreed-upon understanding of "a better state of life," it can be observed throughout human history that human beings engage in activities aimed at bettering their status. The better status may be perceived in terms of material or psychological wellbeing of people. One fundamental way of achieving psychosocial wellbeing is the attainment of peace. However, peace remains an ideal which humans continue to strive for as is indicated by the following observation by Ian Harris:

> Here we are in the 21st century. We have put a man on the moon and can communicate instantaneously with our brothers and sisters all over this planet, but we have not figured out how to live in peace. Why not? (Harris, 2004).

The question to ask at this point is, "what is peace"? In answer to that question (Howard 1987, 10) states that "peace is something that can mean all things to all men and even more to women." This statement raises the question of what peace means to children. The analysis of internally displaced narrated experiences will perhaps lead to an understanding of displacees' perception of peace. Harris identifies two levels of peace; personal and interpersonal (social). Personal peace is a state of individual consciousness and of quietness and calm on an inner state which many do not achieve. Yet it is possible to have inner peace in a world torn by strife. One's capacity to achieve a degree of personal tranquillity, balance and calm is an essential prerequisite to creating peaceful social relations.

In ordinary perception, peace denotes the absence of conflict. However, there is a distinction between positive peace and negative peace. Negative peace refers to the absence of war, but scholars assert that though it is good, the absence of war is not enough in the peace endeavour. Such scholars see war not merely as a state of hostility but an inclination thereto. According to Howard, peace is a balance between order and justice.

It should be noted here that this balance is an ideal which individuals and societies strive towards achieving throughout their lives. Human beings are constantly consciously or unconsciously balancing between how much injustice they are prepared to tolerate in the interest of order and how much disorder they are prepared to provoke injustice. Macquarrie emphasizes the centrality of justice in the pursuit of peace by asserting that there be wholeness where injustice persists.

Pazahayampallil (1984) defines peace as "the tranquillity of order. It is the right relationship between God and people and between people and people. The right relationship consists in the observance of love for one another". Bansikiza (2004) echoes this definition by asserting that peace is both a gift from God and a product of people's efforts. He argues further that peace must be constructed based on central human moral values which include justice, truth, freedom and love. According to him, peace is not an event; it has to be continually sought after. "Its dynamism implies building bridges that unite divided people, heal inflicted wounds and remove bitterness harboured". From the previous, it is clear that peace is a complex concept. Perhaps it is best understood by focusing on its varied attributes including order, justice, love and balance between individual good and collective good.

As the discussion of peace necessarily subsumes the concept of conflict, which focuses on this point. A basic definition of conflict is "the pursuit of incompatible goals." This can be at various levels including personal, interpersonal, national and international. Hall (1996) defines conflict as "power struggles over differences: differing beliefs, interests, values or abilities to secure needed resources". Lederach (1996) deals with conflict from a Social Constructionist perspective and argues that conflicts emerge and develop based on meanings and interpretations people attach to actions and events. Lederach argues further that conflicts do not just happen; the people concerned are active participants in creating them. What emerges from the foregoing arguments is that differences greatly influence conflict in perceptions and interpretations?

Howard also sees conflict as part of life, not something unnecessarily, arising from extraordinary pathological conditions. "Conflict bubbles up naturally, almost necessarily, within societies". Therefore, he asserts the need to understand the sources of conflict, the hidden roots and dynamics that create conflicts whether they erupt into wars or not. According to him, peace is not natural to humans and has to be constructed. Hobbes (1992) in his work *The Leviathan* argues that humans are brutish and selfish and need a powerful state (the leviathan) to curb their selfishness. Schomookler (1984) in *Parable of the Tribes*, argues that the roots of human violence are civic and political; human communities war against each other to gain resources and plunder treasure.

From this discussion, three features develop as the key drivers of conflict: the pursuit of mismatched goals, differences of perception and interpretation and disagreements about sharing resources. One factor that is not brought out in the foregoing arguments but is an underlying factor in fueling conflict is self-perception. A perception of self that largely excludes "the other" has a great potential for creating conflict. The us/ other dynamics in sociopolitical relations usually produces conflicts that are self-perpetrating. This is because as Lederach has observed, "conflict transforms perceptions of self, others and the issue. This usually leads to reduced accuracy in understanding the other's intentions and decreased ability to articulate one's intentions" (1996, 18).

When conflict is not positively transformed, we realise that when conflict is not positively transformed, it may eventually erupt into physical violence, which in many cases leads people to seek safety by fleeing their homes. When such people cross a national border, they become internally displacees. Currently, Africa has about 8 million internally displacees. According to Jesuit Refugee Services (JRS), internally, displacees are part of a complex global migratory phenomenon. "Many people are prompted to leave their own country by a mixture of fears, hopes and aspirations which can be very difficult if not impossible to unravel" (2000, 122). When mass displacements occur, providing relief is, understandably, the immediate preoccupation becomes the international internally displacees regime. However, there is a need to look at a displacement from other perspectives in the longer term. Therefore, this study focuses on another perspective by understanding the internal displacees' perception of the reality of displacement by focusing on their narratives performed in the camps. Therefore, the study intended to produce useful insights about internally displacees whether children, adults, and their perception of peace, harmony, conflict, and displacement.

Studies done on urban internally displacees in Uganda focused on social issues affecting people populations. Kinyeki (2006) studied the survival strategies of displacees and discovered that internally displacees meet their basic needs through hardship. They survive without legal rights to work, and they are forced to cope with an angry host community with more conflicting issues. Kanyeki's study mainly handled related matters affecting urban internally displacees, but the current study of squares harmony through the narrative argues that displaces can turn against each other unless a sense of harmony is created from within through narratives.

A study conducted by PHARP (Peace Building Healing and Reconciliation Programme) on NGO working among internally displacees revealed that internally displacees live under the constant fear of police harassment. They also feel psychologically disturbed due to the apathetic and sometimes hostile attitude of colleagues and others. His scholarship discussed the need for trauma healing sessions trough narration of experience (Bukuru et al., 2006). PHARP has also researched internally displaced children in which they collected oral narratives from among themselves and narrated to each other (PHARP, 2006). This anthology has fifteen stories by internally displaced children from the Great Lakes Region. There are questions based on the story with a broad perspective of peacebuilding at the end of every story. This project's objective was to provide a tool that teachers and caregivers dealing with children traumatized by conflict could employ to pursue healing. Ndirangu (2007:111) conducted a study on the internally displacees in Kenya and focused on the perceptions of their problems. She concluded that the internally displacees desire local integration into the host country and harmony as a solution for healthy living.

Polkinghorne (1988) studied the nature of narrative meaning and discovered that a narrative is a scheme utilizing which human beings make sense of their experience of temporary and personal actions. Salomon asserts that the importance of the role played by historically rooted collective narratives in a community's sense of identity and way of interpreting reality can be seen in the way new state schemes new narratives or change old ones, thus not only offering the root for collective narratives but for colouring them. Arguably, the collective narrative is more fundamental than historical facts in creating a nations' sense of individuality.

Salomon argues that collective narratives enable people to know who they are, what they are suffering from, why they are labelled under the despised "others" and the experiences that lead them to the entire complication. Collective narratives seem to be the coping mechanisms for displaces.

Salomon points out an aversive feature of collective narratives in intergroup conflict:

> By necessity, the collectives of groups in conflict contradict each other...thus, whereas a group's collective narrative bolsters the groups self-identify and justifies its role in the conflict, it also, invalidates the other side's collective narrative and its role in the conflict: if "we" are victims "they" are obviously the perpetrators (277).

The significance of creative expression in helping internally displacees and immigrant to adjust in their new culture was affirmed in a quantitative study conducted among internally displaced children in Montreal in 2005. The use of an artistic expression in classrooms helped the self-esteem, expression of emotions, problem-solving and conflict resolution among internally displacees (Rousseau et al., 2005, 180).

This study applying within the context of other narrative studies on internally displacees reveal that most of these studies Africa (Uganda) and a review of the available literature shows the need for such studies in the Ugandan context. This is why the current study proposed the analysis of harmony among the internally displacees' narratives to discover what they reveal about their lives' perception in relation to their internally displaced position.

4. Research Questions

1. What sort of harmony created by narratives exists among the internally displacees in Gulu?

2. Is there a relationship between the harmony and the human emotions expressed in narratives of displacees' in Gulu?

3. What is the perception of displacement in the narratives among the internally displacees in Gulu?

5. Research Design

This study on internally displacees in Uganda Gulu employed three main methods: evocative survey, narrative survey and content scrutiny. The survey method enabled interviews of a sample of the internally displacees in Gulu. The purpose was to understand the situation through an actual collection of narratives from these internally displacees. The narrative survey informed the process of gathering relevant information through storytelling. The observation and recording of narratives were done in the camps, especially through created focus groups. These narratives were then critically examined as phenomenal literary objects and the concept of harmony derived by structuralism literary theory.

6. Study Area and Population

The target population of the study was internally displacees in Gulu. The sample was arrived at through the uneven sampling technique rigorously applied to the different camps. The narratives performance was delivered in focus groups where narratives were amassed using an audio recording. During recording, the researcher observed the respondents' performance cues and noted anything in the narrative situation pertinent to the research. The respondents' cues were the tone of voice, posture, gestures, head nodding hand clapping and foot stamping. We read through all the data collected to familiarize ourselves before transcribing the collected points and the recorded narratives. The data was then screened to eradicate irrelevant information in the study. The data in the research study was threefold: ground notes, interview notes and recordings. This information was ordered in order, checked in order to identify the idea of harmony among displacees. The data used was related to the research questions because it was assumed to draw general observations and interpretation to address the research problem; appropriate data sets must be edited. The data interpretation was made though the structuralist literary theory. We grilled how internally displacees reconstruct their world to create sense and existence.

7. Results and Discussion

To answer the research questions critically, a structural literary theory was used within the calculative qualitative research design. The data collected was analysed based on how the internally displaced Gulu's internal displacees performed the narratives revealing their social behaviour, feelings, perceptions, and the relations between what they were telling vis-a-vis their actual physical dispositions.

7.1 Harmony Created by Narratives Among the Internally Displacees in Gulu

From the data collected, it was argued that through performing narratives, the internally displacees get to enact a unity of their human experiences and learn to reorder their history as a vital constituent of the coherent whole. For instance, listening to the young man's story performed in the field and presented here below, one realises that a humanitarian act of solidarity tends to create harmony among people who have lost both home and a sense of identity:

> I was at home, building my first personal hut when five fierce people (men) arrived from nowhere in particular. They asked me to put down my tools, including the poles I had lifted over my shoulder for roofing my hut. One man asked me to tell him where my father had gone or else he would cut me into small pieces like 'simsim' if I did not inform him. I answered that I did not know where my father had gone, but he could not accept my answer. These five furious men then grappled my hands and bound them at my back. They slapped me on both sides of my head till my ears were blocked. I unconsciously fell on the ground, and one of them shouted: "kill this dog with a stick". "I felt hopeless and gone but was later awakened by some kind of noise from pacing up and down of human feet in someplace. It was in the camp.

The narrator and the audience have one thing in common "transposition" within their own country. Even though the narrator sounds traumatised and haunted by his bad experience, this narrative's performance humanises the casualties caused by the political tensions brought about Lord Army Rebels (LRA). According to the structuralist theory, the young man's narrative structure commences with humanity's antiquity code. It makes the other displacees mind their own unique experiences and language of expression since no humanity lacks language or narrative. Therefore, a narrative is able to order any of peoples' thoughts or those of any human groups irrespective of gender disparities. Through a structuralist's eye, whereby every structure exemplifies either the wholeness or a sense of internal coherence or transformation, harmony is reached among the internally displacees. Harmony is confirmed by the fact that the capacity of every structure or the transforming substance and its self-regulation generates meaning without appealing to its outside influences. Hawkes (1989) confirms the research by proposing that a narrative usually relies on its internal nature and not on actuality for it to make sense. Narratives by the internally displacees make independent meaning capable of harmonising the agony experienced through their endurance and conflicts caused by scramble for space in the camp.

Even though the most central consequence of a structure or an ordering of reality is an instilling of events in narratives with moral meaning; narratives may soothe the internally displacees to transfer their core experience of reality to a non-chaotic or a non-arbitrary order. This may also be demonstrated by a mother who narrated her incidence most emphatically:

> I had bought two kilos of meat for supper and had seasoned it very well so that my children would for once have enough proteins for their growing bones. Their father lived and worked in Kampala city, but he had sent enough cash to treat our children. We were going to taste new millet bread. Little did I know it was going to be a delicious dinner for Kony rebels. No sooner had I served the excited children than a stream of people dashed in our small sitting room. All they shouted was get out "get out everyone before we shoot". We stood up at once and left without even a small piece of meat for my youngest daughter, who valued meat so much. They then sat down to dine. I wondered how they had learnt about my children's delicious meal that evening. What was going to happen to us as we were not allowed time to pick anything from our house which was burnt down immediately after their supper and looting.... In a trickle of an eye, we had lost everything we worked so hard to acquire.

In light of a structuralist perception the mother of children laments how they lost their precious home, their daily farming occupation, their easiness of family gesture of sharing a meal and their expressions of feelings as language peculiar to their family. Despite all the sadness, however, she expressed secret joy for having escaped with all her children alive. We noted that so many internally displacees seemed to emphathise with her during the performance, hence creating a sense of harmony within their category. Applying a structuralist viewpoint, we realise that the performer and the audience generally demonstrate harmony since there was a sense of courage, resilience, hope and power to live having escaped alive as illustrated and derived from their personal speeches.

The footballers called Northern Under Cranes were exercising in the trading Centre field to equip ourselves for a game with Soroti Cotton Team the following Friday. All of a sudden we looked to the east of the field and we saw men in full football uniform approaching us, and we were about to mock and cheer them thinking that they were our opponents who had contemplated serious rehearsals with us to gauge our strength before the main game. 'They were not I tell you' as we had to be forced to line up in a straight line and stand still for hours like in the movement army, they started to train us to match militarily. "Left, right ... about turn "!Northern boys oyoye!!! oyoye!!! Some of our boys demonstrated some attitude of escape or rebel-ism. At once, they were separated from us and beaten to terribly. I tried to dash off the line objecting because one of the boys being beaten was our gifted goal post keeper who had made the team survive in and out of season. What I thought was a rescue plan became a fatal scheme for talented members. A mental-like man pulled me by the hand and forced me to shout in the air, but all of a sudden diverted the gun to aim at my friend and to kill him at once. I feel so bad about the things that I did. What I did disturbs me so much that I inflicted death on own people my team member. When I go home, I must do some traditional rites because I have killed. I must perform these rites and cleanse myself. I often dream about the goalkeeper from my village whom I killed. I see him in my dreams, and he is asking me why I killed him for nothing. I cry a lot, and I am not myself any longer.

The above narrative concerns the rethinking about but terrible act in a displacee's story where he was forced to kill his best friend. Here, this narrative acts as prose of despair because it dwells on the rebels' morale hypocrisy (LRA). The narrator's tone depicts unending traumatic events and a call for urgent interference to respond to all displacees' crises. In the spirit of the structuralists, 'the performer's attitude in the narrative reaches quite beyond the past, beyond nostalgia, beyond trauma and also beyond the present consolation to suggest future consolation with the hope of healing: 'What I did disturbs me so much in that I inflicted death on my people, my team member. When I go home, I must do some traditional rites because I have killed. I must perform these rites and cleanse myself."

Another young person also narrated his sad experience as follows:

> I knew a boy all my life but was told to attack and kill. We were from the same village. I refused to kill him, and they told me they would shoot me. They pointed a gun at me, so I had to kill him in cold blood. The boy was asking me, 'Why are you doing this?" I said! I had no choice. After I killed him, they made me smear his blood all over my arms. I felt dizzy. There was another dead body nearby, and I could smell the body. I felt sick. They said you must do that not to fear death or kill since you are yourself a rebel.

This narrative illustrates how literary perspective can give his complex picture of total confession of all the experiences that have led to a diminished life living in displacement in your own country. Displaced murderers are usually portrayed as downtrodden, voiceless victims who cannot reject a degrading situation, such as having the will to kill their loved ones. Thus, it is important to consider how literary narratives attempt to give a voice to displacees to express regrets and renounce evil things they did without willpower or rational authority. Narrative delivery also enables internally displacees to mark their severe exclusion from home and wish to return whenever opportunity chances.

In cases of murder above, the two performers reported having been forced to kill their best friends and were now yet each of them was living with a severe sense of guilt as if they had murdered out of their wills. Consequently, their experience became compatible with the structuralist view that humans cannot understand things in isolation; they understand by recognizing or creating new structures. Therefore, human beings do not observe a whole universe, but on the contrary, they create their own. Therefore, through structuralism, we concluded that many people share similar challenges when displaced. When the chance is given to amplify their voices and experiences through narrative performance, they gain supportive powers that enable them to meet their learning needs to overcome enormous hurdles, thereby achieving harmony.

> My husband was trying to take a glimpse of me while experimenting with his new camera he had just afforded after very hard work when we managed to sell our four bags of shelled groundnuts.

We had been given a small gift on top of the usual price as our nuts proved healthier than those of others peasants. Our house's building was always shielded by some homegrown forest where my husband and I teased each other with snapshots. Suddenly, two men popped from a place of hiding in our forest and captured my husband, who was following me right inside the sitting room as I was picking our car keys. I made a shout for help, but one of the men dragged me into the children's room and started to insult me. After a terrible abuse, the other also arrived and started to abuse me afresh. I continued screaming, but my husband could not manage to come to rescue me from the monsters since he had been shot in both legs and was left alive to experience the suffering of my abuse helplessly.

The above narrative performer clarifies that women are the most delicate category of all the internally displacees. A woman could not be allowed time to be loved or even enjoy the fruits of her labour in front of her husband amid all sorts of threats. Women, as victims of sexual abuse, have had to suffer a lot due to their gender. Literature is a witness to history in the past, now and in the future, to bring scrutiny and humanity through narrative performances. Narratives constitute an imperative feature in displacees' lives because they bring about social cohesion among them. According to the structuralists, displacees have a particular common civilization, and they look at themselves as one people, one love and one heart established by other beings. This sense brings about peace and stability in among them and can even lead to development. Oral narratives are a source of unity and harmony among displaces because they make each displacee realise that some peoples' experiences are perhaps worse than their own after all. This may make displacees visualise a sense of hearing or as structuralists argue to reconstruct meaning in their terms based on what they have seen performed or heard narrated in their presence.

7.2 Relationship Between the Harmony and Human Emotions: in Narratives of Displacees

There is a strong relationship between the narratives commonly narrated in everyday language in the camp and the emotions triggered among the internally displacees. For instance, in the case of the young man who was displaced while building his house/hut, some portion of the conceptual performance system is given structure. In the narrative, the act of destruction compared to conventional food crop of the area 'simsim'. The relationships in these narratives are supported and given credence by articulated human speech, oral or written, or image whether still or cause and effect one, including gesture, posture and another organized blend of various substances. This question posed by the rebel; "where is your father" declares the relationship and purpose of the occasioning. This expression commonly used in everyday language among the Acholi communities where children are supposed to substitute their parents or vice versa. This situation of a child being beaten instead of a parent suggests a significant correlation between harmony and human emotions likely to raise among the audience who may wonder how one character has to suffer because the intended one is missing. In fact, among many African communities, a mother might be forced to be arrested instead of her daughter or son, and no one might be expected to question.

According to structuralists, there is a link between what is being said and the participant's traditional or cultural disposition. Indeed, as the narrator explained, displacees used to sit around a bonfire at night not just to warm themselves but to decide important issues concerning who they are. Therefore, this metaphor is conventional since it was commonly be used in everyday language to give structure to some portion of the Ugandan culture's conceptual system. These findings are then in line with the structuralism which claims that: "viewed in the context of performance the narrative arouses some emotional feelings of affection of love toward each other in a camp or among families, friends, duties and responsibilities. Through structuralism theory guiding this research, the analysis shows that a vital link of relationship exists between the oral texts and the emotional involvement of the internally displacees. There is a strong link between texts and their specific socio-cultural context of production. It is the knowledge of this link that helps the audience to interpret and understand better texts produced by the performer and to connect the object mentioned or the person compared to it.

7.3 Perception Revealed Through Narratives Performance of the Internally Displacees

Narratives among the displacees had an original comparison that calls attention to the camping situation's entire experience. The narratives' description demonstrates how the researcher, in the current study, could appreciate how the internally displaces manage to coop with each other. It was established that the internally displacees' perform with a view of making each other as the audience to laugh but with an idea behind drawing the audience's attention to immortalise their unique experience in the camp. According to the structuralists, the narratives of the internally displacees performer must draw images of the person being talked about so that the utterance becomes original and poetic in its structure and meaning. Linguistically and structurally analysed narratives have the power of uplifting everyone in the camp.

The linguistic and structural analysis of the internally displaced' reveals a positive attitude of how people, especially performers and audiences, can recreate a language, sense of identity pretending that they are referring to somebody or something else whereas they address their interlocutor directly. There was care in performing narratives to ensure that they sought (intentionally) to avoid the fact that the other within in the audience should feel humiliated rather than feel relieved or even feel like laughing with the others at all humorous acts by rebels such sending owners in the camps and resorting to filling their stomachs with the residents' supper. The creative performance may lead to humour as the positive emotion of mirth invoked in a social context by the perception of playful incongruity expressed through laughter-related behaviours. Structuralists studies tend to highlight the positive impact of humour on listeners in a communicative event. Logically, humour forms an obligatory part of human communication and behaviour, in that every individual at one point in time must be satirised or mocked or tricked. The internally displacees ought to naturally express or react with humour in their interactions in the camp to coexist coherently and in peaceful harmony. The narrative's creative and structural features being significantly performed rely on the exaggeration performers create an exciting atmosphere to make the delivery colourful and memorable despite forced camping in one's state.

Conclusion

The study sought to understand how harmony is created among the internally displacees through narrative performance sampling Gulu Uganda. Therefore, this study captures some experiences observed in this induced state of the internally displaced in Gulu (Northern Uganda). The experiences that shout up concerning the harmony created by narratives told among the internally displacees in Gulu communities ranged from devastation due to loss of proper shelter and loss of respect by one's children to lack of privacy. The displaces narrated that even though harmony existed among themselves, there was no respect of generation gaps within the camps. Parents and children lacked freedom from each to express their age differences. Distancing between one's children and the parents was impossible due to Kony human raids' expected re-occurrence in the camps. Parents preferred to remain inseparable with their children than risk them for further loss and damage. Respondents argued that being landlessness, jobless, homeless, marginalization, food insecurities, increased loss of access to common national property and assets including loss of African community expression muted displacees' sense of harmony which could have been real.

Concerning the experiences with the relationship between harmony and human emotions: in narratives of displacees in Gulu, some of the respondents wept at repeating painful situations still prevalent in their lives. There was much desperation among these people who were forced to leave their normal dwelling place because of internal conflicts and useless wars in Uganda. It was observed that harmony among people who can no longer advance a secure livelihood in their homelands due to power struggle was further fetched. Most displacees appeared to have already despaired realizing that they had no alternatives and northern conflict seemed to have no limit.

The experiences that came up concerning perception revealed through narratives performance of the internally displacees had to do with the styles of illustration of the displacees' state of displacement and the impression such depictions had on displacees. Displacees wondered whether the repeating of their unique stories and narratives performances aimed to raise awareness about the life of displacement. They would have been better narrated that reported if their unique, disturbing condition could prevent future wars in such extreme circumstances experienced by those fleeing their homes steads in their own country. They shared in general how their lives were full of uncertainties for unification with their clan lands, how their teenage daughters were being threatened with sexual abuse, emotional distress, disability, illiteracy and poverty and the like. They regretted how their abducted youths had been forced into being gorilla soldiers, human shields and hostages or coerced sexual objects. The internally displacees in Gulu seemed to harbour more negative feelings than harmony. Displacement had brought about more psychosocial effects such as family and social breakdown, increased resentment and violence, persistent insecurity, fear and despair than harmony. Parent displacees reported that the blame game peddled by politicians who thought that the youth, in particular, Ugandans, in general, were lazy and that is why they were being abducted was a mere escapism approach, one which was baseless and misconceived.

Precisely, three questions conceptualized the study that investigated harmony among the internally displacees through a narrative performance. The study found out basically that through the eye of a structuralist, there is a point whereby in every structure the totality of internal coherence or transformation, brings about harmony among the internally displacees. Harmony is visualized in a narrative performance and can order any class of peoples' thoughts or any human groups. A healthy relationship exists between the narratives commonly narrated in everyday language in the camp and the emotions cherished displacees internally. The linguistic and structural analysis of the internally displacees narratives reveals a positive attitude of how people, especially performers and audiences can recreate a language, and sense of identity pretending that what they are narrating are mere stories. The narratives by the internally displacees enable them to make independent meanings leading to harmonizing coexistence in the new environment. Narrative performance and emotional effect of the internally displaced are birds of feathers, therefore excluding one from the other renders both useless and not capable of being enacted or performed. Moreover, the internally displacees are eager to hear each other's narrative, hence harbouring performance. Upon this discussion, the researcher recommends that the internal displacees' narrative performance be structured, ordered, and upheld more future researchers should focus on the relation between cultural lag and the internally displacees' special needs.

References

Bukuru, Sebastian, et al. *Peace and Conflict for Urban Refugees: Analysis of Refugee Peace Initiatives in Nairobi, Kenya.* Nairobi: Pharp and Kurve Wustrow 2002.

Harris, Ian, Book review of The Ideal of Peace. Oxford: Blackwell Publishing, 2004.

Hawkers, Terence, *Structuralism and Semiotics,* Routledge 1989.

Kreitzer, L. *Liberian Refugee Women: a Qualitative Study of their Participation in Planning Camp Programmes. International Social Work.* May 2002.

Landy, Alice S. *The Health Introduction to Literature* D. C. Health and Company, 1980.

Lederach, John Paul, *Preparing for Peace.* New York: Syracuse University Press, 1996.

Ndiragu, B. Kirigo, *In search of durable solutions to the refugee problems in Kenya. An analysis of the traditional solutions from the refugee's perspective.* 1996 to 2006. M.A Thesis. Nairobi: Catholic University of Eastern Africa 2007.

OAU 1969 Convention, Art. 1

Pavlish, C., Narrative Inquiry into Life Experiences of Refugee Women and Men. *International Nursing Review.* March 2007.

Polkinghorne, D., *Narrative Knowing and the Human Sciences.* Albany: State University of New York Press 1988.

Salomon, Gavriel, A Narrative based View of Coexistence Education, *Journal of Social Issues,* June 2004.

Sperl, Stefan, *Evaluation of UNCHR's policy on refugees in Urban Areas: A case study Review of Cairo*, 2001 in www.unhcr.org accessed on 18th June 2007.

Steele Q. Mary, *Realism, Truth and Honesty,* Monterey Brooks Cole 1999.

Verdivame, Guglielmo and Barbara Harrel Bond, *Rights in Exile Janus faced Humanitarianism.* New York: Berghahn Books 2005.

UNHCR *Refugee Children: Guidelines on Protection and Care.* Geneva, 1994.

UNHCR *Population Data Unit Refugee children in Africa.* Geneva 2001, www.unhcr.org. Accessed on 18th June 2007.

UNHCR. *Strategy and Activities Concerning Refugee Children.* Geneva 2005.

UNHCR. *Policy on Refugees in Urban Areas.* Geneva 1997

UNICEF, *Children in Situations of Armed Conflict,* UN Document. E/ICEF/1986/CRP.

About the Author

Dr Lucy after graduating from Formation house of my Order, the Sisters of Mary in 1996, she embarked on studies in Education and Theology at Christ the Teacher Institute for Education and St. Mary's University of Minnesota. Four Makerere University earned a degree in English Literature and studied Literary theories and Ugandan Literature, acting, poetry and narrative voices and became University lecturer at the Catholic University of Eastern Africa and Tangaza College. She has published articles in Kenya and Uganda and a poem entitled "African Psalm" in Aachen-German. Dr Lucy's teaching experience is balanced as she has taught in University for 14 years and four years in colleges and HSCs. She was the Congregation's Justice and peace representative (1994 – 2006).

Challenges of Refugees in an Integration Challenged Community: Refugees in the USA

Henry Poduthase[13] & Genevieve Sabala[14].

Abstract

This chapter focuses on how US Federal and State agencies collaborate with voluntary agencies (VLOAG) to implement the refugee resettlement process to integrate into the community. Failure to recognize refugees' credentials, in addition to individual and institutional barriers, contribute to economic and integration challenges. However, change in societal attitudes, and economic empowerment programmes show that adapting innovative hands-on practices, from sustainable employment to unlocking entrepreneurial potential, is transformative. The chapter narrates an in-depth perspective of the refugee community's economic and integration challenges in the US. The study uses recent and relevant research about refugee settlement and challenges faced, focusing on the United States. Integrating relevant theories and empirical research, the authors depict the refugee community's social and economic reality in the country. The authors explore empowerment programmes by VOLAGs, including Journey's End Refugee Services in Buffalo NY, Peace of Thread in Clarkson GA, International Institute of Minnesota, and Global Talent Boise, ID. Using case examples, theories, and a synthesis of existing literature on refugees' economic and integration challenges are examined. The findings show that refugees in the country are predominantly located into urban areas and relocating to new locations are discouraged by the US refugee policy based on a perceived challenge of secondary migration and community

---

13   Associate Professor and Director, Graduate Social Work Programme, West Texas A&M University, Canyon, TX-79016, Email: hpoduthase@wtamu.edu

14   Assistant Professor, Department of Social Science, University of Wisconsin Stout, 712 South Broadway Street, Menomonie, WI 54751, Email: sabalag@uwstout.edu

integration. However, there is a disconnect between US resettlement policy and refugee secondary migration where the refugees move to various rural locations for employment opportunities, welfare benefits, reunification with relatives, and a more congenial climate. Later, in achieving economic stability, refugees must face challenges like language skills, mental health, individual challenges, whereas recognition of qualifications and negative cultural bias/ discrimination are common institutional challenges. Failure to recognize refugees' qualifications and previous work experiences, limited language skills, societal and cultural biases, and regulatory barriers in the host country affect refugees' ability to achieve economic sustainability. The importance of recognizing the impact of both individual and institutional challenges on refugees' economic success must be underscored during the resettlement process. Ultimately, using the strengths and empowerment approach to support and promote entrepreneurship, is an alternative to employment among refugees, increases economic and social benefits for the host country.

Keywords: Refugees in the United States, Economic Challenges, Integration Challenges.

"No one puts their children in a boat unless the water is safer than the land." *Warsan Shire*

Introduction

According to the Department of Health and Human Services report, refugees brought in $63 billion more revenue to the federal, state, and local governments than the cost incurred, for them, for the period of 2005-2014. Since refugees come to the country with nothing, this achievement is critical and substantial. When the refugees move to the country, they mostly rely on public funds during the country's initial years. However, this investment is paid back several times during their lifetime in the country, and hence, the core goal of economic self-sufficiency of the United States refugee settlement programme is achieved to an extent. Refugee resettlement is conducted by the collaboration of public and private non-profit organizations. These organizations are critical in the resettlement process of refugees. While long term resettlement resources are provided through the Office of Refugee Resettlement (ORR), their sponsoring agencies provide them with essential services for a period of no less than 30 days that may extend up to 90 days.

This chapter focuses on how US Federal and State agencies collaborate with voluntary agencies (VLOAG) to implement the refugee resettlement process to integrate into the community. Failure to recognize refugees' credentials, in addition to individual and institutional barriers, contribute to economic and integration challenges. However, change in societal attitudes, and economic empowerment programmes show that adapting innovative hands-on practices, from sustainable employment to unlocking entrepreneurial potential, is transformative. Using case studies and other empirical research, the chapter narrates an in-depth perspective of the refugee community's economic and integration challenges in the US.

1. Refugee and Refugee Resettlement

According to the United Nations High Commissioner for Refugees (UNHCR), a refugee is someone who has been forced to flee his or her country because of persecution, war, or violence. A refugee has a well-founded fear of persecution for reasons of race, religion, nationality, political opinion, or membership in a particular social group (UNHCR).

Defined in the 1951 U.N. Refugee Convention as people who are outside their homeland and are unwilling to return because of "a well-founded fear of being persecuted for reasons of race, religion, nationality, membership of a particular social group or political opinion," refugees face an uncertain future (Singer & Wilson, 2006). The U.N., therefore, recognizes three "durable solutions" for refugees, in order of preference: voluntary repatriation to their homeland, integration into the host society (known as the "country of first asylum"), or resettlement to a third country. This last option is pursued when the first two options are not feasible, and less than one percent of the world's refugees are referred for resettlement (Singer & Wilson, 2006).

The United States had previously led the world on this measure for decades, admitting more refugees each year than all other countries combined (Krogstad, 2019). During the 1980s and 1990s, the United States accepted an average of 100,000 refugees for resettlement annually. After the terrorist attacks of September 11, 2001, levels were curtailed as security and background checks were enhanced (Singer & Wilson, 2006). However, since 2017, that number significantly dropped, and the demographics have changed. The number of Muslim refugees admitted to the United States in the first half of fiscal 2018 has dropped from the previous year more than any other religious group, falling to nearly 1,800 compared with the roughly 22,900 admitted in all of fiscal 2017, according to a Pew Research Center analysis of U.S. State Department data (Connor & Krogstad, 2018). The data shows about 10,500 refugees, including about 6,700 Christians, entered the U.S. from Oct. 1, 2017, to March 31, 2018 – far behind the 39,100 admissions at this point in fiscal 2017 (including 18,500 Muslims and 16,900 Christians). The United States plans to admit a maximum of 18,000 refugees in the fiscal year 2020, down from a cap of 30,000 in the one that ended Sept. 30, 2019, under a new refugee admissions ceiling set by the Trump administration (Krogstad, 2019). According to the Pew Research Center analysis of the U.S State Department data, this would be the lowest number of refugees resettled by the U.S. in a single year since 1980, when Congress created the nation's refugee resettlement programme (Krogstad, 2019).

Refugees are admitted to the United States via the Refugee Act of 1980 when potential refugees are screened outside of the United States and must be determined by an officer of the Department of Homeland Security or by the United Nations High Commission for Refugees as meeting official refugee criteria (Singer & Wilson, 2006). When it comes to resettlement, using data from the Office of Refugee Resettlement (ORR) on the location of initial settlement of refugees arriving between 1983 and 2004, Singer and Wilson (2006) found that: a) More than 2 million refugees have arrived in the United States since the Refugee Act of 1980 was established, driven from their homelands by war, political change, and social, religious, and ethnic oppression; b) Refugees have overwhelmingly been resettled in metropolitan areas with large foreign-born populations; c) In medium-sized and smaller metropolitan areas, refugees can have a considerable impact on the local population, especially if the total foreign-born population is small; and d) The leading refugee destination metro areas have shifted away from traditional immigrant gateways over the past two decades, while newer gateways are resettling proportionally more refugees.

2. Refugee Resettlement Programmes (ORR) in the US

The resettlement system is a public-private programme run by the Department of State Bureau of Population, Refugees, and Migration and the US Department of Health and Human Services Office of Refugee Resettlement (ORR). These federal agencies work with nine national resettlement agencies (or "voluntary agencies") that provide services to newly arrived refugees through a network of local affiliates in communities across the US (Bernstein & DuBois, 2018).

2.1 Federal and State Agencies

The Office of Refugee Resettlement (ORR) provides new populations with the opportunity to achieve their full potential in the United States. These programmes provide people in need with critical resources to become integrated members of American society (ORR, 2018). To better serve those in need, ORR collaborates with Federal Agencies, State Partners, Training and Technical Assistance Providers, and Resettlement Agencies (ORR, 2018).

Federal agencies include 1) the Department of Health and Human Services specifically Office for Civil Rights, Center for Disease Control, Substance Abuse and Mental Health Services Administration (SAMHSA), and HHS Lesbian, Gay, Bisexual and Transgender (LGBT) Health and Wellness Resources; 2) HHS Administration for Children and Families (AFC) through Early Childhood Development's office of Child Care and Office of Head Start, Office of Community Services; 3) Department of Homeland Security including Customs and Border Patrol, Immigration and Customs Enforcement, and US Citizenship and Immigration Services; 4) Department of Justice including Bureau of Citizenship and Immigration Services, Executive Office of Immigration Review, Office of Special Counsel for Immigration-Related Unfair Employment Practices (OSC), Human Rights and Special Prosecutions Section; 5) Department of State through the Bureau of Population, Refugees, and Migration (ORR, 2019).

Partnership with States is made possible by a State Refugee Coordinator, a State Refugee Health Coordinator and a managed State website (ORR, 2019) with detailed information on the services, policies and procedures, and employment opportunities. ORR also has a one-stop hub under the Refugee Technical Assistance Programme (RTAP) and one specialized organization with technical assistance expertise in services for survivors of torture known as Switchboard. Switchboard engages a network of subject matter experts to provide tools and materials, learning opportunities, research, and technical assistance on resettlement-related topics, including employment, education, health, and monitoring and evaluation (ORR, 2019).

ORR works closely and directly with Voluntary Agencies (VOLAGs) that operate at international, national, and state levels. ORR works directly with nine international refugee resettlement agencies across the world including Church World Services (CWS), Ethiopian Community Development Council (ECDC), Episcopal Migration Ministries (EMM), Hebrew Immigrant Aid Society (HIAS), International Rescue Committee (IRC), US Committee for Refugees and Immigrants (USCRI), Lutheran Immigration and Refugee Services (LIRS), United States Conference of Catholic Bishops (USCCB), and World Relief (WR) corporation (ACF, 2019) that ensure successful completion of a two-year screening process prior to any travel plans of selected refugees. Applicants are screened, interviewed, and selected by the United States Citizenship and Immigration Services (USCIS) officers. These officers conduct a 24 months long extensive screening of applicants before they are ready to travel and be resettled in the United States. Upon completing this process, the international agencies communicate with ORR providing them with individual refugee information to identify a Resettlement Agency (RA) or affiliate that will receive and resettle the refugees.

2.2. Non-profit Organizations

Resettlement Agencies or affiliates or local VOLAGs work directly with a parent VOLAG operating at State level. They are mostly nonprofits within the 50 States dedicated to serving newly arriving refugees from airport arrival, housing, employment, and continuous support through the integration process. For example, Bethany Christian Services in Grand Rapids Michigan is an affiliate and resettles referrals by Church World Services; International Institute of Wisconsin is an affiliate for U.S Committee for Refugees and Immigrants; Lutheran Social Services of

Wisconsin's parent VOLAG is Lutheran Immigration and Resettlement Services; and Hebrew Immigrant Aid Society is a parent VOLAG for Jewish Social Services (Wisconsin DCF, n.d). Refugee Services of Texas as an affiliate of Church World Services, Episcopal Migration Ministries, and Lutheran Immigration and Resettlement Services resettles refugees across the state of Texas.

Zucker (1982) affirms that these agencies cope with the myriad resettlement problems of adjustment and acculturation. They instruct refugees in the naturalization process. Moreover, when the refugee is no longer a refugee, but a citizen, some voluntary agencies continue to provide psychological and material help (Zucker, 1982). They continue to help them navigate economic, social, and cultural challenges. Their services range from governmental and quasi-governmental functions to purely private aid activities; they receive public monies under sundry contractual arrangements, primarily from State and Health and Human Services (Zucker, 1982).

3. Policies that Inform Refugee Economic Resettlement

In the Immigration and Nationality Act of 1952 that is amended several times in subsequent years defines a refugee as an alien who, generally, has experienced past persecution or has a well-founded fear of persecution on account of race, religion, nationality, membership in a particular social group, or political opinion. Authorization for domestic resettlement programmes and assistance to refugees, following details, support the refugees for their economic self-sufficiency. There are specific sections that discuss the economic self-sufficiency of the refugees in INA of 1952. Under the Act in conditions and considerations:

(1)(A) In providing assistance under this section, the Director shall, to the extent of available appropriations, (i) make sufficient available resources for employment training and placement in order to achieve economic self-sufficiency among refugees as quickly as possible, (ii) provide refugees with the opportunity to acquire sufficient English language training to enable them to become effectively resettled as quickly as possible, (iii) ensure that cash assistance is made available to refugees in such a manner as not to discourage their economic self-sufficiency, following subsection (e)(2), and (iv) insure that women have the same opportunities as men to participate in training and instruction.

(B) Congress intends that in providing refugee assistance under this section-

i. Employable refugees should be placed on jobs as soon as possible after they arrive in the United States;

ii. Social service funds should be focused on employment-related services, English-as-a-second-language training (in non-work hours where possible), and case management services; and

Furthermore, with regards to settlement region of the refugees, the INA clearly states that,

(2)(C) Such policies and strategies, to the extent practicable and except under such unusual circumstances as the Director may recognize, shall-

i. Ensure that a refugee is not initially placed or resettled in an area highly impacted (as determined under regulations prescribed by the Director after consultation with such agencies and governments) by the presence of refugees or comparable populations unless the refugee has a spouse, parent, sibling, son, or daughter residing in that area,

ii. Take into account-

a. The availability of employment opportunities, affordable housing, and public and private resources (including educational, health care, and mental health services) for refugees in the area,

b. the likelihood of refugees placed in the area becoming self-sufficient and free from long-term dependence on public assistance, and

c. The secondary migration of refugees to and from the area that is likely to occur.

Hence, the INA provides specific details in creating an environment for the economic self-sufficiency of the refugees who are settling into the United States. Later in the year of 1980, another act was signed into law called the 1980 Refugee Act. This Act established a process for resettlement for refugees. Primarily, the act served two significant purposes 1) to provide a uniform procedure for refugee admissions and 2) to authorize federal assistance to resettle refugees and promote their self-sufficiency. Based on the provisions of these two acts, the following areas of services are provided for the newly coming refugees in the United States of America for their economic self-sufficiency:

Orientation: Once a refugee has entered the country, they are provided with an orientation about the community that includes information about the sponsoring agency. Other agencies were assisting them in public services and facilities, personal and public safety, public transportation, the importance of learning English, personal finance, information regarding legal status in the country, and various other services available for the refugees.

Housing: A decent, safe, and sanitary accommodation will be provided for the refugees upon their arrival into the country based on the guidelines established by the Department of State. Furthermore, ORR provides cash assistance to eligible refugees to cover basic needs such as food, clothing, and housing for up to eight months. These initial supports provide the foundation for any newly came refugee to understand the country and the culture to move towards economic independence.

Health: Upon arrival, the agencies involved refer the refugees to conduct a comprehensive health assessment to identify any health problems and treat it if needed to help them find employment and resettle effectively. This comprehensive health assessment is offered free of charge for refugees, and additionally, they are eligible to apply for Medicaid or Refugee Medical Assistance to cover basic health care costs.

English as a Second Language Training (ESL): For an effective integration into the United States, learning English is essential as English is the country's popular language. Hence, refugees are provided with various options to learn English as a Second Language (ESL). Several organizations, including, local public libraries and sponsoring organizations, offer these courses for the refugees to learn ESL. These training would ultimately help refugees be hired or help them establish their own business in the country.

Education: Yet another service available for the economic self-sufficiency is that of school education. Public school education is free for grades Kindergarten to 12 and is operated by local governments. Refugees could enrol their children in the local public school, and Office of the Refugee Resettlement (ORR) supports these children to integrate into the American school system.

4. Integration in U.S Communities

Resettled refugees are an incredibly diverse group (Capps et al., 2015). Given this diversity, there is not just one "refugee experience" in the US, but many (Bernstein & DuBois, 2018). Refugees come in with different backgrounds and have different starting points and trajectories in the US (National Academies of Sciences, Engineering, and Medicine 2015). They range in educational background, English proficiency, mental and physical health condition, age, and many other characteristics that, like any immigrant or native-born individual, shape their outcomes and experiences in the US (Bernstein & DuBois, 2018), especially their ability to fully integrate.

Integration of refugees happens through various forms. According to Puma, Lichtenstein, and Stein (2018), integration has been explored through research, policy, and practice as a framework for gauging the extent to which refugees successfully navigate the economic, social, and cultural dynamics of their new country. However, they argue that the definition and assessment of integration remain elusive. Center for American Progress reports shows that while new arrivals face challenges, in the long run, all groups achieve significant levels of integration (Kallick & Mathema, 2016). According to Kallick and Mathema (2016), educational attainment, English language skills, homeownership, intermarriage, and citizenship contribute to refugees' integration in the United States.

An analysis of 2014 American Community Survey, 5-year data for Somali, Burmese, Hmong, and Bosnian refugees shows that: 1) Refugee groups are gaining a foothold in the labour force whereby refugee men quickly move into the labour force, and refugee women become increasingly integrated into the labour force over time; 2) Refugee groups are advancing in their careers (substantial gains in earnings, moving up the occupational ladder) and starting businesses; 3) Refugees integrate into American Society overtime, i.e. learn English, buy homes, become citizens; 4) As part of economic revitalization, refugees make the most difference in States and metropolitan areas such as Minneapolis and St.Paul, in Minnesota (Kallick & Mathema, 2016).

The integration of refugees is a dynamic and multifaceted two-way process which requires efforts by all parties concerned, including a preparedness on the part of refugees to adapt to the host society without having to forego their own cultural identity, and a corresponding readiness on the part of host communities and public institutions to welcome refugees and meet the needs of a diverse population (UNHCR Nicosia, 2014). The integration process is complex and gradual, comprising distinct but inter-related legal, economic, social and cultural dimensions, all of which are important for refugees' ability to integrate successfully as fully included members of the host society (UNHCR Nicosia, 2014). These economic successes among refugees do not come easy. There are substantial obstacles that refugees encounter before they gain this economic success.

5. Economic Opportunities for Refugees in the United States

Refugee resettlement programme envisions to provide a safe and sustainable economic growth of refugees coming into the country. In this regard, refugees' various positive economic effects on receiving communities are well established and well researched (Legrain, 2016). Research has found that there are multiple times returns on the amount spent on the refugee resettlement programme when they economically established. A study conducted by Chmura Economics and Analytics (2013) concluded that $4.8 million spent on refugee services of Cleveland, Ohio, yielded $50 million of economic returns by way of refugee-owned business and household spending. Thus, the impact of initial support provided for refugees has a much more profound impact on the economy. In addition to $50 million impacts, state tax revenue was $1.8 million, and the local government earned $900,000.

There are several employment promotion-specific programmes within the country. Among them, vocational training is something various resettlement agencies promote and help the refugees to attain. Several community colleges and technical institutions and higher education universities could help refugees identify specific employment-generating training that could eventually secure a job. Furthermore, ORR employability training services enhances the refugees to attain economic self-sufficiency sooner. Under the ORR employability training, various aspects of developing a self-sufficiency plan, job orientation, job referral, job development, job placement, follow-up, English language training, and employability assessment services are included to help the refugees to be economically independent.

6. Factors affecting Economic Achievement among Refugees

The main goal of the U.S refugee resettlement programme is the achievement of self-sufficiency. Therefore, most of the resources are directed toward employment through job training skills, language proficiency through English language classes, and educational attainment, especially for those who acquired formal education in their home countries. However, the Migration Policy Institute (MPI) reports that this minimal level of support for employment, education, and language services provided through resettlement programme may be insufficient to meet these groups' more significant needs. Only a small share of refugee adults (5-10 percent) advance their education once in the United States (MPI, 2020).

Unlike economic migrants who typically have time to plan and organize their departure, to save money, learn the local language or prepare beforehand for the cultural changes that await them (Lyon, Sepulveda & Syrett, 2007; Wauters & Lambrecht, 2006), refugees are a vulnerable group that is less prepared, lack personal connections to the host country, and have low self-confidence due to their traumatic experiences. Compared to other migrant groups, refugees tend to be slower to "close the gap" with the rest of society regarding labour market outcomes (Scholten et al., 2017). Nevertheless, some research shows that past engagement in entrepreneurship and cross-cultural experiences results in a high entrepreneurial spirit amongst refugees, and migrants more generally (Rengs et al., 2017; Vandor & Franke, 2016) be harnessed if some of the barriers could be removed.

6.1 Limiting Factors

Through their journey to achieve economic success, refugees encounter individual challenges, institutional challenges, or a combination of both. Individual challenges range from low levels of human capital and entrepreneurial skills, lack of language skills, undercapitalization to difficulties accessing finance. Institutional barriers include the inability to gaining access to the labour market, difficulty obtaining recognition of their diplomas and previous experience, distrust in public services, business regulatory barriers, and negative cultural bias and discrimination.

1) Individual challenges to economic sufficiency

Due to their lived experiences with war, trauma, and years of living in camps of substandard conditions, refugees' previous skills and knowledge prior to these experiences are highly impacted. They are individually disadvantaged and viewed generally as possessing *low levels of human capital and entrepreneurial skills. Lack of language skills* is a multifaced barrier in entrepreneurship, including a challenge in completing administrative steps necessary for starting a business, i.e. registration, tax, payroll accounts (OECD, 2011), especially for non-English speakers. This increases difficulty understanding legal and regulatory obligations; identify and build relationships with partners, suppliers, and customers; build networks, access finance, and seek other support services.

Another challenge faced by all entrepreneurs is a *lack of capital and difficulties accessing debt or equity finance.* This challenge is more significant for refugees than for most entrepreneurs because many lack access to a bank account (Lyon, Sepulveda & Syrett, 2007). Consequently, they cannot demonstrate a credit history. They also often lack savings and collateral, which hinders their access to traditional bank loans (Betts, Omata & Bloom, 2017). A lack of stable residence status also affects refugees' access to external finance (European Commission, 2016), operating a business in low-growth sectors (Wauters & Lambrecht, 2008). As a result, migrants and refugees tend to seek finance through other channels, including informal loans and community-based mechanisms. These finance types tend to provide access to small amounts of funding, limiting the scale of operations they can support and are often much more expensive than formal loans. This propensity to rely on informal networks for financing is also found in migrants, notably due to biases encountered in the banking sector (OECD, 2011).

Under-developed entrepreneurship networks (OECD, 2011) is another factor. Forced migration is much less coordinated and less driven by social networks in the receiving country than other migration forms. Refugees tend to have small social networks, yet social interactions are at the centre of entrepreneurial networks. It is usually difficult to distinguish between personal and business networks for an entrepreneur, and separating them is somewhat artificial (Halabisky, 2015). Small social networks mean that some refugees will have no one to turn to for support or assistance when looking for help in setting up a business (Wauters & Lambrecht, 2008), affecting their chances to thrive economically.

Refugees interested in running a business often have *difficulties in securing operating premises* (OECD, 2011). Access to material resources, such as physical working spaces or storefronts to run their business, is also an obstacle that disproportionately affects refugee entrepreneurs. This is due to difficulties in identifying appropriate locations and financial constraints (European Commission, 2016; Lyon, Sepulveda & Syrett, 2007). Lack of knowledge on the importance of location as a success factor for businesses is also an issue for refugee entrepreneurs (Wauters & Lambrecht, 2008).

Mental health challenges count as another restraining factor in the life of the refugees. A significant number of refugees experience traumatic events in their country of origin or during their journey, and the prevalence of post-traumatic stress disorder (PTSD) and depression are significantly higher than in the general population (UNHCR, 2002). Besides, the journey of a migrant seeking international protection is often long, and reception procedures are rarely swift. Stress and other mental health issues are among the greatest barriers in integrating refugees into employment within the

EU (Scholten et al., 2017) and the United States. This has also been shown to be a significant barrier for business creation due to low self-confidence (Lyon, Sepulveda & Syrett, 2007; Wauters & Lambrecht, 2006).

Gender-based cultural norms can influence the likelihood of refugee women starting a business (Rath, 2011). There are very few women refugee entrepreneurs (Wauters & Lambrecht, 2006), partly due to their lower human and financial capital and work experience. In addition, social attitudes in some cultures may discourage women from working on starting and operating businesses because they are expected to allocate the bulk of their time towards family responsibilities and childcare (Kooy, 2016; Rath, 2011; Lyon, Sepulveda & Syrett, 2007).

2) Institutional challenges

The host institution is governed by laws and policies that inform its political, educational, and economic structures. These standard regulations automatically apply to all residents; hence refugees are no exceptions. *Recognition of qualifications* (OECD, 2011) of educated, employed, or ran their businesses in their home country is a major challenge that affects refugees in entrepreneurship, and in the labour market more generally. The regulations make it challenging to recognise their diplomas, qualifications, and previous work experiences abroad for those lucky to have them. Others often find it difficult to produce certifications and documents as they are frequently left behind or lost in travel (Wauters & Lambrecht, 2008). As a result, refugee entrepreneurs may find themselves unable to start a business related to their experience or expertise, particularly in regulated professions (e.g. health sector, accounting).

Distrust of public services is another frequently cited difficulty for refugee entrepreneurs experience with public services. Initial negative experiences with state services upon arrival tend to breed distrust among refugees towards the state in the future (Lyon, Sepulveda & Syrett, 2007). For example, in the United States, refugees must simultaneously fulfil specific requirements such as attending English classes, job training, and or community services, as they work toward self-sufficiency within 180 days of arrival. Considering their experiences, these six-month unreasonable expectations sometimes result in refugees losing their benefits for those who fail to meet them. This increases the likelihood that refugee entrepreneurs will not use public support programmes (OECD, 2011) to boost their businesses.

Speaking of businesses, *business regulatory barriers* (OECD, 2011) vary across countries, which can add to the confusion as others in an entrepreneur's personal or family network may have a very different regulatory environment based on their resettlement country. Moreover, there are challenges in seeking support to meet regulatory obligations due to insufficient or inappropriate communications about regulations and related support services (Berns, 2017; Lyon, Sepulveda & Syrett, 2007; Rath, 2011).

In a world dominated by Eurocentric cultures and structures, we must underscore the impact of *negative cultural bias and discrimination.* Refugees may have trouble establishing themselves as entrepreneurs due to discrimination. Press coverage of refugees has recently focused on host countries' costs, rather than the potential benefits they can bring (OECD, 2011), and anti-immigration policies perpetuate discrimination. A study of five EU countries commissioned by the UNHCR found that humanitarian themes and security concerns were omnipresent in press coverage on refugees (Berry, Garcia-Blanco and Moore, 2015). As a result, there are low levels of awareness about the potential of refugees as entrepreneurs. Previous studies have described how discrimination can reduce chances of integration in the job market (Kloosterman, 2010; OECD, 2013) and securing loans (Wauters & Lambrecht, 2008).

6.2 Enhancing Factors

A combination of factors has proven to enhance the economic success of refugees across the country. The use of multiple support, personalized assistance, and tailored delivery methods (OECD, 2019) builds on individuals and community strengths. Many nongovernment organizations offer programmes on a small scale and focus primarily on entrepreneurship training and coaching, while financial support is still a relatively underserved area (OECD, 2019).

In the United States, microenterprise Development (MED) Programme provides financial support and training to refugees. The MED programme provides grants to organizations supplying aspiring refugee entrepreneurs with business training, and microloans of up to USD 15 000 (Office of Refugee Resettlement, 2017). Under the responsibility of the Office of Refugee

Resettlement (ORR) of the Department of Health and Human Services, these programmes provide support in the shape of short-term training, individual counselling, business technical assistance (including business plan preparation) and services (ORR, n.d). In 2016, 22 programmes were supported across 17 states and the District of Columbia for a budget of USD 4.5 million. These programmes disbursed 645 loans and contributed to 1160 jobs (Office of Refugee Resettlement, 2018b).

Through MED, both public and nonprofit organizations have creatively innovated ways that help refugees achieve economic success by tapping into their client's cultural and inherent strengths. The following organizations combine multiple types of support, tailored to the refugee community they serve as they progress to achieve economic success.

Journey's End Refugee Services (JERS) in Buffalo New York, and Bethany Christian Services (BCS) in Grand Rapids, Michigan engage their clients in childcare microenterprise project that provides access to licensed businesses in family childcare, and they learn how to navigate mainstream childcare services. A case example is of Lisa (not her real name), a refugee from Congo, who went through childcare, was licensed, and started running her childcare centre that provides affordable services for her fellow refugee families and community in Grand Rapids. Her multilingualism makes her a top choice by many new families whose children do not understand English yet, besides the adults. The result shows increasing economic self-sufficiency for women in the local refugee community and creating stable childcare options for other working families enhances economic success for both service providers and their clients who concentrate on their jobs with a peace of mind knowing their children are in trusted care. Additionally, both BCS and JERS offer interpreter training that opens employment opportunities in hospitals, schools, employers, courts, etc. Health Care interpreter earned through a medical interpreter training is the most marketable (JERS, n.d). Finally, like BCS's Hope Farms, JERS offers

Green Shoots, urban farming that taps into adult farming and marketing skills (JERS, n.d). Farmers provide food for their families as well as sell their fresh produce at the local farmer's markets. These farmers are trained about season extension, composting, and urban farming practices to apply at the community shared agriculture programme (JERS, n.d).

Peace of Thread is another non-profit organization in Clarkson, Georgia that empowers women who have come to the United States seeking refuge from war, persecution, and poverty to make a new life for themselves and their family (Peace of Thread, n.d). Most refugee families with a single mother whose husband was the breadwinner might have been killed in the war struggle most, especially if the women stayed at home mothers. Peace of Thread is a handbag company that makes high-quality bags that employ unemployable women in vulnerable populations, hence providing them with a sustainable source of income, practice in English, mentorship, and job skills (Peace of Thread, n.d).

International Institute of Minnesota (IIM)offers a variety of employment security to refugees through their Hospitality Careers Pathways programme in St. Paul. Training is offered to refugees in Housekeeping, Dietary Aide, and Supervisor Training. The Housekeeping Training helps New Americans to overcome barriers and secure much-needed employment. Dietary Aide is a 4-week, 80-hour class that provides students training in food safety, infection control, special diets and patient orders, dialogues with patients, American foods, customer service practices and practical experience serving and communicating with elderly. Through Supervisor Training, IIM helps experienced workers in customer service fields gain the skills needed to move into a supervisory or training positions.

Through classes and collaborative workshops with our Hotel Housekeeping and Dietary Aide classes, students will learn positive feedback and teaching techniques and develop supervisory skills. The Pathway's Dietary Aide and Supervisor Training help build a career to advance to earn a sustainable living (IIM, 2020). According to OECD (2019), between 1991 and 2015, the MED programme has provided 24000 refugees with micro-loans, amounting to USD 10.03 million. Repayment rates are higher than average, and so are survival rates of participating businesses; they outperform the national average and that of businesses in other microbusinesses programmes (Collins, 2017). Although the evidence-based on the impact entrepreneurship initiatives for refugees is thin, recent evaluations suggest that the most successful programmes combine multiple support types and offer personalized assistance. Another key success factor is the use of tailored delivery methods, including specialized staff that can speak the relevant languages and are knowledgeable about the local entrepreneurship support system and the challenges faced by refugees (OECD, 2019). An ongoing need to develop a more substantial evidence base on entrepreneurship among refugees, especially on programmes' effectiveness and efficiency (OECD, 2019).

Conclusion

In 2015, there were more than 65.3 million people who were forcibly displaced from their country, and only 107,100 people were resettled to another country. This wide gap of millions who live in a foreign country deprived of many of their rights and privileges is ever-increasing, and the alarming rate is seen when United Nations High Commissioner for Refugees report that nearly one out of every 100 people are displaced from their homes. In the United States, refugee settlement began with 250,000 refugees from Europe after World War II. This resettlement was conducted in the light of the 1948 Displaced Persons Act. After initial resistance, the US became the global leader in accepting refugees to the country from then onwards. However, after the 1980s, there was a decline in the US's responsiveness towards the international refugee crisis. After the 2016 election, several policies purposefully targeted to bring down the total number of refugees resettled into the country.

Since the Refugee Act of 1980, there has been a substantial success among the refugee resettlement programme to reach the goal of economic self-sufficiency. For instance, in 2015, among the 29,765 refugees served by the programme, it helped achieve economic self-sufficiency for 67% within 120 days of arrival in the United States. Further, the percentage went up to 82% reporting economic self-sufficiency within six months. However, even with these successes, there are several occasions where refugees are underemployed due to the difference in the culture and complications regarding accepting foreign certifications. Hence, failure to recognize refugees' qualifications and previous work experiences, limited language skills, societal and cultural biases, and regulatory barriers in the host country affect refugees' ability to achieve economic sustainability. The importance of recognizing the impact of both individual and institutional challenges on refugees' economic success must be underscored during the resettlement process. Ultimately, using the strengths and empowerment approach to support and promote entrepreneurship, as an alternative to employment among refugees, increases economic and social benefits for the host country.

References

Berns, J. (2017), *Killing two birds with one stone: Exploring refugee entrepreneurial intent in the Netherlands*, Radboud University.

Berry, M., I. Garcia-Blanco and K. Moore (2015), *Press Coverage of the Refugee and Migrant Crisis in the EU: A Content Analysis of Five European Countries*, United Nations High Commission for Refugees

Betts, A., N. Omata and L. Bloom (2017), "Thrive or Survive? Explaining Variation in Economic Outcomes for Refugees", *Journal on Migration and Human Security*, 5(4), 716-743.

Capps, Randy and Kathleen Newland with Susan Fratzke, Susanna Groves, Gregory Auclair, Michael Fix, and Margie McHugh. 2015. The Integration Outcomes of U.S Refugees: Success and Challenges. Washington D.C. Migration Policy Institute.

Collins, J. (2017), *Private and Community Sector Initiatives in Refugee Employment and Entrepreneurship*, Lowry Institute for International, Sydney.

Connor, P. & Krogstad, J, M. (2018, May 3). *The number of refugees admitted to the U.S has Fallen especially among Muslims*. Pew Research Center. Retrieved from https://www.pewresearch.org/fact-tank/2018/05/03/the-number-of-refugees-admitted-to-the-u-s-has-fallen-especially-among-muslims/

European Commission (2016), *Evaluation and Analysis of Good Practices in Promoting and Supporting Migrant Entrepreneurship Guidebook*, European Commission, Brussels.

Halabisky, D. (2015), "Entrepreneurial Activities in Europe – Expanding Networks for Inclusive Entrepreneurship", *OECD Employment Policy Papers*, No. 7, OECD Publishing, Paris. Retrieved from http://dx.doi.org/10.1787/5jrtpbz29mjh-en.

Harvard Immigration and Refugee Clinical Programme. (2017). Fulfilling U.S. commitment to refugee resettlement: Protecting refugees, preserving national security, and building the U.S. economy through refugee admissions. Retrieved from https://harvardimmigrationclinic.files.wordpress.com/2017/06/syria-final-draft-v9.pdf

International Institute of Minnesota (2020). Hospitality Careers Pathways. Retrieved from https://iimn.org/programmes/workforce-development/hospitality-careers/

Journeys End Refugee Services (n.d). Urban Farming to Feed a Community. Retrieved from https://www.jersbuffalo.org/brewster-street-farm

Kallick, D.D. & Mathema, S. (2016, June). Refugee Integration in the United States. Center for American Progress. Retrieved from https://cdn.americanprogress.org/wp-content/uploads/2016/06/15112912/refugeeintegration.pdf

Kloosterman, R. (2010), "Matching opportunities with resources: A framework for analyzing (migrant) entrepreneurship from a mixed embeddedness perspective", *Entrepreneurship and Regional Development*, Vol. 22/1, pp. 25-45.

Krogstad, J, M. (2019, October 7). *Key Facts About Refugees to the U.S.* Pew Research Center. Retrieved from https://www.pewresearch.org/fact-tank/2019/10/07/key-facts-about-refugees-to-the-u-s/

Legrain, P. (2016). Refugees work: A humanitarian investment that yields economic dividends. Retrieved from http://www.opennetwork.net/wp-content/uploads/2016/05/Tent-Open-Refugees-Work_V13.pdf

Lyon, F., L. Sepulveda and S. Syrett (2007), "Enterprising refugees: contributions and challenges in deprived urban areas", *Local Economy*, Vol. 22/4, pp. 362-375.

Migration Policy Institute (2020). Retrieved from https://www.migrationpolicy.org/

OECD (2011), "Migrant Entrepreneurship in OECD Countries", in *International Migration Outlook 2011*, OECD Publishing, Paris, https://dx.doi.org/10.1787/migr_outlook-2011-8-en.

OECD (2019), Financing SMEs and Entrepreneurs 2019: An OECD Scoreboard, OECD Publishing, Paris, https://doi.org/10.1787/fin_sme_ent-2019-en.

Office of Refugee Resettlement (2018), *Annual Report to Congress Office of Refugee Resettlement Fiscal Year 2016*, Office of Refugee Resettlement, Department for Health and Human Services. Retrieved from http://www.acf.hhs.gov/sites/default/files/orr/arc_16_508.pdf.

Office of Refugee Resettlement (2018a). Retrieved from https://www.acf.hhs.gov/orr/resource/federal-agencies

Office of Refugee Resettlement (2019). Retrieved from https://www.acf.hhs.gov/orr/about

Office of Refugee Resettlement (2018b), *Annual Report to Congress Office of Refugee Resettlement Fiscal Year 2016*, Office of Refugee Resettlement, Department for Health and Human Services. http://www.acf.hhs.gov/sites/default/files/orr/arc_16_508.pdf.

Peace of Thread (n.d). Our Mission. Retrieved from https://www.peaceofthread.com/our-mission

Perez, A. D., & Hirschman, C. (2009). The Changing Racial and Ethnic Composition of the US Population: Emerging American Identities. *Population and development review*, 35(1), 1–51. https://doi.org/10.1111/j.1728-4457.2009.00260.x

Puma J.E., Lichtenstein G., & Stein P (2018, December). The RISE Survey: Developing and Implementing a Valid and Reliable Quantitative

Measure of Refugee Integration in the United States, *Journal of Refugee Studies*, Volume 31, Issue 4, Pages 605–625, https://doi.org/10.1093/jrs/fex047

Rath, J. (2011), *Promoting ethnic entrepreneurship in European cities*, Publications Office of the European Union, Luxembourg. https://www.eurofound.europa.eu/sites/default/files/ef_publication/field_ef_document/ef1138 en.pdf.

Rengs, B. et al. (2017), "Labour Market Profile, Previous Employment and Economic Integration of Refugees: An Austrian Case Study", *Vienna Institute of Demography Working Papers*, No. 13/2017

Scholten, P. et al. (2017), *Policy innovation in refugee integration? A comparative analysis of innovative policy strategies toward refugee integration in Europe*, Erasmus University Rotterdam.

Silja K., Lee S.K., Downs-Karkos S., Taylor M.B (2013). Adult Education and Immigrant Integration: Networks for Integrating New Americans (NINA). Boston, MA: World Education, Inc.

Singer, A. & Wilson, J. H. (2006). *From "There" to "Here" Refugee Resettlement in Metropolitan America*. Living Cities Census Series. The Brookings Institution.

UNHCR (2002), "Planning for Optimal Mental Health: Responding to Refugee-related", in *UNCHR Resettlement handbook*, United Nation High Commissioner for Refugees, Geneva. http://www.unhcr.org/3d98623a4.html.

UNHCR (2020). USA for UNHCR. Retrieved from https://www.unrefugees.org/refugee-facts/what-is-a-refugee/

UNHCR Nicosia (2014, July). The Integration of Refugees: A Discussion Paper. https://www.unhcr.org/cy/wp-content/uploads/sites/41/2018/02/integration_discussion_paper_July_2014_EN.pdf

UNHCR. (n.d.) Internally displaced people. Retrieved from https://www.unhcr.org/sy/29-internally-displaced-people.html

UNHCR Resettlement Handbook. (2018). Country chapters-The United States of America. Retrieved from https://www.unhcr.org/3c5e5a764.pdf

U.S. Department of State. (n.d.). Refugee admissions. https://www.state.gov/refugee-admissions/

Van Kooy, J. (2016), "Refugee women as entrepreneurs in Australia", *Forced Migration Review*, Vol. 53, p. 71.

Vandor, P. and N. Franke (2016): *Why Are Immigrants More Entrepreneurial?*

Wauters, B. and J. Lambrecht (2006), "Refugee entrepreneurship in Belgium: Potential and practice", *The International Entrepreneurship and Management Journal*, Vol. 2/4, pp. 509-525.

Wauters, B. and J. Lambrecht (2008), "Barriers to refugee entrepreneurship in Belgium: Towards an explanatory model", *Journal of Ethnic and Migration Studies*, Vol. 34/6, pp. 895-915

Welch, K. (2017). A pivotal moment for the US refugee resettlement programme. Retrieved from http://haasinstitute.berkeley.edu/sites/default/files/haasinstitute_usrefugeeresettlment_june2017_publish.pdf

Wisconsin Department of Children and Families (n.d). Path to Resettlement. https://dcf.wisconsin.gov/refugee/resettlement.

Zucker, N.L. (1982). Refugee Resettlement in the United States: The Role of Voluntary Agencies. *Michigan Journal of International Law.* Vol 3. Issue 1, (155).

About Authors

Dr Henry Poduthase is the Director of the Graduate Social Work Program at West Texas A&M University and teaches Research and practice courses at the graduate level. He has authored several peer-reviewed (in international journals) research articles and book chapters. He serves as the editorial board member of an international journal and peer reviewer of four reputed international journals. He has presented papers in various international and national conferences. His research interests extend from psycho-social challenges of children, adolescents, and families to refugees and social policies.

Genevieve M. Sabala is currently an Assistant Professor of social work at the University of Wisconsin-Stout, while concurrently pursuing a PhD in conflict resolution and peace studies at Nova Southeastern University. She previously taught at West Texas A & M University. She also worked in the nonprofit sector serving refugees through Bethany Christian Services, and West Michigan Refugee and Education Center. She has served as a board member for Sow Hope and Holistic Global Partners as well as an advisory board member for Refugee Services of Texas in Amarillo. She continues to serve on the advisory board for Kenya Matters.

Social Support to Adolescent Mothers' for School Re-Entry: Kakuma Refugee Camp-Kenya

Charity Kola[15]

Abstract

Teenage pregnancy is a worldwide phenomenon with a broad effect on education, leaving juvenile mothers exposed to other forms of abuse and segregation that on many occasions, results to school drop-outs. The numerous health issues associated with adolescent pregnancy tend to eclipse the education-related effects of this dilemma. Refugee adolescent mothers are exposed to a wide range of distress, including poverty that forces them out of school. Adolescent mothers are influenced by their social contexts and understanding the relationship between these contexts and their enrollment in school, retention, and transition is paramount. This chapter highlights the degree to which social support, including family, school, peer, and community, is accorded to adolescent mothers returning to school in Kakuma Refugee camp Kenya. A mixed-method study approach was employed, and a descriptive survey was utilized to collect quantitative data while phenomenology design was used to collect qualitative data. The study targeted adolescent mothers, caregivers, headteachers, local government administration and NGO representatives. This study's findings indicate that refugee adolescent mothers received little support from their families, schools, and communities. Family support is minimal, as was indicated by 85 (65.9%) of the refugee adolescent mothers with the main form of support given by families being material support 55 (42.6%). A majority of the adolescents 72 (55.8%) indicated that local schools did not support teenage mothers' school re-entry and that the local community

---

15   Advisor-Africa, Regional Community Accountability Reporting
     Mechanism(CARM). Email: charity.kola@gmail.com

accorded little support to adolescent mothers' school re-entry as indicated by 63 (48.8%). Adolescent mothers involved in study 101 (78.3%) indicated that their relationship with their peers changed due to pregnancy and parenthood. However, peer groups remained an outstanding support group for refugee adolescent mothers. School guidance and counselling departments need to be well established in learning institutions while the community and the local government administration should take collective action and embrace girl child education, ensuring re-entry of adolescent mothers to school.

Key Words: Adolescent mothers, Social support, Re-entry; Refugee, Kakuma-Kenya

Introduction

Teenage pregnancy is recognised as a worldwide marvel with an overall effect on education. It leaves juvenile mothers exposed to other forms of abuse and segregation that bring about school dropouts on many occasions. In the United States, adolescent mothers are excessively found in poor communities characterised by poor housing, poor schools, high criminal activities and inadequate health centres. Due to this, poverty is a great challenge to the adolescent mothers in schools and their community since they face increased health problems, decreased educational attainment and an increased chance of living in poverty (Darroch et al., 2016).

Almost 20% of kids born in Brazil are by adolescent mothers through unplanned births in high-risk areas, approximately twice as high as the world average (11%) in this age category (SINASC, 2014). Each year, above 560,000 children are born to teenage mothers in Brazil, with most births occurring in the most populated southeastern states (WHO, 2014). In Jamaica, high school pregnancy's pervasiveness among 15-19 age group and young ladies transcends from poor financial, rural, and downtown communities. These communities are portrayed with increased destitution, wrongdoing, gang fighting, and single-parent and extended families with relatively low incomes (Dasmine, 2017).

The difficulties that girls face in educational participation varies, every year in developing countries, roughly 16 million girls between 15 to 19 years and 2.5 million girls under 16 years conceive an offspring (Neal et al., 2015; UNFPA, 2015). In Uganda, the challenge of girls dropping out of school due to pregnancies has been explained by a mix of socio-cultural views, perceptions and practices surrounding early pregnancy. In a survey conducted in 20 districts of Uganda, it was established that; the leading cause for girls to drop out of school is pregnancy (34%), followed by poverty (28%) and engagement in early sex/marriage (11%) (Josephine & Madanda, 2011).

Fewer than one in three Zambian youth complete secondary school (UNESCO, 2016). Just 38% of pregnant girls who leave primary school and 65% of those who leave secondary school return to school after giving birth (Zuilkowski et al., 2019) highlighting the persistent school dropout problem Zambia, with exceptionally high rates for girls and rural youth. Preliminary findings from an ongoing study by the Population Council in Homabay County, Kenya on expanding access to secondary school education for teenage mothers in Kenya identified pregnancy as the most common reason for girls being out of school accounting for nearly 70% of all female school dropout cases (Undie et al., 2015).

Adolescent pregnancies are mostly compelled by poverty, lack of education and employment opportunities which are more likely to occur in relegated communities (UNFPA, 2015). Pregnancy and childbirth are deliberate for some adolescents, while in some backgrounds, there is social pressure for girls to get married and bear children. Every year, about 15 million girls under 18 years are married globally (UNFPA, 2015; UNICEF., 2013). In developing countries, fifty per cent of pregnancies among adolescent girls are estimated to be accidental; thus, for several adolescents, pregnancy and childbirth are neither wanted nor planned (Darroch et al., 2016). This problem has worried most parents, social workers, policymakers and other human service providers from the developed to the developing countries due to its adverse consequences on the girl's education (Cowan & Cowan, 2019). It is projected that by 2030, the number of adolescent pregnancies will escalate globally with the most significant comparative rises in West, Central Africa, Eastern and Southern Africa (UNFPA, 2015).

The numerous health issues associated with adolescent pregnancy tend to eclipse the education-related effects of this dilemma. Yet, early and unintended pregnancy leads to a considerable loss of educational opportunities, which in itself results in recurrent limitations on female life chances (Nazar et al., 2018).

Their social contexts influence adolescent mothers, and there is a need to understand the relationship between these contexts and their enrollment in school, retention and transition (Dennis et al., 2005). Therefore, social support is provided to these adolescent mothers with a sense of protection, which, in turn, helps them to address education distractions as opined in social capital theory. Social support has been proven to improve school attendance for learners already in school (Rueger et al., 2010). However, refugee adolescent mothers are exposed to a wide range of distress that forces them out of school.

People that have been displaced by war move to safer countries for protection and access to lifesaving support. After achieving the lifesaving support and assurance of security, they seek education for their children (UNESCO, 2015). The living conditions in the countries of asylum for these refugees are not favourable, especially for girls. The situation in refugee camps in countries like Kenya enforcing encampment policy characterised by food rationing, restricted movement and limited access to livelihood opportunities results in high poverty situations among the refugees. Poverty and teenage pregnancies are the main factors contributing to education disruption, especially among girls in developing countries. The refugee camps are situated in the remote areas of the country where movement is restricted, and they host populations from cultures characterised by forced early marriages hence exposing the girls to teenage pregnancies and adolescent motherhood.

In Kakuma, the area under study, 91 girls out of 18,189 got pregnant while in a primary school in 2018, and there is no data on the number of girls who returned to school after delivery (UNHCR, 2019). In Kakuma International NGOs have put in place strategies to offer social support to these adolescent mothers as well as re-admit them to school. However, quite a few adolescent mothers go back to school as they are in most instances vulnerable to further abuses and societal stigma such as family rejection, societal segregation, forced child marriage and SGBV among others.

Policies formulated for students who become pregnant vary widely in Sub-Saharan Africa (Carrington, 2011; Harriet et al., 2015; Molosiwa & Bernard, 2012; Obonyo & Thinguri, 2015; Zuilkowski et al., 2019). Regardless of the policy's specific nature, these regulations rarely result in large proportions of young mothers returning to school (Catherine et al., 2015). The re-entry policy provides adolescent mothers with an opportunity to complete their education and enjoy its benefit. However, adolescent mothers who have taken advantage of this policy have contended with a hostile school environment, where they are isolated, humiliated and stigmatised by their fellow pupils and students without any effective interventions from the teachers.

The re-entry policy is not ample and may not safeguard the teenage mothers from the challenges related to nurturing and their wellbeing within the school, at home and within the community. However, vital information and awareness on social support systems surrounding re-entry of adolescent mothers in school help them overcome barriers and inform the adoption of relevant strategies by stakeholders including the community, schools, department of education and Non-Governmental organisations working among refugee communities.

1. Social Support for Adolescent Mothers

Social support is outlined as an element of a strong interrelation and a healthy mind. It is made up of a network of friends and family that offer support when a need arises. Literature has shown that adult pregnant women receive more social support than pregnant teenagers (Patrícia et al., 2017). Among refugees, four social support groups could offer assistance to adolescent mothers; family, school, local community, and peer groups.

Family social support to adolescent mothers is vital in the growth of both the teenage mother and their children. The family is also a comfort source; emotional, financial, and physical support, especially for young mothers who deliver during their teenage years. When parents and other family members fail to support them socially, it may lead to stress and depression. This affects their lives (Cox et al., 2008) indicating that increased parenting stress with decreased social support leads to higher dejection levels in adolescent mothers at baseline (Huang et al., 2014).

A holistic and tailor-made program should be available at the family level to support young mothers. This is because of their newly acquired roles that require practical support. For instance; these young mothers will need money to buy babies' clothes and other requirements for the new baby, and sound advice on breastfeeding which is primarily offered within the family setups (Chase et al., 2006).

Schools play a significant role in supporting adolescent mothers who return to finish their education after a maternity break. The kind of support offered here can either make these young mothers complete their schooling or drop again all together (Yungungu & Wambua, 2006). A teacher's job is to convey information and help students grow to be promoters of life transformation. Therefore, school re-entry cannot be complete without teachers' active involvement. A study by (Kurgat, 2016) noted that school principals and teachers could be more patient in answering girls' questions about their growth and development and their encounters. The assumption here is that teachers have all it takes to guide young mothers who come back to school and offer moral support. However, other studies have indicated that most teachers deem the situation of young mothers to be personal and of no interest to them hence they face bullying, exclusion and lack of teachers' assistance within the school environment (Olivier, 2000; Chigona & Chetty, 2008).

Health education in schools equips young mothers with requisite knowledge of these individuals' general well-being and babies. A study conducted in the US, Finland and Australia by (Strunk, 2008) on the impact of school-based health clinics providing therapy, health care, health education, and childhood development education explicitly for teenage pregnancy demonstrated decreased absenteeism and dropout rates among parenting adolescents.

Young teenagers getting pregnant when still in school find it difficult to fit well in the community. Therefore, to go back to school, the community must be involved and offer necessary support without looking at these young mothers' age. Adolescent mothers and their young ones are extremely endangered groups whose long-term life prospects are intertwined and can influence healthy growth, prosperity and competitiveness or deprivation and reliance (Stephens et al., (2003). The community can develop mechanisms to help young mothers care for their kids while attending school at the same time. Aiding adolescent mothers in an academically meticulous job can be better positioned to obtain the knowledge and expertise they require to build a sustainable future for themselves and their children (Zachry, 2005).

Young mothers wishing to go on with their studies need people to take care of their children when they are in school (Phillips & Straunars (1991; Stroble, 2013). Community daycare is one way to reduce school dropout rates for young mothers and increase their child's positive results. This, however, depends on the family backup and the financial capabilities of young mothers since such services are never free. Adolescent mothers are confronted with unexpected budgets linked to the mother's expenses and childcare; therefore, they have to seek financial assistance from the community.

Peer groups support consists of young mothers, who offer moral support to each other regarding aspects such as child-rearing, material support, among others. According to Stevenson et al.., 1999, unofficial support systems seem to be the most prevalent among parents and pregnant adolescents, and network composition depends on several features such as age, race, or ethnicity. Such groupings offer necessary support to its members and enable them to cope with the new challenges of raising a child and balancing it with going back to school.

Peer support can safeguard against postpartum depression, relieve stress symptoms, and ease social isolation (Dennis et al., 2009). Within peer relationships, empathy also plays an important role. Young mothers can use such avenues for emotional recollection to reflect and empathise with each other regarding maternity hood and schooling's double burden. Getting overlooked or neglected by peers makes teens feel isolated or aggressive. Such exclusion and neglect by peers are also related to the subsequent mental health and individual's criminal issue (Kupersmidt & De Rosier, 2004). Implying that adolescent mothers are likely to feel alienated and fail to cope well in school and upbringing their children.

A young mother in early teens, for example, often needs to be "babysat" by her mother or an individual in her life who serves as her mother (DeVito,

2007). Therefore, adolescent mothers have unique needs to help them navigate effectively through the combined demands of youth development and their position as a new parent. In scenarios where such links are missing, adolescent mothers are likely to turn to their peers for solace and support. Researchers pinpoint the importance of role identity, social assistance relationships and cognitive viewpoints for the teenage mother as she adapts to parenting requirements, a factor which is often present in peer support groups.

Adverse reactions from peers can cripple the school re-entry of adolescent mothers (Wanjiku, 2015). A study carried out by (Chigona & Chetty, 2008) to identify how much support offered to teen mothers to facilitate their schooling in South Africa revealed that many adolescent mothers described their adolescent peers as teasing, bullying, and alienating them. The investigator asserted that the adolescent mothers were bothered and victimised by the treatment, which contributed them to ignore school and, in several scenarios, utterly drop out of school for good.

Adolescent mothers with low motherly and peer backing have a greater sense of alienation and less educational ambition (Valaitis & Sword, 2005). Adolescent mothers in steady peer relations are often inspired to raise their standard of living demonstrated by increased attendance at school, improved grades, and better interpersonal relationships Ormrod (2006). Therefore, peer groups are seen as vital forums where adolescent mothers can confide to each other and make something out of their lives.

2. Material and Methods of Study

The study was guided by one research question; how do those living with and around them support adolescent mothers? A mixed-method study approach was employed. A descriptive survey was utilised to collect quantitative data while phenomenology design was used to collect qualitative data. The study targeted adolescent mothers, caregivers, headteachers, local government administration, and NGO representatives within the Kakuma refugee camp. The camp is established due to the arrival of the "Lost Boys of Sudan" in 1992. By August 2019, Kakuma and Kalobeyei incorporated settlement had a population of 191,000. With a new arrival flow, Kakuma exceeded its capacity in 2014 by over 58,000 individuals, leading to congestions (UNHCR, 2019). This led to the identification of a new settlement created in Kalobeyei, 20 kilometres from Kakuma town. The expert purposive sampling technique used to sample 100 adolescent mothers to collect quantitative data using self-constructed interview schedule and qualitative data was collected ten key informants and 50 caregivers as participants of the study using the in-depth interview. Quantitative data was collected and analysed using descriptive statistics with the Statistical Package for Social Sciences (SPSS version 20). Whereas qualitative data was transcribed using express scribe. The data was then coded into themes, and the codes were analysed using NVIVO 12.

3. Results and Discussion

The study results disclose that a majority of the adolescent mothers were aged 15 – 18 years. This was indicated by 62 (48.06%) of the participants that were involved in the study similar to the case in South Africa (Jochim et al.,2020; Undie et al., 2015), having unintended pregnancies some while in their upper primary level schooling while some in their early secondary schooling. On the other hand, most of the caregivers were aged 30-39 years old, 31 (24%) of the study respondents. It is evident that more so the adolescent mothers had acquired secondary level education, although most of them had dropped out due to pregnancy. They comprised of 61 (47.3%) of the respondents involved in the study.

Majority of adolescent mothers, 77 (88.51%) got their firstborns at the age of 15 to 18. The findings point 63 (48.8%) adolescent mothers were still unmarried. They had gotten pregnant from fellow schoolboys, camp and surrounding host community men, who longed for pleasure and did not bother the act's consequences. Furthermore, 33 (25.6%) of the respondents indicated that they were cohabiting with their partners. This finding was similar to the baseline study report of teenage mothers in Kenya, indicating 48% of adolescent mothers lived with their parents and 20% lived with a spouse (Undie et al., 2015).

3.1 Family Support for Adolescent Mothers

The family is a comfort source; emotional, financial, and physical support, especially for young mothers who deliver during their teenage years. Family support to adolescent mothers in the Kakuma refugee camp is necessary for these young mothers to go back to school and finish their education; however, it was minimal at Kakuma refugee camp. This was shown by 85 (65.9%) of the respondents involved in the study. A majority of the adolescents 62 (48.1) indicated that their mothers were responsible for families' support. The support offered to adolescent mothers by their families covered a broad spectrum, ranging from financial, material, psychological and emotional, among others. However, the respondents identified material support 55 (42.6%) as the primary form of support of vital essence. The adolescent mothers had difficulties raising their children, affording their day-to-day necessities, and even faced hostilities. Such eventualities restricting receiving support on food, clothing and medicine only, to enable them effectively raise their child. Undie et al. (2015) concurred with this study opined that the significant stress that confronts young mothers is the lack of support from their families. However, this is expected because refugees have little even support to offer since they are hosted in the countries; they seek refuge. Conditions in these camps want to warrant them to give any adequate support to their members.

Table 1: *Extent of Family Support According to Adolescents Mothers*

Factors Extend	Frequency	Percent
Great extend	6	4.7
Moderate Extend	9	7.0
Little Extend	85	65.9
Not at all	29	22.5
Total	**129**	**100.0**

Source: Field Data, 2020

3.2 School support for Adolescent Mothers

School environment created by both teachers and peers provides both moral and psychological support needed by young mothers in school re-entry process, determining whether refugee adolescents complete their schooling or drop again all together. In this study, most of the respondents 72 (55.8%) indicated that local schools did not support teenage mothers' school re-entry. They suggested that the school management viewed the adolescent mothers as spoilt and immoral, and hence held the view that whenever they were re-entered in the schools, they would spoil the rest of the students. This contributed to school re-entry being lower than it ought to be. However, 57 (44.2%) of the respondents involved in the study indicated that some schools embraced adolescent mothers' school re-entry and supported them. These findings were in tandem with Olivier (2000), who stipulated that teachers deem young mothers' situations personal and of no interest to them.

Factors that could discourage school re-entry among adolescent mothers include discrimination, stigmatisation from teachers and fellow students, poor social support, negative attitude towards these teenage mothers, and adolescent mothers' own poor academic attitude. Local schools' social support systems to support adolescent mothers were sex education, remedial classes, guidance and counselling, exemption from school manual work, and releasing adolescent mothers earlier than the usual school leaving time to ensure that they breastfed their children. This was adapted from a respondent who was quoted saying, "Local schools around here have put various measures to support adolescent mothers. These include sexual and reproductive education, guidance and counselling." (Interview, 20 February 2020). Another respondent said, "Adolescent mothers are exempted from routine school manual work and released earlier than the usual school leaving time to enable them to breastfeed their children." (Interview 21 February 2020). According to Wanyama & Simatwa (2011) schools should receive these girls and modify their view of them as mothers through their counselling and therapy program and give help and inclusion which is in line with these study findings.

3.3 Local Community support to Adolescent Mothers

The study findings indicate that the local community accorded little support to adolescent mothers' school re-entry, indicated by 63 (48.8%) of the adolescent mothers

Table 2: *Extent of Local Community Supporting to School Re-entry According to Adolescent Mothers*

Extend	Frequency	Percent
Great extend	12	9.3
Moderate Extend	34	26.4
Little Extend	63	48.8
Not at all	20	15.5
Total	129	100.0

Source: Field Data, 2020

Adolescent mothers indicated that community members considered them as ridicule and gossip subjects, without assuming they had to go back to schooling. The respondents highlighted that some community members would support the adolescent mothers by offering material, psychological and even financial support, to ensure that their education was catered.

These findings agree with Taherdoost's (2016) study that, in the community, the two extremely vulnerable groups whose long-term life prospects are intertwined and can be influenced towards a healthy development, prosperity and competitiveness or deprivation and reliance are the adolescent mothers and their children. The researcher further explored the local community's contribution to adolescent mothers' school re-entry from key informants. The respondents interviewed indicated that the local administration was keen on ensuring that every child was in school, whether they gave birth or not. Some community members also gave donations like books, pens, school uniforms and finances to adolescent mothers to support their education. This was evident from various respondents interviewed; a respondent is quoted saying, "Here, the local administration including the area chief, the assistant chief and the village elders are vigilant in ensuring that every child goes to school, irrespective of whether or not, they gave birth." (Interview 23 February 2020). Another respondent expressed similar sentiments, "We are given donations like books, pens, school uniform and some fees in case we are sent home, by some of the sympathetic community members." (Interview, 24 February 2020).

3.4 Peer group Support to Adolescent Mothers

Adolescent mothers involved in the study indicated that their relationship with their peers changed due to pregnancy and parenthood. This was represented by 101 (78.3%) of the respondents. It is indicated that their peers now considered them as having moved to another level and hence were no longer free to mingle with them. Further highlighting that the quality times initially spent with their peers were no longer there suffering solitude, and were in one way or the other captives as a result of the parenting role they had. Rubenstein (2018) points out that most new mothers and their young children suffer social isolation in the modern household. Reactions from friends like the ones indicated in table 5 can result in the adolescent mothers' low esteem and discourage them from rejoining schools. Such consequences might affect their entire future economic as well as social wellbeing. Such can only be resolved by changing our attitudes towards early pregnancies and accept them as unintended.

Conclusion

Concerning family support to adolescent mothers, the study showed that family members offered little help to refugee adolescent mothers. This is because they felt disappointed and therefore lost hope and trust in the adolescent mothers. However, despite little support from family members, mothers were more supportive of teenage mothers than their fathers. Although the family offered refugee adolescent mothers a little help, the largest support provided was material support. Various family-level factors determined refugee adolescent mothers' school re-entry. These included adolescent – family head relationship, family head characteristic, cultural practices, and negative attitudes towards adolescent mothers. Parents and family members should be aware of the importance of supporting refugee adolescent mothers in their households and the various forms of support accorded at the family level.

School administration plays a crucial role in ensuring that refugee adolescent mothers are enrolled back to school after child delivery. The social support systems put in place by the local schools to support adolescent mothers include sex education, remedial classes, exemption from daily school routine manual work, guidance and counselling, releasing adolescent mothers earlier than the usual school leaving time to ensure that they breastfed their children, and offering medical attention.

Although some of the respondents stated that teachers were supportive about their going back to school, the results showed that a high percentage of the respondents revealed that the school staff did not support adolescent mothers' school re-entry. These refugee adolescent mothers were termed as spoilt and immoral, and hence held the view that whenever they were re-entered in the schools, they would spoil the rest of the students. This contributed to school re-entry being lower than it ought to be. Stakeholders shall aspire to build linkages between schools and homes to support the school re-entry process and to conduct follow-ups in cases where refugee adolescent mothers dropped out of school due to pregnancy. Schools should carry out sex education to ensure that adolescents are free to talk about their sexuality, and are aware of risks associated with premarital sexual intercourse and multiple sexual relationships.

The local community accorded little support to refugee adolescent mothers' school re-entry. Community members considered them as subjects of ridicule and gossip having to go back to school. Nevertheless, some community members support the refugee adolescent mothers with psychological, and even financial support, to ensure that their education was provided. Community-level factors like culture, education, the poverty level remains a barrier to school re-entry support. Community entry points like the local authority, namely the area chief, assistant chief, and village elders, need to take collaborative action to ensure all children, irrespective adolescent mothers or not, attend school and create awareness of the re-entry process the government.

Refugee adolescent mothers' relationships with peers' changes as a result of pregnancy and parenthood, their peers now considered them as having moved to another level. They hence were no longer free to mingle with them. The quality times they had with their peers no longer exist. This made them suffer from solitude and were in one way or the other captives as a result of the parenting role they had. However, the peer group remained the outstanding support group for refugee adolescent mothers. Some peer members embraced and assisted them, even when no one else would do. Whenever they went back to school, peer groups would encourage them, motivate them to study hard, and even take them through revisions and discussions.

Recommendation for Future Studies

This study was limited to refugee adolescent mothers who delivered before completing their primary education. The respondents' sample was drawn from adolescent mothers residing in Kakuma refugee camp, who had gone back to school to finish their education at the time of the study. The future research needs are broad considering this study's limitation to the refugee population. A nationwide survey on various aspects concerning adolescent mothers' school re-entry process, highlighting the support system in multiple regions is paramount. Another priority is on studies on adolescent mothers' performance who manage to go back to school, highlighting within school barriers.

References

Carrington, D. (2011). Why women's education in Tanzania is critical for slowing population growth. Global Development. http://www. theguardian.com/global-development/2011/oct/24/women-education-tanzaniapopulation.

Cathcrine, B. K., Jonah, N. K., & Joseph, K. L. (2015). Impact of teenage motherhood on academic performance in public primary schools in Bungoma County, Kenya. International Journal of Educational Administration and Policy Studies.

Chase, E., Maxwell, C., Knight, A., & Aggleton, P. (2006). Pregnancy and parenthood among young people in and leaving care: what are the influencing factors, and what makes a difference in providing support? Journal of adolescence, 29(3), 437 451.

Chigona, A., & Chetty, R. (2008). Teen mothers and schooling: Lacunae and challenges. South African Journal of education, 28(2), 261-282.

Cowan, C. P., & Cowan, P. A. (2019). Enhancing Parenting Effectiveness, Fathers' Involvement, Couple Relationship Quality, and Children's Development: Breaking Down Silos in Family Policy Making and Service Delivery. Journal of Family Theory & Review, 11(1), 92-111.

Cox, J. E., Buman, M., Valenzuela, J., Joseph, N. P., Mitchell, A., & Woods, E. R. (2008). Depression, parenting attributes, and social support among adolescent mothers attending a teen tot program. Journal of Pediatric and Adolescent Gynaecology, 21(5), 275-281.

Darroch, J., Woog, V., Bankole, A., & Ashford, L. (2016). Adding it up: Costs and benefits of meeting the contraceptive needs of adolescents. New York: Guttmacher Institute.

Harriet, B., Chi-Chi Undie, I. M., Anne, K., Francis, O., & Patricia, M. (2015). Education Sector Response to Early and Unintended Pregnancy: A Review of Country Experiences in Sub-Saharan Africa. Population council, STEP UP and UNESCO Research Report.

Huang, C. Y., Costeines, J., Kaufman, J. S., & Ayala, C. (2014). Parenting stress, social support, and depression for ethnic minority adolescent mothers: Impact on child development. Journal of child and family studies, 23(2), 255-262.

Jochim, J., Groves, A., & Cluver, L. (2020). When do adolescent mothers return to school? Timing across rural and urban South Africa. South African Medical Journal, 110(9), 850-854.

Josephine, A., & Aramanzan, Madanda. (2011). A Survey On Re-Entry Of Pregnant Girls In Primary And Secondary Schools In Uganda. Commissioned by FAWE.

Kurgat, J. J. (2016). Administrative Support Factors Influencing Re-Admission of Teenage Mothers in Secondary Schools in Kenya: A Case of Baringo County. Journal of Education and Practice, 7(30), 208-211.

Molosiwa, S., & Bernard, M. (2012). Girl-pupil dropout in secondary schools in Botswana: Influencing factors, prevalence and consequences. International Journal of Business and Social Science 3(7):266-271.

Nazar, R., Chaudhry, I. S., Ali, S., & Faheem, M. (2018). Role Of Quality Education For Sustainable Development Goals (SDGs). PEOPLE: International Journal of Social Sciences, 4(2).

Neal, S., Matthews, Z., Frost, M., Fogstad, H., Camacho, A. V., & Laski, L. (2015). Childbearing in adolescents aged 12–15 years in low resource countries: a neglected issue. New estimates from demographic and household surveys in 42 countries. Acta Obstetricia et Gynecologica Scandinavica, 91(9), 1114-1118.

Obonyo, S. A., & Thinguri, R. W. (2015). A Critical Analysis of The Extent to Which The Education Policy On Re-Entry Of Girls After Teenage Pregnancy Has Been Implemented In Kenya. Researchjournali's Journal of Education 3: 4. ISSN 2347-8225.

Patrícia, J. P., Christian, L. d. M., Mariana, B. d. M., Fábio, M. C., Karen, A. P., Ricardo, A. d. S.,... Luciana, A. Q. (2017). Association between perceived social support and anxiety in pregnant adolescents.

Rubenstein, J. F. (2018). Exploring the Challenges of Refugee Camp Education: Kakuma and Buduburam Refugee Camp. Nairobi: United Nations.Brazilian Journal of Psychiatry. Print version ISSN 1516-4446On-line version ISSN 1809-452X.

SINASC. (2014). Information system on Live Births in Brazil.

Stroble, C. M. (2013). A phenomenological study: The lived experience of teen mothers who graduated from high school and attended or completed college. The University of North Carolina at Charlotte,

Strunk, J. A. (2008). The effect of school-based health clinics on teenage pregnancy and parenting outcomes: An integrated literature review. The Journal of School Nursing, 24(1), 13-20.

Taherdoost, H. (2016). Sampling methods in research methodology; how to choose a sampling technique for research. How to Choose a Sampling Technique for Research (10 April 2016).

Undie, C.-C., Birungi, H., Odwe, G., & Obare, F. (2015). Expanding access to secondary school education for teenage mothers in Kenya: A baseline study report.

Undie, C., Birungi, H., & Obare, F. (2015). Expanding access to secondary school education for teenage mothers in Kenya: A baseline study report. Nairobi: Population Council.

UNESCO. (2015). Education for All 2000-2015: Achievements and Challenges

UNESCO, A. (2016). Teachers Guide to the Prevention of Violent Extremism. In: Paris: UNESCO.

UNFPA. (2015). Girlhood, not motherhood: Preventing adolescent pregnancy. New York: UNFPA.

UNHCR. (2019). Kakuma and Kalobeyei camps population statistics.

UNICEF. (2013). Ending child marriage: Progress and prospects. New York: UNICEF.

Valaitis, R. K., & Sword, W. A. (2005). Online Discussions With Pregnant and Parenting Adolescents: Perspectives and Possibilities. Health Promotion Practice, 6(4), 464-471. doi:10.1177/1524839904263897

WHO. (2014). Health for the world's adolescents: A second chance in the second decade [Internet]. Department of Maternal, Newborn, Child and Adolescent Health, WHO.

Yungungu, M., & Wambua, K. (2006). The Perception of Society on The Education of Girls in Kenya: A Case Of Secondary Schools in Ainabkoi Division, Uasin Gishu District, Kenya. Educator (Eldoret, Kenya), 1(1), 145-152.

Zuilkowski, S. S., Henning, M., Zulu, J., & Matafwali, B. (2019). Zambia's school re-entry policy for adolescent mothers: Examining impacts beyond re-enrollment. International Journal of Educational Development, 64, 1-7.

About the Author

Charity Kola holds both Masters and Bachelor's degrees in Arts and Social Science. Diplomas in Project Management, Mass Communication, Community Development and Social Work, and short management courses. She has a professional experience working with Refugees and IDPs in Africa and the Middle East, with various International Humanitarian and Development Organizations. She has supported programs in: Communication with Communities, Accountability and Community Based Protection. She currently serves as a Regional Community Accountability Reporting Mechanism (CARM) Advisor-Africa with Mercy Corps. Her career interests are gender and protection for the forcefully displaced and disadvantaged populations.

The Human Cost of Development: Displacement and Resettlement Experiences from India

Shreya Mitra[16]

Abstract

India has rich mineral, gas, forest, and other natural resources; these are found in the lands where tribal, indigenous and the poor reside. These lands' rich natural resource base makes them a potential site for establishing development projects and industries. While these development projects can significantly benefit society, these projects often come at human costs, where the poor and the indigenous people are the victims and merely share the benefit of the development. Displacement has a social-economic impact on the lives of the poor; the loss of traditional livelihood, culture, food security, ownership rights over resources, and land alienation are the most prominent among other issues they face. India has experiences where displacement and resettlement issues have taken a violent turn and increased mass protests and movements. In this chapter, the author critically appraises the consequences of development-induced displacement in India through secondary data analysis. This paper aims to determine the issues and challenges related to displacement, reallocation, and resettlement to be addressed to attain inclusive development. The findings suggest that displacement and resettlement pose enormous risks for the poor who are uprooted from their native places and put into a new place with limited or no ownership of resources. Displacees are not entitled to any legal rights over the land and lack access to basic amenities like health, sanitation, education and secure livelihood. Displacement must be done with informed choice and consent of the communities. They should be included in the decision-

---

16 Research Scholar, Department of Social Work, Visva-Bharati University, Sriniketan, West Bengal India. Email id – mailtomitra85@gmail.com

making process when reallocation and resettlement measures are determined. Resettlement mechanism should not restricted to compensation and allocation of housing but focus on the specific needs of various communities, cultures, and ecosystems and ensure a sustainable livelihood for the displaced.

Key Words: Displacement, Development, Livelihood, Food security, Resettlement

Introduction

'Development', a commonly used word in our day-to-day conversation, encompasses social, economic, political, and cultural procedures of human civilisation enhancement. Infrastructural development and projects like dams and mines have an important implication in human life, contributing to its growth and progress. India has focussed on developmental projects since independence and presently stands as one among the fastest developing countries. India has a rich cultural heritage and rich mineral, gas, forest, and other natural resource bases. The rich resource base areas attract and make them potential sites of development projects and industries.

Post-independence, India's nation-building tasks were flagged off with the launching of five years plans. The situation then compelled the Government to focus on economic development. Hence the emphasis was on the construction of dams, mega projects, factories, mining etc. India's introduction to the neo-liberal economy was through the New Economic Policy in 1991, where the main focus was growth centred. The adoption of new liberal reforms created avenues for foreign investors, multinational companies, and corporates to set their foot in the country. In India, 354 zones have been notified as Special Economic Zones (SEZs) under the Special Economic Zones Act, 2005 (Ministry of Commerce and Industries, 2020). With the identification of SEZs, the Government promoted corporate-led growth, where land was acquired and handed over to corporates and private developers to set up their establishments. The corporate-led industrialisation claimed to attract foreign capital, create job opportunities with efficiency and competition, reduce poverty, and enhance economic growth. However, the reality is that the corporates' profit motive gives little attention to most of the poor population (Siddiqui, 2012).

While these development projects have enormous benefit to society, these projects often come at human costs where the people reside in the area are forcefully displaced with mere compensation and/or unplanned rehabilitation and resettlement. Displacement has a social-economic impact on the lives of the poor; the loss of traditional livelihood, culture, food security, ownership rights over resources and land alienation are the most prominent among other issues they face. It is a fact that the rich resource base areas are where the indigenous, tribes and poor reside and are dependent on the natural resources for their survival. The benefits of the development projects are hardly percolated to the displaced population; instead, they are exposed to vulnerabilities like loss of traditional livelihood, culture, food security, ownership rights over resources and land alienation. The existing literature on the issue has highlighted that in India, rehabilitation and resettlement have not been given adequate attention, which further exacerbates the plight of the displacees.

1. The Displacement Scenario

Displacement means dislocation of human population from their native place or region due to various reasons like natural calamities, social or political unrest, for setting up power projects, mining, mineral extraction to number a few. Displacement for mining, industries, building dams, urbanisation and other infrastructures is known as development-induced displacement. Often, development-induced displacement is forced wherein the people are compelled to vacate their residential places and social systems as they are uprooted from their homes and their homelands they attached to, from generations after generations (Lone, 2014).

Due to land acquisition for various India's developmental activities, people's forced displacement is significant. There has been a rise in protests across the country by the indigenous people, the tribes, farmers and the poor. Past experiences have shown that these kinds of displacement affected the poor sections of the society mainly the tribal population and with displacement, they were pushed to further marginalisation and trapped in the vicious cycle of poverty (Siddiqui, 2012). Although there is no exact data on the number of development-induced displacees, India's Government admitted that several million people have been displaced due to developmental activities and are still waiting for rehabilitation (Lone, 2014). The global report of Internal Displacement Monitoring Centre's (IDMC, 2020), data of India mentions that there were 5 million disaster displacement and 19000 conflicts and violence triggered displacement during 2019-20. The report does not have any mention on development induced displacement in the country. The working group on Human Rights in India and the UN report stated that India has the highest number of populations displaced due to development projects globally, and those displaced mostly belonged to traditional forest dwellers and the Scheduled tribes (WGHR, 2012). States like Odisha, Jharkhand, Chhattisgarh, Andhra Pradesh and the Northeastern States face the threat of development-induced displacement. The 11th Five Year Plan identified that compulsory land acquisition, using the Government's land acquisition process, was the leading cause of the alienation of tribal land in Scheduled areas. It also highlighted the arrangement of resettlement and rehabilitation of those affected were detrimental and prejudicial to the interest of the tribal. The erosion of the corpus of tribal land continues at an accelerated pace under the new economic reforms while the policy options are debated (Housing and Land Rights Network, 2012). Rajagopal (2000) has laid down the human rights challenges that arise due to development-induced displacement. The challenges are:

1. Right to Development and Self-Determination: The Universal Declaration of Human Rights (UDHR) states that every human being is entitled to participate in and contribute to, and enjoy economic, social, cultural, political development in which human rights and freedoms can be fully realised. It further asserts people's right to self-determination and their inalienable right to full sovereignty over their wealth and natural resources.

2. Right to participation: The tribal and indigenous shall participate in the formulation, implementation, and evaluation of the national and regional development plans that affect them.

3. Right to Life and Livelihood: Forced eviction and use of security forces to evacuate people from their land often lead to a threat to

the right of life. The right to livelihood is threatened by the loss of home, occupation, farmlands and other means to livelihood.

4. Rights of vulnerable groups: Development-induced development poses a threat to the indigenous groups, primitive tribes, women, elderly. Displacement pushes them to further marginalisation and vulnerabilities (Paul, 2020; The Wire, 2019).

5. Right to Remedy: This right is asserted in Article 8 of UDHR and International Covenant on Civil and Political Rights (ICCPR) Article 2. The development projects' decision is taken at the top level without consultation and consent of the project affected people and the poor come to know about the actions after the decisions are already taken. In these cases, they need a quick and effective remedy to pause an ongoing project and prevent future violations. Other authors like Downing added such risks as loss of access to public services, disruption of formal educational activities, and loss of civil and human rights (Terminski, 2015).

There has been disagreement regarding the exact number of people displaced due to development process as neither the State nor the Central Government has any database on displacees (Mishra, 2002). The resettlement of displacees in monetary compensation is arbitrarily decided, and a lump sum amount is paid to the displacees. The attitude of the project authorities towards these poor and marginalised are apathetic and negligent. Research shows that even to get the compensation, the poor have to face many hurdles like bribing Government officials, recourse to lawyers and intermediaries (Kumar & Mishra, 2018). These people take advantage of the uneducated poor who lives in the interior pockets with limited interaction with the market forces. Compensation to displacees is limited to individual landowners who have land titles. The tribals/poor people have a simple living. When they get the cash compensation in bulk, they fail to channel it properly and spend the amount in alcohol & substance abuse, medical expenses, marriages, or frittered away, without investing it in rebuilding assets livelihoods. Resettlement, only in cash leaves them in the mercy of the market forces about which they do not know (Mohanty, 2005; Vanclay, 2017). Often, they fall prey to fraud land brokers; microfinance companies lure them to double the amount invested with them within a short time. Cases were reported from Jharkhand, where hundreds of illiterate tribals were cheated by middlemen's compensation amount (Hindustan Times, 2015). In 2019, the Nilgiris district's twenty-one tribal families alleged that they were duped of compensation they received for relocation from Tamil Nadu's Mudumalai Tiger Reserve, by property dealers allied with forest officials (Down to Earth, 2019).

The literature on development-induced displacement, over time, have documented the adverse effect of development-induced displacement and livelihood of the displacees. Pandey, 1996 noted in a study that unemployment among the tribal population shot from 9% to 43.6% in Talcher of Odisha. People had to shift from their primary occupation to tertiary occupations, which resulted in a reduction in income from 50%-80% among the scheduled tribes and the scheduled castes (Pandey 1996 as cited in Mohanty, 2005). There has been a steep rise in the number of landless people after displacement in many places, which further pushed the displacees to marginalisation and trapped them in acute poverty. The project authorities claim to provide employment opportunities to the displacees, but the job creation for this section of the people, who lack education and skills, was far from expected. The high mechanisation and automation in the establishments reduce the demand for labour; hence guaranteeing jobs before displacement remains an unfulfilled promise. The unskilled labour (if employed) are always at a loss and are devoid of the labour rights: job insecurity, prevention from unionisation, extensive casualisation and contractualisation of labour, lack of benefits, unjust wages, and overtime without pay are some of the rights which are curtailed (Pandey,2015). The Uranium Corporation of India's mining project in Jharkhand displaced around 400 households, predominantly the Scheduled Tribes, with more than 2000 population. They were poorly compensated, and jobs were restricted to only those families who had land ownership. Even the rehabilitation was mismanaged, and complete rehabilitation could not be done as the host community voiced their discontent and refused to accept the displacees. The lack of transparency and accountability of the agencies responsible for resettlement aggravated the miseries of the displacees. There were increasing vulnerabilities among the displacees trapped in the vicious cycle of poverty, chronic malnourishment, and food insecurity. The social and psychological stress and undernourishment led to the worsening of health standards of the displacees (Kumar, 2013: Paul, 2020).

The Scudder-Colson theory 1982 states that relocation, whether voluntary or compulsory, is a stressful experience. People who are relocated react in predictable and broadly similar ways partly because the stress of relocation limits the range of coping responses of those involved. The most stressful period is in the early phase, where they have to begin from scratch. The risk factors associated with displacement and relocation are landlessness, homelessness, joblessness, food insecurity, marginalisation, loss of access to natural resources, morbidity, and social disarticulation (Cernea, 1990; Rao, 2013). The displacees face many difficulties adjusting to the new environment with socio-economic disturbance as they are forcibly resettled without psychological and cultural preparedness, resulting in distressed and depressed conditions. The kinship relationship is also affected, as the family starts living in scattered locations, the social fabric is also disrupted, and their cultural identity is often lost, leading to social disarticulation (Paul, 2013, Kumar & Mishra, 2018). The displacement experience of the Singrauli region of Uttar Pradesh and Madya Pradesh border due to dams and mining shows how forced displacement had affected those displaced' social fabric. The worst affected were the elderly population who could not adjust to the new social setting. There was a breakdown in the family norms, kinship solidarity and disintegration of village solidarity. Tribals, who had an honest and straightforward living earlier, were succumbed to greed and became money minded for their livelihood. The implementation of various development projects resulted in quarrelling and conflict among tribals over trivial money matters. The rehabilitation sites also witnessed caste conflicts over common resources, which affected many people's lives and livelihood (Verma, 2004). A Case study on the displacement due to the construction of Hirakud Dam in Odisha reveals that forced displacement and unplanned resettlement had upsurge conflicts among the host community and the displacees over-sharing natural resources and livelihood opportunities. The displacees are often subjected to social alienation on caste issues, ethnicity, cultural clashes, political problems and demographic imbalances. The displacees lost their livelihood and wealth and their liberty, identity, opportunities, and their basis of self-respect (Nayak, 2013).

In a new location, the women are subjected to face an additional burden of workload. In their native, they were acquainted with the natural resources and the social environment; hence they were comfortable fetching water, collecting firewood, and other livelihoods. Nevertheless, in the new location, they are under fear while going out for water, firewood or work, there are threats of molesters, thieves, and looters. They also feel alienated from their close kin, neighbours and other relatives. Displacement also gives rise to other social problems like alcoholism, domestic violence, gambling, theft, prostitution, etc. (Kumar & Mishra, 2018). The displacement due to the Mumbai Urban Transport Project brings forth the faulty and unplanned resettlement arrangements. The houses provided were unfit for a decent living; they lacked access to civic amenities, water, proper sanitation, public transportation, the heightened sense of insecurity and lack of adjustment among new neighbourhoods. The buildings were constructed too close to each other with no ventilation. The dark spaces of these buildings became breeding grounds of diseases and petty crimes. Women in the site complained of losing jobs due to the commuting problem affecting their income, autonomy, mobility and freedom. They narrated how it has pushed them and their families to mental and financial stress. Class and caste conflicts were a regular phenomenon as the displacees belonged to various religions, castes, classes, and social backgrounds (Ayyar, 2013). The resettlement sites of Bagri Dam (1992) have also shed light on the dreary condition of the displacees. The Independent People's Tribunal report on Environment and Human Rights reported cases of starvation deaths resulting from faulty planning at the end of the project authorities (Ghosh et al., 2015).

The displacees lack access to adequate information regarding the proposed development projects, its purpose, the actual benefit, the resettlement, and rehabilitation packages, instead they are misled by exaggerated benefits of the project, and false hopes by the project authorities, creating distress and anguish among the people. The Internal Displacement Monitoring Committee and Norwegian Refugee Council's report in 2016 findings mentioned that in all the nine locations where they conducted the study, no public consultations were held before eviction and no community participated in the resettlement process (Walicki & Swain, 2016). Unethical business practices result in overexploitation of natural resources for more production affecting the peripheral locality where resettlement is often done. Drying up of streams, lowering of groundwater leads to acute water shortage. An increasing trend in the number of diseases has been observed in the relocated sites due to the industries' release of effluents and air pollution (Mohanty, 2009). The Land Acquisition, Rehabilitation and Resettlement Act (LARR) 2013 made it a mandate to consent to the local people to go ahead with the land acquisition: 70% in a public-private partnership project 80% in case of private companies. Siddiqui (2018) believes that though the LARR 2013 has laid down some beneficial provisions in terms of fair compensation yet, it completely ignores the socio-economic issues related to compensation. There remains a possibility of Government favouring the corporates. The Act talks of determining compensation based on 'market value' of the land/property, whereas in practice these market values are based on the 'circle rates' and the sale deeds of the similar property and these 'circle rates' fixed by the Government are often outdated and below the market price.

With globalisation and the new economic policy reforms, the Government opened its gate to multinational companies to industrialise India. Special Economic Zones (SEZs) were notified, and the entire process was done in haste without looking into any social and environmental considerations. Parwez and Sen (2016) in their paper computed a data by Ministry of Rural Development (2010) which estimated that 114000 farming households along with 82000 families of farmworkers dependent on these lands would be displaced due SEZs all over India. Till January 2015 the number of formally approved SEZs is approximately 491, notified and in principle approvals are 352 and 33 respectively, and operation SEZs are 196. SEZs' total area is 0.058% of the total land area and 0.317% of agricultural land. The lands acquired were predominantly agricultural, most of it was multi cropped lands. Conversion of these land to industrial purpose means reduced production of millions of tons of food grains which implies the significant rise of food insecurity (Verma, 2016). Pandey (2015) viewed the SEZ policy to be biased, anti-poor, and anti-nature. He affirmed that human labour is treated as a commodity in the unregulated markets, and SEZs' creation has led to structural violence and exclusion of people who do not have the means to participate in the market. This entire process leads to the accumulation of material wealth through deprivation and inequality.

2. Some Experiences of People's Protest to Development Projects

The past displacement, resettlement, and rehabilitation experiences are not very decent in India. It has raised equity, justice, and equality before the law shares the projects' benefit and burden. The project affected people were not ready to suffer displacement and concomitant consequences (Mohanty, 2009). Hence, the rampant and forced land acquisition process agitated the people, and they started protesting against the unruly and unjust development projects. Below mentioned are some of the protests against forced displacement and land acquisition which gained support from various corner of the Nation:

Narmada Bachao Movement: One of the oldest and still ongoing protests against development-induced displacement in India. In 1979 the Narmada Valley Development Project was launched. The movement's main aim was to protest against large dams in the Narmada river and its tributaries in the States of Madhya Pradesh, Gujrat, and Maharastra (Shrivastava, 2007). In 1985, the World Bank agreed to provide 450 million dollars for the Sardar Sarovar Project (Samling, Ghosh et al., 2015). The Sardar Sarovar Project saw the largest ever displacement in India, affecting around 300 villages, displacing a population of 163000 (Parasuraman, 1999 cited in Lone, 2014). Without considering the human rights and prior consultation with the displacees, the resettlement and rehabilitation packages were determined. The packages were determined in terms of land ownership, but most of the tribals did not prove their landholdings. Though they have been living there for generations after generations, they were considered encroachers and hence packages offered to them were negligible. 96% of the population displaced in Gujrat under the project have complained that relocation has worsened their living condition because of the poor amenities in the relocated areas and the degraded quality of agricultural land in the site (Garikpati,2002).

Looking at the intensity of protests and the legal complications, the World Bank withdrew its support from the project in 1993. The controversy over the Narmada dams has continued for years, and the project's damage was beyond the projected. Anticipating the project's economic benefit and several years of negotiation, the Supreme Court allowed the Sardar Sarovar Dam construction with certain prerequisite conditions and the project revived in 2000. Mahmood and Dalal (2019), has examined the quality of life among Bhil and related tribe after resettlement due to the Sardar Sarovar Dam. His study reveals that the redistribution of land and labour has affected the displaced families' socio-economic conditions. Due to the decreased size of the given land holding, there is a shift in their occupation from cultivators to agricultural labour. There has been a drastic decline in animal husbandry (except poultry farming) as a livelihood source. These factors have resulted in decreased food consumption of the families and increase in health-related issues. Similar findings were noted by Sikka (2020). In his study on the socio-cultural impacts of displacement by the Sardar Sarovar Dam, the displacement has resulted in breaking the social networks, losing tribal folk art, marriage customs, and dressing patterns.

Even though the project has completed, the Narmada Bachao Movement is still active; the affected people and the activists' stage protests on the project's issues like nonpayment of compensation, unfulfilled promises, rehabilitation, and submergence of areas. In 2019, several agitations were staged demanding complete rehabilitation before submergence, as Gujrat Government decided to fill up the reservoir on Sardar Sarovar Dam to the maximum limit, resulting in submergence of many areas. They also put their demands on resolving pending issues of rehabilitations, compensating crop loss of the submerged areas, compensating and rehabilitating genuinely affected people, and constituting a committee that would assess the dam's benefits and losses dam (Sarkar, 2019; Newsclick, 2019). This protest movement entered its 35th year in 2020. With the third generation of leaders taking the responsibility, the movement is continuing with full zeal, momentum and determination with which it was initiated and stand firm on voicing the rights of the affected population.

The POSCO Project Odisha: In 2005, a memorandum of understanding was signed between the Government of Odisha and the South Korean company named Pohang Steel Company (POSCO) for setting up an integrated steel plant, captive power plant, and marine port near Paradip, Jagatsinghpur district. It was considered the largest foreign direct investment in India, with USD 12 billion. The Government of Odisha agreed to grant mining lease right for 30 years to POSCO and 4000 acres of land earmarked to establish the project, which would adversely affect 11 villages with an estimated population of 22,000 and further disrupt the livelihood of 30,000 people in the district. The livelihood of the families depends on betel vine cultivation, pisciculture, cashew cultivation, and fisheries. The project faced a massive protest from the villagers over the years. They were subjected to violence and forced eviction by police and paramilitary forces, sent by the Government with collusion with POSCO. There were numerous incidences of violations of Human Rights by police, including beating, shooting, arbitrary arrests, torture, and filing false cases. In 2007 a peaceful protest was attacked by corporate goons where many protestors were injured. The villagers' protest was so intense that in 2010, the Ministry of Environment and Forests formed a four members committee to investigate the implementation of existing legalities on environmental issues, including the Forest Rights Act (2006) and the Coastal Regulation Zone rules by POSCO India Private Limited. The committee reported a grave violation of environmental laws, the Forest Rights Act, fabrication of evidence, and information suppression. Irrespective of the committee's findings and recommendations, the POSCO project was given Forest and Environment no objection certificate in 2011, which later in 2012 was suspended by the National Green Tribunal (Housing and Land Rights Network, 2012). The villagers' miseries did not end there; in 2013 the police troops surrounded the village threatening the community people of forced eviction, there were cases of bombing in the community, which again stirred the protest.

In 2010, the research examined and predicted the impact of the project on the community. The study's findings highlight that the small betel vine provides a sustainable and steady income for the families, which is three times the average Indian income while cultivating land plots is less than the one-tenth size of an acre. The betel vineyards gave the families an average monthly income, of Rs.20000. More than 30000 small scale fisherpersons would also lose their livelihood. POSCO's compensation would not be adequate for the loss of their homeland and their livelihood; hence, they rejected the State Government's offer of Rs.70 crore rehabilitation package. The forced eviction would have led to grave violations of human rights including housing, health, food security and livelihood. The project was also considered to harm the environment and local biodiversity.

Furthermore, after more than a decade long people's resistance and fight for their rights, POSCO officially withdrew its project from Odisha (Business-Humanrights, 2013; Sahoo, 2017). Presently, the land acquisition process has been stopped, and POSCO remains a stalled project. People have gone back to their livelihood and rebuilt the destroyed betel vines to construct the project and earn a good income. Further, those compensated and moved to the rehabilitation centre are returning to their villages (Mallik & Parida, 2020).

Save Niyamgiri Movement: The Niyamgiri hills are a mountain range in Odisha, home to the Primitive Tribal Groups[17] namely the Dongaria Kondh and Kutia Kondh. These tribals share a critical and symbiotic relationship with the Niyamgiri forests, which is the prime source of their living. In 2003, Vedanta Resources, a UK based company, signed an MoU with Government of Odisha to construct an alumina refinery and thermal coal plant at Lanjigarh in Kalahandi District. The alumina refinery would require around 3 million tons of bauxite per annum, which was proposed to be mined from the Niyamgiri hills. With clearance by the Government of Odisha, Vedanta acquired 58 acres of forest land for building the refinery. In 2004 the clearance was challenged by local activists and the tribal people. While the legal battle was ongoing in the Supreme Court, Vedanta continued the construction of its refinery.

With the violation of various environmental laws, mining also had human costs. The mining would affect 28 Kondh villages covering a population

---

17   As per Ministry of Tribal Affairs, 'Primitive Tribal Groups' are communities among the Scheduled Tribes that live in near isolation in inaccessible habitat and thus eligible for special protection.

of 5148 persons intrinsically tied to the Niyamgiri forest-economically, religiously, and culturally. The tribes depend predominantly on forest produce and loss of forest cover would hamper their livelihood. These people's cultivable land is located in proximity to the project location; hence, the mining activities would deny them access to their lands that they have used for generations. The streams and other water resources would also be dried up or contaminated, and the ecological balance would be disrupted due to loss of biodiversity (Bal, 2020). The protest by the Dongria Kondhs and mass support to the protest compelled the Government to send a team of experts to the hills in 2010, and the report suggested that the proposed bauxite mining would be detrimental to the existence of the tribals. The tribal protest and the legal battle continued over the years. In 2013, the Supreme Court ruled that mining should rest on the local inhabitants, after which the majority of the villages rejected the mining project and won over the mining giants. In 2016 the Odisha Mining Company submitted a petition to the Supreme Court pointing flaws and technical issues in the village assemblies' resolutions, but the apex court rejected the plea. This again resulted in a clash among the tribals and the State authorities. In 2018 the villagers set to protest against the fresh proposal by Vedanta for further expansion of its refinery. The people of Niyamgiri live with the fear of permitting mining in the area, resulting in the degradation of the natural resources hence they are still fighting for the cause of protecting Niyamgiri (Paliwal, 2019). The Niyamgiri hill ranges are of religious importance to the Dongarias hence they are adamant in their stand. With support from civil societies and NGOs at the local, national and international level, the Dongarias are attempting to claim their community rights over the entire Niyamgiri range under the Forests Rights Act, 2006 (Borde & Bluemling,2020).

Singur and Nandigram Protest against Land Acquisition: Singur and Nandigram of West Bengal saw mass protest against forceful land acquisition for industrialisation. In 2006 the Government of West Bengal decided to acquire around 1000 acres of land for setting up a factory of small cars. The project would have affected 6000 families, mostly belonging to the small and marginal farmers, to lose their land and livelihoods. No compensation was decided for the landless and other rural families who were dependent on the agricultural lands. Resistance by the farmers was apparent from the very beginning of the announcement of the projects. The opposition political party ruling then led the protest in West Bengal. The farmers' struggle in forms of marches, rallies, and public hearings continued for more than two years. They faced violence by police and armed forces deployed in the region to resume the factory work. Finally, Tata Motors withdrew their project from West Bengal in 2008, and later in 2011, returning the acquired land to the farmers was initiated (The Hindu, 2016). A similar protest was observed during the same period in Nandigram of West Bengal, where forceful land acquisition for the setup of a chemical hub with financial support from an Indonesian company. There were clashes between the State authorities and the protestors. The inhuman treatment towards the protestors by the authorities, police firing, erupted violently in the area, resulting in loss of life of 14 people, leaving many injured (Livemint, 2007). Both the incidents shook the State and was condemned by people across the country. The two incidents in West Bengal led to the fall of the State's ruling party after 34 years of tenure (Walicki & Swain, 2016). The State Government said that approximately 955 acres of land out of 997 acres' land acquired for the TATA project in Singur, has been returned to the farmers. It also admitted that only 260 acres of land returned is put under cultivation which was previously 640 acres. The data signifies that there is a drastic fall in the land under cultivation in Singur. Though the factory has been demolished, the farmers complained that the debris remains make the land unfit for cultivation. Nandigram witnessed occupational shift among the farmers; most farmers have shifted to fisheries as they consider that it brings them more income than agriculture (Dasgupta, 2019; The Bengal Story, 2019).

The protests across the country against the corporate invasions signify the Government's wrong and unplanned move for industrialisation. The bitter experiences of resettlement and rehabilitation made the poor realise the importance of the land where they belong. The protests are borne out of their conviction that their livelihood loss cannot be compensated only by their land valuation. It is a matter of land and a matter of their identity, livelihood, and future. The victory of their struggle inspired many poor across the country and instilled hope in people's power.

3. Implications of Displacement

Based on the shreds of evidence of the literature referred, the study intends to develop a comprehensive picture of development-induced displacement and its implications. The above discussions indicate that during any development project is planned the focus is solely on the economic benefit, anticipated by the authorities. It neglects the tangible and intangible social aspects, which further leads to the people's marginalisation. Policymakers, authorities and civil society must frame strategies for socio-cultural and psychological rehabilitation of the affected people. The Human Rights aspect of the people affected should be considered, focusing firstly on identifying and recognising the rights of the displacees and, secondly, ensuring the protection of those resettled. There is a need to apply context-sensitive approaches in terms of compensation, appropriately compensating those who do not have entitlement to land, sharecroppers, artisans, wage labours, etc. The poor's livelihood is also dependent on the community's common property resources, which are not compensated when a community is displaced.

The land is the primary source of livelihood of the people in rural India; it is also a politically sensitive issue. The laws related to land and land rights are complex, protracted and ambiguous. In the present context, the two fundamental laws that protect land rights are (i) Forests Rights Act (FRA), 2006 and (ii) Land Acquisition, Rehabilitation and Resettlement (LARR) Act, 2013. The FRA grants the Scheduled Tribes and other forest dwellers rights of cultivating in the forest land, collect and dispose of minor forest produce, use grazing land and water bodies, and protect and manage their forests. It also states that no development project can be carried out without the approval of gram sabha. The LARR 2013, emphasised on increasing the compensation, necessitates social impact assessment and taking consent of the people affected 70% in public-private partnership and 80% in private projects. The Government should ensure that the legislation related to land and land rights is effectively implemented and pro-poor. There is a strong need for maintaining a database of people who are displaced due to development projects at State and National level; to understand the dynamics of development-induced development.

Displacement and resettlement plans should be implemented thoroughly and adequately. Monitoring the resettlers' socio-economic condition should be done for a considerable period after displacement to limit displacement risks. Private companies cannot shed their responsibilities only by compensating the people affected; instead, they should provide social security services to those affected by their Corporate Social Responsibility funds. The authorities should integrate the displacees with those already residing in the communities where they are resettled to avoid conflict. Kumar and Singh, 2020 have stated that "there is a need for a paradigm shift and the focus of resettlement and rehabilitation policy should consist of the livelihood reconstruction components which should consider: from landlessness to land-based resettlement; from joblessness to reemployment; from homelessness to house reconstruction; from marginalisation to social inclusion; from increased morbidity to improved health care; from food insecurity to adequate nutrition; from loss of access to the restoration of community assets and services, and from social disarticulation to rebuilding of networks and Communities" (Cernea, 1990).

Civil societies and NGOs can play a crucial role in this aspect. Awareness generation at grassroots on individual/community rights and entitlements can help the people make informed choices and empower them to negotiate the terms of compensation and resettlement. Legal activism is yet another aspect that can protect the rights of the people affected by development projects.

Conclusion

Researches and field-level experiences on displacement have highlighted the impoverishment of the displaced people. It is the poorest and the weaker sections of the communities who bear the highest development-induced displacement cost. These people already live in poverty, prior alienation, but displacement uproots them from their survival foundation. This is not restricted to only material impoverishment but also the social and psychological domain. The development projects deprive these people of their right to live with dignity by affecting their living and sustenance source. Alienation from their land, livelihood, culture, and social resources, devaluation of their assets through low compensation and improper resettlement procedures increase their sense of powerlessness. Consequences like hunger, cultural disintegration and debt-bondage are what they are left. It cannot be denied that the promotion of industries and development is essential for the country's economic growth, but the Government should ensure that these projects' destructive consequences are minimised. In the name of development, the Government should not slide only towards the interest of the corporates. In 'open market' and liberalised economy, the monopolists are given enormous power, which they often misuse and exploit the poor. Transferring the poor's productive resources to the hands of the privileged section augments the gaps in wealth.

The displacees who shares the pain hardly shares the gain of the development projects. The poor are further marginalised and exposed to food insecurity, poor health, loss of livelihood, etc. It can be said that India's displacement and resettlement experiences confirm the justification of Cernea's (1990) impoverishment risks and reconstruction model and Rajagopal's (2000) Human Rights Challenges of displacement. The Government should make it mandatory to provide the displacees with proper shelter, essential services, water and sanitation facilities, medical and healthcare, livelihood sources, educational facilities. It should also ensure the protection of the human rights of the displacees (Hoshour & Kalafut, 2007). Land Acquisition should be consciously made as diverting vast amount multi cropped, fertile agricultural land and converting forest land into industrial would adversely impact the country's food security, which is already in a critical condition. India has been ranked 94 among the 107 countries in the Global Hunger Index 2020, and it continues to be in the 'serious' hunger category. Further diversion of rich natural resource-based land into SEZs would intensify the climate change issue, which is a serious concern globally.

The above analysis depicts that neither the State nor the Corporates take the issue of displacement seriously. Rehabilitation is the least thought of as they consider compensation to be the easiest way. India strongly needs to address the issue of displacement sensitively. A robust legal instrument needs to be framed by plugging the loopholes in the existing laws related to displacement, resettlement and rehabilitation. The land acquisition process must be simplified, and compensation should be determined by landholding and other socio-economic aspects. Gender issues and concerns remain neglected in compensation, resettlement and rehabilitation.

Corporates who acquire land for their establishment should be made responsible and accountable for resettlement and rehabilitation. The community should be consulted before clearance of any project. Their needs and consent must be taken into account before taking any whimsical decision of resettlement and rehabilitation. Many displacees/ project-affected people are illiterate and do not have the technical skills to acquire jobs. However, these people can be trained for semi-skilled jobs and engaged in the projects. The project authorities must focus on resettlement and rehabilitation with adequate necessary service rather than only on the project's financial aspect. The loss of livelihood and other social capitals should be considered while cost-benefit analysis and the loss of assets are viewed as market commodities. The State, in the process of rapid development, should not neglect the welfare of the people. Inclusive growth is the only way towards sustainable development of the country.

References

Arun, Kumar & Singh, Arun. (2020). *Development Induced Displacement: Issues and Indian Experiences.* Retrieved from Researchgate on October 16, 2020. 16https://www.researchgate.net/publication/340771447_ Development_Induced_Displacement_Issues_and_Indian_ Experiences

Ayyar, V. (2013). Caste and Gender in a Mumbai Resettlement Site. *Economic and Political Weekly, 48*(18).

Bal, S. (2020). People's Resistance to Development: A Study of Save Niyamgiri. *Tathapi, 19*(4).

Borde, Radhika & Bluemling, Bettina. (2020). Representing Indigenous Sacred Land: The Case of the Niyamgiri Movement in India. *Capitalism Nature Socialism. 1*-20. 10.1080/10455752.2020.1730417.

Business-Humanrights. (2013). *Impacts of POSCO-India's Project on the Lives of Local People in Jagatsingphur, Odisha, India.* Retrieved from https://www.business-humanrights.org/sites/default/files/media/documents/briefing-note-posco-india-private-ltd.pdf.

Cernea, M. (1990). From Unused Knowledge to Policy Creation: The Case of Population Resettlement. *The World Bank Discussion Paper No. 342*. Boston: Harvard Institute for International Development, Havard University.

Dasgupta, M. (2019, April 10). Nandigram, Singur farmers angry with Mamata as getting land back hasn't improved their lot. *The Print*. https://theprint.in/politics/nandigram-singur-farmers-are-angry-with-mamata-but-trinamool-still-expected-to-hold-sway/219514/

Down to Earth. (2019, October 14). Nilgiris tribals allege they were duped of compensation. Down to Earth. Retrieved from https://www.downtoearth.org.in/news/governance/nilgiris-tribals-allege-they-were-duped-of-compensation-67231

Garikati, Supriya (2002). Resettlement Sites of Narmada Valley Project: Some Revealing Insights. *Economic and Political Weekly,37*(23).

Hindutan Times. (August 2015). *Middlemen duping tribals with hopes of compensation*. Hindustan Times.

Hoshour, K., & Kalafut, J. (2007). *A Growing Global Crisis: Development-induced Displacement and Resettlement*. International Accountability Project, Issue Paper.

Housing and Land Rights Network. (2012). *Human Rights to Adequate Housing and Land in India: Status Update 2012*.

Internal Displacement Monitoring Center (IDMC) and Norwegian Refugee Council (NRC). (2020). *Global Report on Internal Displacement 2020*. Internal Displacement Monitoring Centre (IDMC) and Norwegian Refugee Council (NRC). Retrieved October 15, 2020, from https://www.internal-displacement.org/countries/india

Kumar, P. (2013). Development, Displacement And Human Rights Violations: Two Case Studies in Jharkhand, India. *World Affairs: The Journal of International Issues, 17*(3).

Kumar, S., & Mishra, A. (2018). Development-Induced Displacement in India: An Indigenous Perspective. *Journal of Management and Public Policy, 10*(1).

Livemint. (2007, March). *The Nandigram Story till now.* Retrieved from Livemint.com: https://www.livemint.com/Politics/I1CAfbH2Und58UkVckctVP/The-Nandigram-story-till-now.html

Lone, R. A. (2014). Development-induced Displacement. *Journal of Social Science Research, 3*(2).

Mahmood A., Dalal S. (2019) Resettlement and Quality of Life of the Bhil Tribe in Sardar Sarovar Dam Area, India. In: Sinha B. (eds) *Multidimensional Approach to Quality of Life Issues.* Springer, Singapore. https://doi.org/10.1007/978-981-13-6958-2_10

Mallik, S., & Parida, B. (2020, January). Development and Voices of Dissent in India: Insights from Odisha. *Journal of Politics & Governance, 8*(1), 10.

Ministry of Commerce and Industries. (2020, May 15). *Special Economic Zones in India.* Retrieved from http://sezindia.nic.in: http://sezindia.nic.in/upload/uploadfiles/files/notify.pdf

Mishra, S. (2002). Development, Displacement and Rehabilitation of Tribal people: A case study of Orrisa. *Journal of Social Sciences, 6*(3).

Mohanty, B. (2005). Displacement and Rehabilitation of Tribals. *Economic and Political Weekly, 40*(13).

Mohanty, M. (2009). Development and Tribal Displacement: Reflection on Core Issues. *The Indian Journal of Political Science, 70*(2).

Nayak, A. (2013). Development, Displacement and Justice in India: Study of Hirakud dam. *Social change, 43*(3).

Newsclick. (2019, November 19). Narmada Bachao Andolan Protest enters 4th Day Medha Patkar flays Kamal Nath Government of failing to meet its own deadline for fulfilling promises on compensation.

Paliwal, A. (2019, October). *Tribals in Niyamgiri Protest Against Bauxite Mining by Vedanta Limited.* Retrieved from Land Conflict Watch:

https://www.landconflictwatch.org/conflicts/tribals-in-niyamgiri-protest-against-bauxite-mining-by-vedanta-limited

Pandey, ManishaTripathy (2015) *'New Capitalism and Violence: The Case of Special Economic Zones in India'*. In Verma, Manish K. (ed.); Globalization and Environment: Discourse, Policies and Practices; Jaipur; Rawat Publication.

Parwez, Sazzad & Sen, Vinod. (2016). Special Economic Zone, Land Acquisition, and Impact on Rural India. Emerging Economy Studies. 2. 10.1177/2394901516661104.

Paul, Norvy (2020). *Marginalised Displacees and Development*, Chennai: Notion Express Publishing.

Paul, Norvy (2013). *Development, Displacement and Social Disarticulation: A Kerala Experience*. Germany: Lambert Academic Publishing.

Rajagopal, B. (2000). *Human Rights and Development*, Thematic Review, Working Paper, Vol.4, World Commission on Dams.

Rao, D. J. (2013). Displacement and Protest Movements-The Indian Experience. *International Journal of Modern Engineering Research, 3*(3), 1554-1560.

Sahoo, P. R. (2017, March). *As Posco exits steel project, Odisha is left with thousands of felled trees and lost livelihoods*. Retrieved from scroll.in: https://scroll.in/article/832463/as-posco-exits-steel-project-odisha-is-left-with-thousands-of-felled-trees-and-broken-job-promises

Samling, C.L., Ghosh A.K., Hazra S.,2015.*Resettlement and Rehabilitation: Indian Scenario*. DECCMA Working Paper, Deltas, Vulnerability and Climate Change: Migration and Adaptation, IDRC Project number 107642.

Sarkar, S. (2019, August). Narmada Bachao Andolan starts indefinite agitation as Rajghat Bridge submerges. The Week.

Shrivastava, R. (2007). Environmental Stewardship and Sustainable Development: A Study of the Role of Government in Rehabilitation of

Persons Affected by Sardar Sarovar Dam in India. *The Indian Journal of Political Science, 68*(3).

Siddiqui, Kalim. (2018). Development-induced Displacement of Rural Communities in India. https://www.researchgate.net/publication/326522310_Development_Induced_Displacement_of_Rural_Communities_in_India

Sikka, Gaurav (2020). Moving Beyond Economic Analysis: Assessing the Socio-Cultural Impacts of Displacement and Resettlement by Sardar Sarovar Project, India. Geography, Environment, Sustainability.

Terminiski, B. (2015). *Development-Induced Displacement and Resettlement: Causes, Consequences and Socio-Legal Context.* Germany: ibidem Press.

The Bengal Story. (2019, July 10). Cultivation in Singur on land returned to farmers is reducing, but can't force them to farm: Mamata Banerjee. Retrieved October 8, 2020, from The Bengal Story: https://thebengalstory.com/english/cultivation-in-singur-on-land-returned-to-farmers-is-reducing-but-cant-force-them-to-farm-mamata-banerjee/

The Hindu. (2016). Singur land acquisition issue: A timeline.

The Wire. (2019, February 28). *Eviction of Tribals: Forced Displacement and Its Links with Poor Health.* Retrieved October 10, 2020, from The Wire: https://thewire.in/rights/supreme-court-eviction-tribals-displacement

Vanclay, F. (2017). *Project-induced displacement and resettlement: from impoverishment risks to an opportunity for development?,* Impact Assessment and Project Appraisal, 35:1, DOI: 10.1080/14615517.2017.1278671

Verma, M. K. (2004). *Development, Displacement and Resettlement.* New Delhi: Rawat Publication.

Verma, M. K. (2016). Development-induced Displacement, SEZs and the State of Farmers in India: Some Insights from the Recent Experiences. *Journal of the National Human Rights Commission India, 15.*

Walicki, Nadine, and Marita Swain (2016). *Pushed aside: Displaced for "Development" in India,* Internal Displacement Monitoring Center (IDMC) and Norwegian Refugee Council (NRC), www.internal-displacement.org/sites/default/files/publications/documents/201607-ap-india-pushed-aside-en.pdf

WGHR. (2012). Human Rights in India: Status Report. New Delhi: Working Group on Human Rights in India and the UN.

About the Author

Shreya Mitra completed her Post Graduate in Social Work from Visva-Bharati University (A Central University) India. Presently she is pursuing her doctoral research at the Department of Social Work, Visva-Bharati, India. She has ten years of professional experience in the development sector. She has worked with organizations like the Foundation for Ecological Security and Action Aid Association. She has been awarded Gandhian Practice Model Award for presenting her research paper titled *"Relevance of Gandhian Philosophy in Mitigating Crisis in Stressed Tea Gardens of North Bengal"* in an International Conclave organized by Rajiv Gandhi University, India in collaboration with Gandhi King Foundation, Hyderabad, India and Gandhi-King Global Initiative, Stanford University Centre, USA.

Internal Migration and Women's Health in India: Understanding the Vulnerabilities and Way Forward

Subrata S Satapathy[18]

Abstract

Internal migration, the movement of people within a country, results in a more efficient allocation of human resources to sectors and regions where they are better utilized. In India, as in most countries, there are generally no restrictions on internal movement. The number of internal migrants in India was 450 million as per the most recent 2011 census. This is an increase of 45% over the 309 million recorded in 2001 and far exceeds the population growth rate of 18% across 2001-2011. Internal migrants as a percentage of the population increased from 30% in 2001 to 37% in 2011. Interestingly, the 2011 Census reveals that women form almost 70 per cent of internal migration. Women migrants, in particular, suffer the consequences of being a woman and a migrant. They remain mostly discriminated in the workforce and invariably suffer economic exclusion. In addition to low pay and inhuman working conditions, low-skilled women migrants often get work that is saddled with health hazards. Garment workers in Bengaluru, comprising 90 per cent women migrants, often suffer from "respiratory illness, tuberculosis, ergonomic problems like back pain, mental health problems such as depression... and reproductive health issues. This paper attempts to throw light on the various post-migration health vulnerabilities of India's women's internal migrants.

Key Words: Internal Migration, Women's Health, Vulnerabilities, India

---

18   *Independent Research Consultant, Bangalore, Karnataka. Email: subrata.satapathy@ gmail.com*

Introduction

Migration is the movement of people away from their usual residence place, across either internal (within the country) or international (across countries) borders. In the last few years, various changes in India have likely put an impact on the pace and pattern of migration. In the last two decades, the growth pattern has steadily widened the gap between non-agriculture and agriculture and between urban and rural areas. The growing spatial inequalities in economic opportunities must have also impacted the pace and pattern of migration. Uneven growth and a growing differential between agriculture and industry is a necessary parallel of the development pattern. Migration has historically played a role in reducing the gap in living standards between sectors and areas and fuelling growth in the more dynamic sectors.

The latest government data on migration comes from the 2011 Census. As per the Census, India had 45.6 crore migrants in 2011 (38% of the population) compared to 31.5 crore migrants in 2001 (31% of the population). Between 2001 and 2011, while the population grew by 18%, the number of migrants increased by 45%. In 2011, 99% of total migration was internal, and immigrants (international migrants) comprised 1% (Census, 2011). Internal migrant flows can be classified based on origin and destination. One kind of classification is: i) rural-rural, ii) rural-urban, iii) urban-rural and iv) urban-urban. As per the 2011 census, 210 million rural-rural migrants formed 54% of classifiable internal migration (the Census did not classify 5.3 crore people as originating from either rural or urban areas). Rural-urban and urban-urban movement accounted for around 80 million migrants each. There were around 30 million urban-rural migrants (7% of classifiable internal migration). Another way to classify migration is (i) intra-state and (ii) inter-state. In 2011, intra-state movement accounted for almost 88% of all internal migration (390.6 million persons). There is variation across states in terms of inter-state migration flows. According to the 2011 Census, there were 54 million inter-state migrants. As of 2011, Uttar Pradesh and Bihar were the largest sources of inter-state migrants while Maharashtra and Delhi were the largest receiver states. Around 83 lakh residents of Uttar Pradesh and 6.3 million Bihar residents had moved either temporarily or permanently to other states. Around 6 million people from across India had migrated to Maharashtra by 2011.

As of 2011, the majority (70%) of intra-state migration was due to marriage and family reasons with variation between male and female migrants. While 83% of females moved for marriage and family, the corresponding figure for males was 39%. Overall, 8% of people moved within a state for work (21% of male migrants and 2% of female migrants). Movement for work was higher among inter-state migrants – 50% of male and 5% of female inter-state migrants. As per the Census, there were 45 million migrant workers in 2011. However, according to the Working Group Report on Migration, the Census underestimates the migrant worker population. Female migration is recorded as movement due to family since that is the primary reason. However, many women take up employment after migrating which is not reflected in the number of women moving for work-related reasons (Ministry of Housing and Urban Poverty Alleviation, 2017) Migrants who move within the boundaries of their own country are known as internal migrants. There are four streams of Internal migration: Rural to urban (R-U), Rural to Rural (R-R), Urban to Rural (U-R) and Urban to Urban (U-U).

Human migration involves people's movement from one place to another with intentions of settling, permanently or temporarily, at a new location (geographic region). The movement often occurs over long distances and from one country to another, but internal migration (within a single country) is also possible; indeed, this is the dominant form of human migration globally. People may migrate as individuals, in family units or large groups. There are four significant forms of migration, i.e. invasion, conquest, colonization and emigration/immigration. Persons moving from their home due to forced displacement (such as a natural disaster or civil disturbance) may be described as displaced persons or internally displaced persons if remaining in the home country. A person who seeks refuge in another country can, if the reason for leaving the home country is political, religious, or another form of persecution, make a formal application to that country where the refuge is sought and is usually described as an asylum seeker. As such, migrants are traditionally described as persons who change their residence places for general reasons and purposes. These purposes may include the search for better job opportunities or healthcare needs. This term is the most generally defined one as anyone changing their geographic location permanently can be considered migrants. Nomadic movements usually are not regarded as migrations, as the movement is generally seasonal, there is no intention to settle in the new place, and only a few people have retained this form of lifestyle in modern times.

1. Women and Migration in India

With globalisation, urbanisation and accompanying socio-economic changes, rural women are attracted to urban areas for better livelihood opportunities and an elevated standard of living. The emerging migration pattern poses various challenges, including health-based vulnerabilities. Female migrants, including young girls, are often exposed to challenging and unsafe conditions, face occupational hazards, live in poor conditions, and face sexual abuse. As a consequence, they are susceptible to several categories of health problems. Census 2011 revealed that women form almost 70 percent of the internal migrant community.

Table 1: Types of Migration with Reasons

Type of Migration	Reason for Migration			
	Work Employment		Marriage	
	Male	Female	Male	Female
Rural to Rural	31.5%	1.2%	7.6%	88.7%
Urban to Rural	31.8%	2.7%	2.8%	74.9%
Rural to Urban	55.9%	3.7%	1%	63%
Urban to Urban	34.9%	3.1%	1%	58%

Source: Census of India 2011

The contrast between the numbers reflects a pattern: men migrating for work/employment, and their wives migrating. While it is probable that these women may have found employment later, work was not the trigger for their migration. One could speculate based on these numbers that while the Indian community has not resisted the idea of women moving out of their native homes to other regions, the resistance for women's mobility arises when the reason is non-marriage related. Challenges surrounding migration and the subsequent hesitation to migrate are often cited as the main bottlenecks that affect educational and employment initiatives like Skill India, for women.

Even though women migrate men likewise, but there is a differential impact on men and women. As noted by the Committee on the Elimination of Discrimination against Women (CEDAW) "to understand the specific ways in which women are impacted, female migration should be studied from the perspective of traditional female roles, gender inequality, the universal prevalence of gender-based violence and the worldwide feminization of poverty, a gendered labour market and labour migration". All of these together have affected migrant women's health. Their physical and socio-economic well-being has also been destabilized by the intersecting types of discrimination linked to race, ethnicity and poverty. Such circumstances are particularly right for the women who remain undocumented, i.e. those women whose productive work is not accounted for in any official record. For those migrant women in the absence of a status of residence record, or whose residence status is unstable or uncertain, the insecurity of their situation and legal barriers to obtaining health services are themselves drivers of poorer health outcomes. Migrant women who face exclusion from the health services implies that those undocumented women (without a residence proof) face the issues like delayed access to screening, treatment and the subsequent care. They also face limited access to pregnancy termination and contraception. By facing heightened discrimination levels and gender-based violence, the migrant woman's health is damaged, and health inequalities are perpetuated. Thus, the study found poor pregnancy outcomes and critical pregnancies, including low birth weight, infant and maternal mortality and the increased likelihood of migrant women delivering their babies without any professional medical assistance.

2. Vulnerabilities of Migrant Workers

While migration is an important livelihood strategy for many and has social and economic benefits, it also has serious negative repercussions, especially on women. A mixture of factors at the destination area complicates the susceptibility, which is principally premised on the alien status of the migrants. Reduced capacity to negotiate and limited choices end up in increased discrimination in life chances. A migrant is considered an 'outsider'. Various surveys and studies have shown that migrants are disadvantaged relative to the native population regarding education, employment and health. It is hard to identify particular reasons for this, like low-grade health care provision, deficient education, poor wages, initial prejudice and sustained discrimination, but these factors reciprocally reinforce each other. For instance, a bias against the migrants may translate into health providers' neglect, which perpetuates poor migrant health. The degree of vulnerability in which migrants find themselves depends on various factors, ranging from their legal status to their overall environment. The irregular situation wherein the hiring of migrants takes place allows employers to escape providing health coverage to them, and then the labour force becomes cheaper than recruiting locals/natives. In the case of internal migrants, their fluidity in terms of movement and their working conditions in the city's informal work arrangements expel them from adequate curative care access.

Migration leads to various types of vulnerability among internal migrants. The common determinants of health risks among migrants are the motivational factors (reasons for migration, occupations at the source of origin) and occupation-related factors. Besides, the living conditions of migrants' affect their health, and these factors are inter-correlated these being:

- Poor environmental sanitation

- Overcrowding living conditions in the urban slums that act as a catalyst in the higher transmission of infectious diseases

- Poor nutritional status leading to low immunity making them susceptible to diseases

- Inadequate quantities and quality of water to sustain health and allow personal hygiene

- Inadequate or no shelter without sanitation facilities

- Occupational Choices and precarious working conditions

3. Rationale of the Paper

Massive migration has taken place in the last few decades in India. During the lean season of the year, people move to urban areas as a daily wage earner. Many are permanently shifting to urban areas as it provides wage-earning opportunities. Rapid urbanization in consumption with industrialization has resulted in the emergence of slums in cities/towns. The number and population of slums are rapidly increasing due to the shortage of developed land for housing, the high cost of land, and house beyond the urban poor's reach (Census of India, 2011). Slums are the areas characterized by shelter crisis, population congestion, unsanitary and poor living conditions, malnutrition, infant mortality morbidity, poverty, inadequate water supply, lack of facilities of underground drainage, the problem of garbage disposal, absence of a pukka road, lavatories, and other civic amenities.

The migrated women experience a series of problems relating to housing, infrastructure, occupation, health and social support mechanisms. They face socio-cultural and livelihood risks in the new setting. The widespread consequences of displacement include dismantling production systems, desecration of ancestral sacred zones or graves and temples, scattering kinship groups and family systems, and disorganising informal social networks. There is a net loss of valuable "social capital," that has compounded the loss of natural, physical, and human capital. For indigenous women, loss of their land and traditional resource base is not merely economic.

They lose a fundamental part of their culture; in many cases contacts with ancestors or other deities are severed, traditional political structures are broken, and the people lose their position in the social system (because they are physically away from the neighbourhood in which their family and friends and kinship matrix have lived). Changes like these often represent stress and adaptation problems for the people, and may even cause a complete breakdown of their culture. Food insecurity and undernourishment are the results of inadequate livelihood options. Nutrition-related risks further reinforced the morbidity and mortality risks of women and children. The displacement seriously declined the level of health of the women. It is a double burden on them. Unsafe drinking water (contaminated) and impoverished sewerage systems increased vulnerability to malaria, chronic diarrhoea, dysentery, etc. The weakest segments of the indigenous population – infants, children, and the elderly – became the worst sufferers. Living in the appalling circumstances, the women slum dwellers constitute the most vulnerable section of the urban population. They are often phrased as "living dead" or "half-dead" people in an atmosphere of intolerable obscurity in packed huts. A bird's eye view on cities reveals that city life is dynamic and exciting. But a close observation exhibits that tribal women, especially those living in slums, lead a very precarious life. In countless slums, manhood is unquestionably brutalized, women are dishonoured, and childhood is poisoned at its very source.

Women migrant's health has been a cause of concern post-migration, in a study done by Oberai and Singh (1983) in Ludhiana district of Punjab, which included the question regarding the effect of rural-to-urban migration on fertility. They found generally higher fertility among migrants, especially, longstanding in-migrants, than non-migrants. However, recent in-migrants have lower fertility than urban non-migrants due to the initial separation between spouses and uncertainties and costs involved immediately before and after the migration. The fertility among the migrants was also lower than the rural residents. Thus, they conclude that migration has the effect of reducing completed family size and lowering fertility during the period immediately following migration. It is reported that the infant mortality rate among the migrant children is usually high because of the lack of proper child care facilities and support. A study conducted by Kaushlendra Kumar and R. K. Sinha (2009) on nutritional status of women in slums of India, found that the percentage of undernourished women is higher (25.5 percent) among the tribal women in comparison to other caste women. Similarly, the prevalence of anaemia is high among the tribal women residing in the slums. (Among the scheduled tribes the percentage of undernourished women are 27.6 in slum areas and 23.9 in non-slum areas whereas 21.6 percent in other castes in slum areas and 16.6 percent in non-slum areas).

A study conducted by the National Family Health Survey (NFHS), found that less than half of the women from the slum areas were currently using contraceptive methods, and discontinuation rate was higher among migrant women. Sterilization was the most common method of contraception (25%). Among slum women, the proportion of skilled attendants' deliveries was low, and the percentage of home deliveries was high. The use of skilled delivery care was significantly associated with age, education level, economic status, parity, and prior antenatal visits. Women from slum areas depended on the government facilities for reproductive health services. The study's findings suggest that significant differences in reproductive health outcomes exist among women from slum and non-slum communities in India. Efforts to progress towards the health MDGs and other national or international health targets may not be achieved without focusing on the urban slum population (Hazarika, 2009). Barros & Pereira (2009) conducted on the health performance of immigrants relative to natives. It finds that women migrants' health is worse. Women are less intensive about visiting physicians than native, except for women from Eastern Europe. When women go to the doctor, they tend to do if more often. Women and people employed are likely to have less risky behaviours, but women with more years of completed schooling are more likely to consume addictive substances. Women are less likely to have additional health insurance, except if they completed more years of schooling or born in the LAC region. Except for older women, women have more out of pocket health expenditures.

3. Health Issues Post-Migration

The migrants are often exposed to unsafe and difficult conditions, dwell in poor conditions, face occupational hazards, and live without their societal structure and supportive family. Additionally, several mainstream programmes like those on health and education exclude this migrant population from their ambit. Thus, as a consequence, they are vulnerable to various categories of health problems.

1. **Morbidity pattern among Women Migrants:** Among the migrant women, the morbidity patterns vary with the type of migration and the potential for creating health vulnerabilities. For example, in the case of migration into Bhubaneswar that occurs more or less permanently, the susceptibility of the women migrants to health problems stems from their peripheral socio-economic existence in the host areas. They suffer from infectious diseases, dermatitis, chemical and pesticide-related illnesses, heat stress,

musculoskeletal disorders, respiratory conditions, and traumatic injuries. Migrants working as sugar cane workers face the risk of occupational accidents and are also prone to toxic pesticides exposure. This might lead to an elevated possibility of lung cancer. Affected by chronic infections, workers might face a reduction in productivity. Migrants working in stone quarries face health issues, including tuberculosis (TB) and silicosis's respiratory diseases due to lengthened silica dust's inhalation.

2. **Infectious Diseases:** Poor drainage system, lack of proper water supply appalling sanitary conditions, and harmful practices expose the women migrants to several health hazards determined by their occupation choice and standard of living. Their health behaviours and living circumstances elevate their vulnerability to various infectious diseases like typhoid fever, malaria; respiratory infections and hepatitis are found to have a higher occurrence among migrant women. They could avail curative care, but due to their movement fluidity caused by employment uncertainty, they mostly fall outside the preventive care coverage.

3. **Malaria and Tuberculosis (TB):** In relation to Millennium Development Goals (MDGs) migration is a serious concern for many major diseases. In malaria cases, migration may increase disease exposure, transfer mosquitoes to newer regions or even create habitats that are encouraging to the mosquitoes. The 44th World Health Assembly (1991) recognized the growing importance of TB as a public health problem. In comparison to the general population, the migrants are roughly six times more vulnerable to get tuberculosis. Migration is a significant reason for the existence of the disease. Other additional reasons include population growth, poor management of TB control programmers, poverty, lack of awareness among the women migrants and a considerable rise of TB cases in HIV endemic regions.

4. **Social and Mental Health:** Women migrants face several stress factors like domestic violence, alcoholism of husbands, poverty, job uncertainty, social and geographic isolation, poor housing conditions, intense time pressures, separation from family,

intergenerational conflicts, lack of recreation and health, shelter and safety concerns. The stress gets manifested in substance abuse, relationship problems, fights with spouses, violence on the children and mental illness. The psychological disorders may be attributed to the loss of protective socio-cultural factors (e.g., family ties, cohesive communities based on strong social support, language and group identity). It could represent initially healthy women migrants eventually getting less psychologically healthy with acculturation over a period of time.

5. **Reproductive Health:** One of the major concerns raised in the low health status of women migrants. The key indicators include the prevalence of anaemia, antenatal care coverage, the occurrence of reproductive tract infection and violence against women. Those pregnant women who opt for temporary migration to their native villages for delivery miss out on receiving services from either place of residence. Both the mother and the child do not receive proper health services due to the villages' remoteness, lack of awareness and negotiating capacity and lack of availability of previously received services record. Despite the availability of private and government hospitals at the post-migration destinations, the migrant women opt for going back to villages for home deliveries. Factors for this preference are unfriendly treatment at government hospitals (as perceived by migrant women), expensive private healthcare facilities, emotionally secure home environment and unavailability of caretakers for other siblings in the event of hospitalization. Pregnant migrant women often suffer from malnutrition and lack of immunization, affecting both the mother and child's health, leading to mortality. Other factors such as overexertion, prolonged bending and standing, poor nutrition, dehydration and chemical exposure in the factories elevate the risk of miscarriage, premature delivery, growth retardation and fetal malformation and anomalous postnatal development. Women migrants are also vulnerable to urinary tract infections due to the absence of clean and safe toilets at the workplace and rigorous working conditions leading to chronic urine retention.

Conclusion and Way Forward

Internal migration can play a crucial role in the reduction of poverty and economic development. Thus, there should be special emphasis on the positive facilitation of safe migration that primarily incorporates access to basic amenities and public services, i.e. education, health and livelihood. Moreover, the increased volume of migration and inter-linkages of the health needs of migrants with all Millennium Development Goals and national policies (National Health Policy, National Population Policy and India Vision 2020) implies success in fulfilling such needs can support the achievement of the MDGs/SDGs and these policies. Increased prominence is requisite for addressing the unique health needs of the women migrant population. Women migrants are uneducated, poor, socially excluded and face a very alien environment when they come to urban landscapes. They have trouble-proving identity/eligibility; language is a barrier, have insufficient awareness of entitlements/rights, little understanding of how hospitals and insurance providers operate, etc. Thus, there is an urgent need to design health policies and programmes that are less complicated and easily accessible.

India faces unprecedented migration challenges and has an increasing need to formulate and implement policies to improve migrants' health. India has few or no structural policies or programmes targeting the migrant issues in totality, and this segment of the population still faces exclusion from the various mainstream programmes. There is a need to modify the existing policy structures and programmes so that this marginalized group's needs are accommodated in the various national policies and programmes. Development of a National Migration Policy would be a proactive step towards it. Effective implementation of the available programmes and their convergence at the source and destination level at both inter and intrastate level would be important to improve migrants' health status. For this, interstate collaboration is required among government departments, to assess and subsequently tackle occupational risks and their health consequences before, during and after migrants' work period, both in their place of origin and destination. Sensitization and capacity building of concerned policymakers and health stakeholders mainly Ministries of Health and Family Welfare, Labour and Employment, NGOs networks,

Urban Development, employers' associations of migrants, insurance companies and financial institutions need to be done large scale. The cadre building among government as well private sector would be critical. The provision of essential services would require better coordination among departments located in different areas and sectors. The central government has a major role in the process, including promoting an alliance among key health services providers and their respective departments, capacity building, and resource allocation. Women migrants have hardly had perceptible champions to take up their challenges. The few struggles and rights movements around migrant issues have focused on survival, livelihood and exploitation issues while health has been given a back seat. It is high time for mainstream health into dialogues' on women migrant's wellbeing.

Women migrant population comprises a considerable proportion of the population in the urban areas, mostly urban slums. They suffer from various health problems and cannot correctly utilize and avail the existing health services. Few of their health problems can be mitigated by providing them with health education about services available. Health care systems should include this vulnerable group, and specific attention is required to educate poor migrant women about the benefits of proper and timely utilization of antenatal and delivery care services. Interventions are needed to control obesity and to decrease the magnitude of non-communicable diseases in this section. Malaria surveillance and control is required in the slums, where the migrant population is residing. Promotion of contraceptive methods must be done at their place of work and in their native place. Interventions must be aimed at lessening their loneliness and isolation. Health care interventions for migrant women to urban areas must be aligned carefully with their existing requirements, not just to target the prevailing conditions, but also to be available and accessible to them at a period without compromising their day-to-day efforts to earn a livelihood.

References

Barone, G., and Mocetti, S. (2011). With a Little Help from Abroad: The Effect of Low Skilled Immigration on the Female Labor Supply. Labour Economics. 18(5): 664675.

Barros, P. P., and Pereira, I. M. (2009). Health Care and Health Outcomes of Migrants: Evidence from Portugal. Human Development Research Paper No. 28. New York: United Nations Development Programme, Human Development Report Office.

Census, 2011, Office of the Registrar General & Census Commissioner, Ministry of Home Affairs.

Chant, S., and Pedwell, C. (2008). Women, gender and the informal economy: An assessment of ILO research and suggested ways forward. Geneva: London School of Economics and ILO.

Curran, S. R., and Saguy, A.C. (2011). Migration and Cultural Change: A Role for Gender and Social Networks? Journal of International Women's Studies. 2(3): 389410.

Hazarika, Indrajit. (2009). 'Women's Reproductive Health in Slum Populations in India: Evidence From NFHS-3', Indian Institute of Public Health, Delhi, India, The New York Academy of Medicine

Jacobsen, J. P., and Levin, L.M. (2000). The effects of internal migration on the relative economic status of women and men. The Journal of SocioEconomics. 29. 291304.

Kaushlendra, Kumar & R. K. Sinha. *(2009) 'Understanding Women's Nutritional Status in Urban India: a Comparative Study of Slum versus Non-Slum Dwellers', Mumbai. International Institute for Population Sciences*

Martin, Susan. (2007). Women, Migration and Development. Transatlantic Perspectives on Migration. 1. Washington, DC: Institute for the Study of International Migration.

Oberai, A.S. and H.K.Manmohan Singh. (1983). *'Causes and Consequences of Internal Migration: A Study of Indian Punjab'*. New Delhi: Oxford University Press.

Ratha, D., Mohapatra, S., and Scheja, E. (2011). Impact of Migration on Economic and Social Development: A Review of Evidence and Emerging Issues. World Bank.

Report of Working Group on Migration, Ministry of Housing and Urban Poverty Alleviation, January 2017, http://mohua.gov.in/upload/uploadfiles/files/1566.pdf

WHO. (2020). https://www.who.int/tb/publications/resolutions/en/

About the Author

Dr. Subrata S Satapathy has experience in Academics and Development Sector. Engaged as Guest Faculty, Course Writer and Independent Consultant in various Research Consultancies (NGO based). She has keen interest in areas like Gender Studies, Women in Informal Sector, Technology and Women Empowerment, E-Governance and Rural Development, Tribal Studies, Tribal Elementary Education, State Budget Analysis for the Social Sectors like Agriculture, Health and Education. She has taught Classical and Modern Sociological Theory, Research Methodology, Sociology of Development, Rural Sociology and Gender Studies at PG level at Utkal University, Odisha.

Where do we Stand among the Marginalized in a Foreign Country?

Henry Poduthase[19] & Lisa Garza[20]

Abstract

Every refugee is moving to a country that has a well-established social hierarchy. These social hierarchies evolve at a languid pace and/or intricately tied into its culture rooted in its own social, political, economic, and religious social fabrics. This chapter would selectively investigate refugees' systematic marginalization in a well-developed social class hierarchy in the United States of America. Furthermore, the chapter would discuss the effect of social hierarchy on refugees' social, economic, and political experiences. Discussing social hierarchies theories, the authors would explore recent and relevant research on marginalization and social hierarchies examining secondary data on refugees' marginalization in the United States. The chapter adopted theoretical, cultural, empirical perspectives on refugees' adaptation to a new country and their challenges in an existing social hierarchy. The study examines various programs and organizations at the state, federal, and charitable level to bridge the marginalisation gap in assimilation and social integration into the mainstream society. Results depict the challenges the refugee population faces to assimilate into the society and how much they stick together as a community for mutual support. Social cohesion among similar refugees is atypical of any minority group behaviour existing within the context of a majority social group. Social, economic, and political marginalization is accepted, to an extent, by the refugees in the process of establishing themselves in their new world of

---

19 Associate Professor and Director, Graduate Social Work Program, West Texas A&M University, Canyon, TX-79016. Email: hpoduthase@wtamu.edu

20 Associate Professor and Head, Department of Psychology, Sociology, and Social Work, West Texas A&M University, Canyon, TX-79016. Email: lgarza@wtamu.edu

already existing social hierarchy. Refugees provide invaluable services and play vital roles in the livelihood of our communities. Every day, refugees work difficult jobs such as providing food to a nation – often putting their health and families' health at risk.

Keywords: Refugees, Displacement, Marginalisation, Social Hierarchy

"We are caught in an inescapable network of mutuality, tied in a single garment of destiny. Whatever affects one directly, affects all indirectly." *Dr Martin Luther King Jr.*

Introduction

Creation of a productive and contributing community of refugees is imperative in The Refugee Act of 1980 that forged a prosperous future for refugees who aimed to create an 'American dream' of their own. A refugee is a person outside of his or her own country and unable or unwilling to return because of persecution or a well-founded fear of persecution on account of race, religion, nationality, political opinion, or membership in a particular social group (ORR, 2007b). While the influx of refugees increased after the second world war, several countries under the leadership of United Nations started to accept people fleeing their home to escape violent conflicts or protect the lives of their family or themselves. It is alarming to know that among the millions of people who had to flee from their country of origin spends long years of life in refugee camps. Among these millions of refugees, only very few have the privilege of relocating to a new country to become part of that country and, sometimes, could become a citizen of that country. According to the United Nations, there were 70.8 million people by the end of 2018 who were displaced due to conflict and persecution worldwide. Among them, the United States of America accepted 22,405 refugees into the country in 2018, and the cap was further reduced to 18,000 in 2020.

This chapter selectively investigates refugees' systematic marginalization in a well-developed social class hierarchy in the United States of America. Furthermore, the chapter discusses the impact of social hierarchy on refugees' social, economic, and political experiences within the country.

We begin with the provisions of The Refugee Act of 1980 that provides the guidelines for the development and integration of refugees to the mainstream of American society.

1. Where are Refugees Located in the U.S.?

The number of refugees coming to the United States has varied over the years, and global and domestic politics have impacted this number. The decision to allow refugees' entry into the U.S. occurs every fall, when the president, in consultation with Congress, determines a "refugee ceiling"; in other words, it determines the maximum number entering the country in every given year (Krogstad, 2019). In recent years, the number of refugees has dropped to an all-time low with a maximum of 18,000 refugees being admitted into the U.S. in 2020 (Krogstad, 2019). This decrease sadly is at a time when the number of refugees, globally is at a peak. The U.S. admits refugees from approximately 60 different home countries; however, we have consistently since 1980, seen a pattern of where refugees immigrate from with 55% coming from Asia, 28% coming from Europe, 13% coming from Africa and 4% coming from Latin America (Krogstad, 2019).

Once admitted into the U.S., refugees settle across the country; however, we have seen a pattern where most refugees have been resettled in five states, Texas, Washington, Ohio, California, and New York. During the 2018 fiscal year, 1,692 refugees settled in Texas, 1,544 settled in Washington, 1,408 settled in Ohio, 1,370 settled in California, and 1,281 settled in New York (National Immigration Forum, 2019).

Refugees may be placed in cities where family members already reside or where there already exists a community where they are from or speak their language. It is critical to keep in mind that this transition can be a traumatic event in that many have experienced violence and trauma in their homeland. Community organizations and agencies are initially responsible for helping refugees obtain resources needed to resettle and work with local and state governments to ensure refugees' needs are initially met. These organizations will help them locate affordable homes, jobs, health care, schools, basic home furnishings, and food.

For refugees, learning English is a priority and enrol in English classes as soon as possible. Social workers and other caseworkers often assist refugees with their transition, including enrolling children in local schools. Refugees are also given a stipend to subsist for three months, and they are required to find work, and most do indeed. It is quite common for refugees to work in some of the most challenging and demanding jobs and often find they are underemployed. In 2015, 62% of refugees participated in the labour force, and during this fiscal year, 2 million were considered highly skilled and educated; however, many were relegated to low-skilled jobs (Kovacs, 2017). Often, refugees find themselves taking jobs as housekeepers, cooks, or working in the agricultural industry; in other words, refugees often find themselves in service jobs.

2. Race and Various Terminologies

Social hierarchy based on race and colour is intertwined in the United States of America culture. This social structural hierarchy is evidently mixed with political, scientific, public attitude, and demographic consideration over several centuries. This spread over centuries is explicitly evident in the census categorization of various races. In the first enumeration of 1790, there were only two categories of civil status: 'free or slave and taxed or untaxed'. Based on these criteria, the system counted for European, African, and Native American (untaxed). However, these three populations have influenced the later stages of racial categorization in the country. Even though there have been several changes to these categories of racial groups within the census over several decades, in 1870 Chinese was added to the census. In the year 1890 'free coloured persons' and Japanese were added. These two additions or a country was an interesting turning point in the country. Until then, the census categorized people based on their skin colour and not based on their country. More specifically, 'whites' were not called European American and or 'blacks' as African Americans. While the census started incorporating race based on country of origin, in 1920 various people from other countries were added like Filipinos, Koreans, and people from India as 'Hindus'.

Interestingly, people from India were counted as 'Hindus in three subsequent censuses and later in the year of 1950 census it was changed to 'whites' and in 1980, again changed to 'Asian'. Similarly, Mexicans were counted as 'white' until 1930. However, when the government of Mexico contested this change of category, it again went back to 'whites.' It was only in 1970 people new category of 'Hispanics' took place in the census. Adhering to the 1997 Office of Management and Budget standards on race and ethnicity, several racial classifications are under the United States Census Bureau. Here are the current (2020) census racial classifications:

- *White* – A person having origins in any of the original peoples of Europe, the Middle East, or North Africa.

- *Black or African American* – A person having origins in any of the Black racial groups of Africa.

- *American Indian or Alaska Native* – A person having origins in any of the original peoples of North and South America (including Central America) and who maintains tribal affiliation or community attachment.

- *Asian* – A person having origins in any of the Far East, Southeast Asia, or the Indian subcontinent, including Cambodia, China, India, Japan, Korea, Malaysia, Pakistan, the Philippine Islands, Thailand, and Vietnam.

- *Native Hawaiian or Other Pacific Islander* – A person having origins in any of the original peoples of Hawaii, Guam, Samoa, or other Pacific Islands.

Additional to the categories mentioned above, since 2000, the census bureau allows individuals to self-identify with more than one race.

The overall effect of the racial terminologies has been highly influenced by the public opinion and has extensively influenced the social stigma attached to it. Popular culture in the country is viewing people based on their race, country of origin, parental country of origin, ancestral country of origin and colour. However, when people's race is attached to a specific country or a continent, there could be a yet another detachment sentiment towards them from other races. Interestingly, only 'whites (Caucasians)' are not called 'White Americans', but almost all other races are called

'Asian Americans', 'Hispanic Americans', and 'African Americans'. Nevertheless, in the modern era, how people perceive their identity has changed, and this is clearly stated in the following statement by Perez and Hirschman (2019):

> Many Americans have multiple identities that reflect complex ancestral origins, tribal and communal associations, and varied ideological outlooks on race and culture. In general, people do not change their ethnicities as a matter of fashion, but they may emphasize different aspects depending on the circumstances. For instance, a person who identifies as Mexican among relatives might identify as Hispanic at work and as American overseas. A person of mixed heritage might be Native American in one context, but white in another. These possibilities exist in census data, just as they do in informal conversations and settings, because of the opportunities for varied responses to different census questions about race and ethnicity (p.1).

3. Refugees in the Social Hierarchy of the United States

The Caucasian American dominance increasingly influences the socioeconomic structure of The United States in the political, economic, and educational structures of the society. This dominance is experienced through several centuries in the country. Within the previously mentioned time frame, a top-down racial hierarchy has created and shaped group relations, the formation of various policies, and political party agendas. These macro perspective developments in a way or other have influenced the concept of oppression and the oppressed within the country. However, even with the acceptance of the reality of racial inequalities, there is still a debate on 'what racial hierarchy are? How do they operate? Why within every race, there are rich and who enjoy socially higher standards? Why there are poor and people who experience lower social status in every race?

Social systems of ethnic and racial stratification are a complex concept that is shaped by various factors. Additionally, there are overt and covert discrimination and prejudice prevalent within the social, economic, and cultural interactions. While the 'White Americans' enjoy privileges of called 'white privilege', they are considered at the top of this racial hierarchy. On the other hand, African Americans are considered at the bottom of this hierarchy and the Native Americans. While Asian Americans enjoy a second position within this racial hierarchy, Hispanic Americans are placed in third place. Among these already existing social and racial hierarchy systems, refugees fall into the already existing racial groups: Asian, African, Arab, and so on. Hence, the concept of advantage or disadvantage has a vital role in the refugee's identity and the multitude of challenges they must overcome in a new land.

4. Challenges Faced by Refugees

Transitioning from a traumatic experience to an entirely new culture itself is a great challenge for refugees. Moving to a new land is rooted in a hope to build their lives together towards a better livelihood. However, these hopes are sometimes shattered due to the obstacles they have to face in a foreign land with a different culture and language. Not surprisingly, several refugees fail to withstand the influx of challenges, and many prove themselves to be successful amid adversities.

Cultural factors: Every refugee family coming to the United States of America are in a dichotomy of two different cultures. The culture of their past country and America's popular culture is continuously pulling them to find common ground. However, while the older generation finds it very difficult to forget their already learned culture completely, their children are open to the new culture leading to a cultural conflict among families. When culture defines the right and the wrong, accepting new norms of a new country, they came to is challenging and demanding for many refugee families. Yet, refugees welcome various aspects of safety, respect for women, and drive towards equality as positive aspects of American culture.

Employment and financial security: Cultural difference, along with the norms of only accepting US education, is troubling for refugees to find work that they have the skillset for. In most cases, refugees are often open to taking up any job as they struggle to settle down in a new country.

However, many of these refugees were trained professionals but cannot find jobs since they prefer US-educated and US experience.

English language: When America predominantly speaks English and is not known for a multilingual, refugee who is not well versed in English or who even knows a very minimum, struggles to survive. During the initial periods of adaptation to a new place, every refugee finds it difficult to communicate to the bureaucrats and even to various professionals. One of the major challenges the parents face is that of their children's performance at school. Due to language limitation, many parents find it difficult to help their students with their academics. Furthermore, these children must experience bullying and other challenges due to cultural differences.

Securing Housing: Securing housing can be a challenge for refugees. It is difficult to obtain affordable housing when refugees take low-paying jobs and are often dangerous, such as working in meat-packing plants. Therefore, refugees often live in households with either multiple families or large families. While these living conditions help refugees maintain minimal financial security, the result can be stressful, and during the current pandemic, can pose a danger for those living in multi-generational homes. The housing problems are undoubtedly real; however, after being in the U.S. for several years, many refugees become successful homeowners.

Mental health and Accessing Services: One of the most challenging services refugees need is mental health assistance. Many refugees come from countries where they have encountered trauma, violence, and exploitation, especially children and women. Consequently, obtaining mental health resources can be a challenge. Many refugees fear being deported or encountering discrimination or rejection and sadly, do not seek the services they need. Besides, language barriers also create challenges in obtaining health and mental health services that are needed. Finally, some refugees obtaining these much-needed services may be taboo in their own cultures and therefore believe it is unnecessary.

5. Contributions of Refugees

The United States is a country of immigrants and certainly has a past of welcoming and giving refuge to individuals who have been displaced.

Furthermore, the US has become a home for those who have sought a better life for themselves and their families. Since 1975, the US has resettled over three million displaced persons (Krogstad & Radford, 2017). While the more recent ideology and climate for refugees have been harmful, the reality is that this population's contributions are stark and the US benefits economically from their presence. Immigrants and refugees often embrace our nation's ideals and principles and contribute to local and state economies by purchasing goods and services that maintain communities.

While refugees have encountered challenging political and economic hardships in their native land, they embrace the opportunities provided them in their new host nation. Refugees have been able to enter the labour force and contribute to society in numerous ways. Kerwin (2018, p. 206-207) found the following accomplishments of 1.1 million refugees who arrived in the United States between 1987 and 2016:

> The median income of refuges is $43,000; 35% of refugee households have mortgages; 63% of refugees have U.S.-born children; 40% of refugees are married to U.S. citizens; 67% have become naturalized; Refugees' labour force participation is 68%; Employment rate is 64%; 10% of refugees are self-employed; 38% of refugees are more likely to be skilled workers.

Refugees are a vital workforce and often take on dangerous, demanding, and necessary jobs for cities and towns to thrive. Male refugees have a higher employment rate than the male U.S. born population, 78% compared to 67.4%, respectively (Bureau of Labor Statistics, 2020). Also, refugees are more likely to be younger than U.S. born workers, which will ensure a more extended period in the workforce, contributing to local economies (National Immigration Forum, 2018). Refugees are more likely to be employed in service jobs than 22.5% compared to 16% of native-born workers (Bureau of Labor Statistics, 2020). This is a significant point since we currently live in an economy driven by the service sector. In other words, our economy today is primarily fueled by jobs that deliver a service to our communities.

Besides, many refugees are entrepreneurs and contribute to their communities' vibrancy, even those that might fail. Refugees begin their businesses and are self-employed. Kerwin (2018), found that 10% of refugees are self-employed. The values of individualism and entrepreneurship are strong values held by refugees and their commitment to their neighbourhoods and communities can be seen by the number of local food stores, clothing stores, and transportation to name a few. The creativity and adaptability of this community is further evidence of the vitality of these communities. While we tend to think about refugee businesses as being small and local; the reality is that some of the most well know U.S. companies are refugee owned. Companies such as Google, WhatsApp, and PayPal are some of the most successful businesses in the U.S. and employ thousands of individuals and contribute to the everyday lives of millions of Americans (National Immigration Forum, 2019).

Perhaps one of the most successful indicators for economic health in communities is the ability to own a home. Refugees do have the capacity to own their own homes. For example, after living in the U.S. for ten years, Burmese and Bosnian refugees have homeownership rates comparable to those of native-born Americans (National Immigration Forum, 2019). The ability for homeownership is consistent with higher median incomes. Yes, it is a fact that refugees upon entering the U.S. struggle with median incomes as low as $22,000, after living in the U.S., the median income increased to approximately $51,000 (National Immigration Forum, 2019). The "American Dream" is homeownership, and refugees certainly strive and have been successful in homeownership. When considering refugees' economic contributions, it is vital to highlight the tenacity, adaptability, and vitality of refugee communities and, ultimately, acknowledge that their economic contributions are significant to the U.S.

Conclusion

As one of the most powerful countries globally and as a leader of the free world, the United States has created a system to provide hope for the millions to aspire for. However, existing political leadership has positively influenced refugees' intake into the country, impacting the country's general population's social and political acceptance mind-set. Hence, even while millions are displaced or have to relocate to a different country due to various reasons, but not of their own, has to wait for the political decision to enter into this country. Even with these limitations, whoever came to this country must undergo another set of the social hierarchy of marginalization to establish and to adapt to this country. Within these struggles to adapt to a new country – culturally and economically, refugees have proved to be successful as responsible citizens by contributing to this country's social and economic development.

References

Bureau of Labor Statistics (2020). U.S. Department of Labor

Harvard Immigration and Refugee Clinical Program. (2017). Fulfilling U.S. commitment to refugee resettlement: Protecting refugees, preserving national security, and building the U.S. economy through refugee admissions. Retrieved from https://harvardimmigrationclinic.files. wordpress.com/2017/06/syria-final-draft-v9.pdf

Kerwin, D. (2018). The U.S. refugee resettlement program – A return to first principles: How refugees help to define, strengthen, and revitalize the United States. *Journal on Migration and Human Security, 6*(3), 203-225.

Kovacs, K. (2017). Refugees in the U.S.: What type of jobs do asylum seekers take in America? Retrieved from https://www.ibtimes.com/refugees-us-what-type-jobs-do-asylum-seekers-take-america-2496242

Krogstad, J. M. (2019). Key facts about refugees to the U.S. Pew Research Center.

Krogstad, J. M. & Jynnah, R. (2017). Key Facts about Refugees to the U.S. Pew Research Center.

National Immigration Forum, 2019. https://immigrationforum.org/article/immigrants-as-economic-contributors-refugees-are-a-fiscal-success-story-for-america/

National Immigration Forum, 2019. https://immigrationforum.org/article/fact-sheet-u-s-refugee-resettlement/

Perez, A. D., & Hirschman, C. (2009). The Changing Racial and Ethnic Composition of the US Population: Emerging American Identities. *Population and development review*, *35*(1), 1–51. https://doi.org/10.1111/j.1728-4457.2009.00260.x

Song, M. (2004). Introduction: Who is at the bottom? Examining claims about racial hierarchy. *Ethnic and Racial Studies, 27*(6), 859-877.

UNHCR. (n.d.) Internally displaced people. Retrieved from https://www.unhcr.org/sy/29-internally-displaced-people.html

UNHCR Resettlement Handbook. (2018). Country chapters-The United States of America. Retrieved from https://www.unhcr.org/3c5e5a764.pdf

U.S. Department of State. (n.d.). Refugee admissions. Retrieved from https://www.state.gov/refugee-admissions/

Welch, K. (2017). A pivotal moment for the US refugee resettlement program. Retrieved from http://haasinstitute.berkeley.edu/sites/default/files/haasinstitute_usrefugeeresettlment_june2017_publish.pdf

About the Authors

Dr. Henry Poduthase is the Director of the Graduate Social Work Program at West Texas A&M University and teaches Research and practice courses at the graduate level. He has authored several peer-reviewed (in international journals) research articles and book chapters. He serves as the editorial board member of an international journal and peer reviewer of four reputed international journals. He has presented papers in various international and national conferences. His research interests extend from psycho-social challenges of children, adolescents, and families to refugees and social policies.

Dr. Lisa Garza is an Associate Professor of Sociology and the Department Head of the Department of Psychology, Sociology, and Social Work at West Texas A&M University. Prior to coming to WTAMU, she was an Associate Professor of Sociology at Regis University in Denver, Colorado. She received a BA in Psychology in 1985 and an MEd in Counseling in 1987 from WTAMU and a PhD in Sociology in 1995 from Texas Woman's

University. Dr. Garza's research interests include the Chicano Movement, Chicanas in the Chicano Movement, Latino education, and first-generation students. She is currently working on research on the Chicano Movement in Colorado and on Radical Tejanas and their influence on the Chicano Movement. Dr. Garza is passionate about issues of social justice, working in her community, and believes it is imperative for individuals to learn their history, culture, and importance of giving back to their communities.

The Transit from the Land Acquisition Act 1894 to RFCTLARR Act 2013 in India – Evaluation of Impact on People Affected

Binod Chandra Mishra[21]

Abstract

Mahatma Gandhi advocated Panchayati Raj as the foundation of India's political system, a decentralised form of government in which each village would be responsible for its affairs. Instead, India developed a highly centralised form of government. On April 24 1993, the Constitutional (73rd Amendment) Act 1992 came into force to provide constitutional status to the Panchayati Raj institutions. This amendment was extended to Panchayats in eight states' tribal areas: Andhra Pradesh, Gujarat, Maharashtra, Odisha, Madhya Pradesh Himachal Pradesh, and Rajasthan beginning on December 24 1996. This amendment contains a provision for devolution of powers and responsibilities to the Panchayats, both for the preparation of economic development plans and social justice, as well as for implementation concerning 29 subjects listed in the eleventh schedule of the constitution, and the ability to levy and collect appropriate taxes, duties, tolls and fees. People's power got strengthened with the PESA Act 1996 followed with FRA Act 2005 and RFCTLARR Act 2013. Thus Indian administration is moving towards power to people. Now, this article is intended to discuss the impact of power to people through RFCTLARR Act over its journey for last five years with a scope to address the livelihood issue and displacement issue by repealing the old Land Acquisition Act of 1984. The article contains the author's experience in a different case study conducted by him and space still available for improvement in the Act for which it has few takers even after five years of enactment.

---

21 Freelance Consultant, Author and Development Specialist, Email: binodbam@ gmail.com

Keywords: RFCTLARR Act, Consent, Gram Sabha, Land Acquisition, Resettlement and Rehabilitation, Livelihood loss, Displacement and Health

Introduction

The most sought after a reform that was witnessed in India is the implementation of The Right To Fair Compensation And Transparency In Land Acquisition, Rehabilitation And Resettlement Act, 2013 (RFCTLARR ACT 2013) Jairam Ramesh the then Union Minister, Rural Development introduced the LARR Bill 2011 in Lok Sabha on September 7 2011.

During initiating discussion in Parliament, he highlighted that:

1. The land acquisition must fully protect the interests of landowners and those whose livelihoods depend on the land being acquired.

2. Land markets in India are imperfect. There is an asymmetry of power (information) between those wanting to acquire the land and those whose land is acquired.

3. Land Acquisition and Rehabilitation & Resettlement(R&R) need to be seen necessarily as two sides of the same coin.

4. New Act is to balance the need for facilitating land acquisition for various public purposes including infrastructure development, industrialisation and urbanisation while at the same time meaningfully addressing the concerns of farmers and those whose livelihoods are dependent on the land being acquired.

5. The draft bill is fully compliant with Panchayats' provisions (Extension to Scheduled Areas) Act popularly called PESA Act 1996, Forest Rights Act 2006, and all such tribal land supporting Acts in force in different states.

When the Land Acquisition Act 1984, which was having a visible amendment in 1984, have the shortfall with the following issues to comply with:

a. Whether the proposed acquisition serves the public purpose

b. Estimation of affected families and families likely to be displaced

c. The extent of lands, public and private, houses, settlements and other CPRs likely to be affected

d. Whether the extent of land proposed is an absolute bare minimum requirement

e. Whether other alternative sites were considered and found not feasible

f. Study of social costs of the project vis-a-vis the benefits that will arise on the project's commission.

g. Arbitrary use of Public purpose and its frequent application for land acquisition of private projects, the applicability of emergency clause, consent of people, calculation of fair compensation for the land and the fixed assets over it, rehabilitation and resettlement of displaced families, addressing livelihood issues and loss of social and economic disjoint due to displacement, timely payment of compensation, amicably address of the family share issues, acceptable rehabilitation colony with all legal rights, stakeholders' management, creating an excellent database to address the grievances.

The government created an impression that the new land acquisition Act will generate more significant gateway for facilitating land acquisition for the industry and mines project in India as the Act will facilitate consent of the people. This impression was based on the assumption that the provision of law will address the livelihood issues and the issue related to employment. The obligatory provision of SIA study is intended not only to recognise the number of landowners and its impact on affected persons through Socio-Economic Assessment (SIA) but also the adherence of the parameters that are generally questioned by activists operating in the acquisition locations to the voice of the agitating people.

It also looked more attractive since it is mandated with public hearing and scope to include the inputs raised during the hearing in the final draft SIA study before being examined by an expert group. The expert committee is required to make a critical assessment of the magnitude of impact on the physically and economically displaced families and the number of an affected household to be physically relocated and those rendered landless or remained with marginal, unviable landholdings. The critical evaluation of social impact management is planned to examine whether the ameliorate measures suggested are adequate to effectively mitigate the adverse impact on individual and community assets, infrastructure and finally the restoration of affected families' livelihood. Even the expert committee is expected to critically access the community's attitude towards the project and reason for the opposition. The expert committee's most exciting and appreciable suggestion is expected to assess physical cost and benefits to arrive at the social cost even if they overlook the tangible cost vis-à-vis project cost to value the project's impact assessment. The district's collector is empowered to ensure that minimum land acquisition and minimum displacement happen and there is no unutilised land to be left after the project is commissioned. However, all these provisions under the Act could not find a taker in the industrial sector or the mining sector, rather the fear of harassment of the private company multiplied with such provisions in the Act. It made a total cessation of greenfield projects in almost all fields. Some of the provisions the new Act proposed, which was absent in the old Act are discussed below to find the differences and its impact.

1. Livelihood Loss and Displacement

When Abhay Sahu could mobilise 200 people in every day to block the road to POSCO proposed Integrated steel project site at Paradeep Odisha, it gave an impression that the money siphoned for the agitation to stop the POSCO India company due to a policy for adequate compensation of livelihood loss of affected families. It was of late detected that POSCO Pratirodha Samiti's agitator was the landless labourers working in the beetle vine coppices and were managing their family. They could be quickly mobilised stating that the land acquisition is intended to compensate landowners and compensate for the structural loss. There is no scope to recognise the landless labourers who were dependent on the beetle vine for their lively hood. They will lose the support soon after the compensation would be paid to the beetle vine landowners, and the orchard will be converted to the green field, facilitating POSCO to commission its steel plant. It is believed by people being affected as the old land acquisition act was silent on supporting the people whose livelihood loss happens in an acquisition which were landless but depended on the land as agriculture labourers/ sharecroppers.

During the acquisition of land for Vedant resources for the Lanjigarh project in Odisha the agitators were against Niyamgiri mines for Vedanta Alumina project. They unanimously opposed the Niyamgiri mines LA in the high profile gram sabha taken up under the direct supervision of Supreme Court on the ground that the people residing in Niyamgiri forest do not win the land. Still, their livelihood is dependent on the forest produce of Niyamgiri. If there had been policy support for negotiation with the villagers on the minimum land, mining the bauxites and a reasonable reclamation and restoration plan with adequate and acceptable livelihood support of the people residing there who do not own any forest land. Still, their livelihood depends on forest could have been mitigated through continuous engagement with SIA study and SIMP and expert opinion provided in the new land acquisition Act. Nevertheless, the question spontaneously comes all such provisions are now in the new Act. If the new Act's provisions can mitigate the livelihood loss issue, a critical parameter for project failure, why new greenfield projects are not showing interest even after almost five years of implementing the new Act?

When people could know that states like West Bengal, Jharkhand and Madhya Pradesh whom the non-congress government ruled took alternative routes for providing land for industries for overall growth without adopting the new Act is not because of the only political opposition of such states to the centre. Still, they did not find any advantage of implementing the new Act. It is also noticed that while opposing to different delicate and new provisions of Act, rules were framed by states which were not in conformity to the requirements made within the Act with a scope to carry on land acquisition. In the conference of Revenue

Secretaries of all states held in ASCI Hyderabad, it was admitted by few of Revenue Secretaries in such states during an informal discussion that it became a political mandate for them to deviate from the provisions of principal Act. The states where Congress party and the regional parties in power who were compatible with the United Progressive Alliance government in the centre took the initiative for framing the regulations under section 109 of the principal Act. The Act has 13 chapters and 114 sections. The calculation of R&R award under chapter five and procedure and manner of rehabilitation and resettlement under chapter 6 in addition to the land acquisition; award means a person who is losing the land is going to get compensation for the loss of land as well as compensation for the R&R as a part of the provision of Act. During Narmada dam height reduction movement or agitation against POSCO proposed steel plant land acquisition, many such affected persons were being ignored to be compensated for their livelihood loss since they do not own land being landless people. Initially, it looked like every aspect of the new Act is self-sufficient to motivate people to agree for land acquisition as all stakeholders' interest are taken care for compensation.

2. Retrospective Effect

The most sought after the impact of RFCTLARR Act 2013, when came into force is the applicability of sections 24 and101 of the Act. On the question what will be the impact of new Act during transit from the old Act to new Act and how the process of land acquisition will continue to be impacted by new land acquisition Act, since many such projects were either at 4(1) or 6(1) or sec 9 or 11 of the old Act at the time of enactment of new Act on January 1 2014. This came to the mind of most of the people involved in it that the abrupt cancel of old Act and the applicability of provisions under the new Act impact the ongoing projects. All these queries are said to be covered U/s 24 of the Act which reads as:

Where no award under section 11 of the said land acquisition Act has been made, then all provision of this Act relating to the determination of compensation shall apply; or an award under said section 11 has been made, (hence such proceedings shall continue under the provisions of the said Land Acquisition Act as if the said Act has not been repealed.

U/s 24(2) – notwithstanding anything in sub-section (1)(b), in case of land acquisition proceedings initiated under the old Act (Land Acquisition Act 1894), where an award under the said Act at section 11 has been made five years or more before the commencement of this Act, but the physical possession of the land has not been taken, or the compensation has not been paid the said proceedings shall be deemed to have lapsed. If it so chooses, the appropriate government shall initiate such land acquisition proceedings afresh in accordance. The provisions of this Act provided that where an award has been made, and compensation in respect of a majority of land holdings has not been deposited in the account of the beneficiaries, then, all beneficiaries specified in the notification for acquisition under section 4 of the said Land Acquisition Act, shall be entitled to compensation following the provisions of this Act.

2.1 Pune Municipal Case

Interestingly the Act came into force on January 1 2014, and the first challenge of such provisions made in case of Pune Municipal case came with an order of adverse judgement u/s 24 of the new Act on January 23 2014. This made all the legal practitioners and the people working in government in LA to be alert to such provisions as Pune Municipal Corporation Vs. Harakchand Misirimal Solanki & Others is a typical case of high handedness and callousness on many District Administrations to deal with the compensation payment in an imaginative manner. Court order recognised that Sec. 24(2) had given an overriding effect u/s 24(1) providing that in acquisition proceeding instituted under 1894 Act where an award has been made five years or more before the commencement of the 2013 Act and where the award is mode five years before and either of the two contingencies.

2.2 Physical Possession of the Land

The compensation has not been paid; such acquisition proceeding is deeming to have been lapsed. In this case, the court upheld the appeal that the Award money was not deposited in an appropriate court. However, Pune municipality has kept the money in Civil deposit, hence contravenes the provisions of sec 24 of the Act and the whole proceeding on old Act was quashed.

The number of cases filed, where the actions under the previous Act is challenged with either to quash the case as it does not comply sec. 24 of the Act and pay the compensation in the new RFCTLARR Act, which is expected to be four times of the compensation fixed under the old Act or Application of Sec.101 for return of the unutilised land.

In Mumbai, whose 5.8 hectors of land was acquired in 1993/4(1) notification was made in 1973. The Evictee argued that he got significantly less compensation, though Municipal Counsel had taken the land to set up a hospital under their jurisdiction. His case was referred to as u/s 18 of the old Act to Court for the challenge against the compensation calculation. He hoped to return unused land during his discussion, which is more than half of the acquired land. It proves that the acquisition of land for the public purpose without actual assessment of the requirement has impacted people like Kharade with a loss of more than 2.5 acres, lying unutilised even after five years of acquisition of value Millions under today's market price. The provision of sec 101 was intended to satisfy such grievances. Similarly, the land acquired for Rourkela Steel Plant (RSP) a unit of SAIL in during 1960 could utilise 25% of the land and rest of the land is either unutilised for the last 60 years or have been encroached not being used by RSP resulted with the agitation of tribal people for the restoration of their land. The offshoot of such grievances, resulted in making provisions for the SIA study before the actual land acquisition process begins to cover the seven factors has some meaning on the feasibility and applicability of the Act and the rules in favour of the people.

3. Consent of People and Power to People

With RFCTLARR Act 2013 made effective from January 1, 2014, under the then UPA government generated a question on the timing of this Act to come into force where land acquisition is mostly dependent on the owner's consent land. Is it a deliberate move to stifle the country's growth through almost a halt in infrastructure support for it? The land is an essential component of the growth of a nation, is there an effort made with deliberate conspiracy to impact the growth of the country. The answer focused on other factors such as (i) precisely seven years back from the date new land Act came in to force that is the year 2007 another landmark Act came into force, Forest Right Act 2006 where the landowners right of the people residing in the territory of the forest were recognised, and the provisions of the law looked antagonised to the conservation of the forest. Gramsabha was empowered to determine the individual right and community right. (ii) It attracted the attention to other people-friendly provisions that is PESA Act enacted in 1996 precisely ten years back the Forest Right Act came into force. It is known to everybody that with the India Forest Act 1927 during British Government, it significantly impacted the primitive civilisation who were mostly living in forest area as the village within the forest, lost their identity as village and land settlement process ignored such villages considering it as part of the forest. Thus the people residing in such locations found ost the right, title over the homestead and agriculture land they possessed from their forefathers' time and were recognised as encroacher by forest officials that lead to the agitation by different tribal communities against the British government with the emergence of great tribal leaders like Birsa Munda and Lachman Nayak in the eastern part of India. British India government was forced to make the provisions of the law in the tribal area where the land rights of the tribal community could not be taken without special sanction through different provisions of the Act like Chotanagpur Tenancy Act (CNT ACT) in Bihar & Jharkhand or Regulation 2 Act in Odisha. It took 60 years to fight in independent India to establish the land right of the tribal communities through PESA Act and Forest Right Act that injustice they experienced since 1927. Hence, RFCTLARR Act 2013 with the multiple provisions of the people's getting consent was a natural outcome of the above historical facts.

Various statistics showed that more than 50 million people were displaced in different parts of India for different development projects like Dam, Industries, and Mines since independence. Hardly 25% people have been suitably rehabilitated, which created pressure in the government to bring the RFCTLARR Act where provision is made not only for enhanced land compensation (fair compensation) and the resettlement rehabilitation was covered under the provisions of the Act. Now the question arises if all such provisions under the new Act are people friendly and have a solution to the issues obstructing the land acquisition, why it has a few takers? It is because people have lost confidence for the delay and forceful acquisition, bad R&R happened in the old Act and the new Act which claims solution related to the issues related to the public purpose, fair compensation, alternate employment, livelihood support to the affected in the process of land acquisition still not able to look to the candid challenges.

There are multiple forums and workshops organised to determine the impact of the new RFCTLARR Act and an expected deliverable that was intended to make through the application of the new Act to acquire land. User agencies, mostly PSUs and the private sector organisations are very apprehensive of the robust process and the consent apprehended to impact their timeline of getting the necessary infrastructure (land) for driving up the greenfield projects. When a forum demanded by user agency and policymakers, the discussion centred at timeline and policy support relating to facilitating user agency to get the land. However, in the forum of various stakeholders involved in land acquisition, the focus of discussion shifted to a question 'can this Act compensate for the livelihood loss and employment generation as is claimed'? The micro issues like displacements, food security, tribal land acquisition, consent from the gram sabha, and conducting public hearing have local issues.

Nevertheless, the magnitude of the impact of such issues on the timeline of completion of land acquisition is linked to the uncertainty of the stakeholder management having no answer in any section of the land acquisition act except the management of landowners. In this context, a case of the land acquisition process, where the author was the lead manager to complete the process. The author experienced specific issues which the new land acquisition Act has failed to capture in its sections. The most critical part of the process involved identifying landowners whose land is acquired and compensated for the land and resettlement and rehabilitation. The second big hurdle was the consent of the landowners. Where there is the least displacement, the consent may be obtained through successful and continuous engagement with the landowners to promise much higher land cost and employment assurance. When there is a question of actual displacement, then the only demand is permanent employment with assured income for all the family's adult members. Contradicting people's expectations may be high profile and require high-tech employment and does not have scope to accommodate a large number of unskilled employment, then assurance to provide employment is not possible. Can a project have the luxury of creating such a large number of unskilled employment, in the competitive world of business and advance technology application which is inversely proportional to each other? The business community also has failed to create a trust in the mind of people involved, village community who may be not losing the land but directly affected on the commission of the project in their locality as regards to the sustenance of community growth and deliverables of which a person can rely upon.

In an instance of interaction while initiating land acquisition pre-feasibility study for a cola block with few of the people present in a meeting in a village told that they prefer the block to be allocated to MCL (Mahanadi Coalfield a subsidiary of Coal India public sector undertaking than SETSPL (Tata Steel & Sasol Joint Venture project, a private company). At Talcher coal mines are mostly operated by Mahanadi Coal Field. Enquiring the opposition, they raised to the Joint Venture to take up mines when both Tata India and Sasol of South Africa are very credible companies, and they instantly replied 'there is some hope of continuity of jobs in PSUs than in the private sector industries'. So people expect not only employment but sustainable long term employment. It guides to conclude that the private sector failed to create trust in general people's minds on the employment assurance in lieu of loss of land. While surveying compensation given to the land losers by MCL in the year 2015-16 and its post-acquisition impact, the MCL offered employment to one of the potential members of the family mostly elder son of the family, who later on shifts to the colony quarters with two bedrooms, and after marriage tries to live independent of rest of the family members. As a result, the old parents and young siblings are deserted and deprived of the benefit of employment given to one family member. The rest of the family members, including the old parents, depending on the cash component received from loss of land and livelihood during rehabilitation. This one-time income mostly had become almost zero deposits as illiterate people had no adequate experience in Financial management.

In such a situation, one family member got a long term livelihood support, but the rest of the families are thrown vulnerable and uncertainty being exposed from the agrarian atmosphere to the urban-focused mindsets. The landowners told that they hardly could understand the plight faced today and it happened so quickly that even it took them a lot more time to understand. They have a firm conviction that their political leaders are hands in glove with the company and the administration is a silent spectator in all the changes with the pretext that policy does not support to come out beyond what is given to the people at the time of displacement. The experience with Nilachal Ispat a Joint venture by MMTC and IPICOL Odisha at Kalinganagar a steel hub of 10 steel companies is equally unpleasant. On the one hand, people working in NINL being involved in one festival occasion of the annual day (inception day) with light and colour in entire campus and enjoying parties and meeting within the campus and on the other land losers of the locality residing around the plant boundary as encroachers were watching to this grand function standing outside the gate being denied entry without permission, as they have the status of temporary workers, working under the vendors with a daily wage. Searching answer to these issues in the new Land Acquisition Act, it is not sure if we find any noticeable change from the 2007 National RR Policy to the Act's provisions. However, addressing the livelihood issue and the change in employment pattern, income generation, social status change, the shift from agrarian condition to urban life, need a greater understanding and superior way of compassionate attitude if we want to solve it right technique.

3.1 Impact of Health Hazards in Resettlement and Rehabilitation

A survey was conducted by XIMB Bhubaneswar at Kalinga Nagar after10 years of land acquisition and part industrialisation in 2003. It was reported that apart from the lifestyle change the disease like diabetics and blood pressure had increased 200% after five years of industrialisation of the locality. These diseases were urban impact and lifestyle diseases for which the displaced people were not exposed earlier. Kalinga Nagar experienced the spread of Dengue in the locality because of poor drainage, and unhygienic atmosphere in the slums created by displaced and migrant labours in search of employment had been noticed by Tata Steel and had taken preventive measures as anchor industry in the complex.

4. R&R, Grievance Redress and Employment

In many R&R colonies, when interacted with the villagers displaced during a study, the common complaint was that they were not provided with land right over the land they had been settled, and their village was not declared as revenue village. The question arises, what was the loss they were undergoing in that change situation. In the absence of land right, they enjoyed in their original village inherited from their forefathers' days; the first and foremost loss was their pride of ownership related to their social status and income and self-esteem of authority in the family. The second significant loss was the right of receiving the social benefits from the government, such as Public Distribution System that provides grains and eatables, old age pension, widow pension and many other benefits as the rightful owner of land/house site, and all development package distributed both by central and state Governments keeping village as the development unit. Any new village notification follows a defined process starting from boundary change proceeding (BCP) to final gazette notification, a standing practice in the new village notification settlement process. It looks at how this critical issue was missed attention, as in many cases. The new village declaration was not made even after more than ten years to 12 years of displacement and rehabilitation. In another study, it was noticed that one villager who was facing double displacement because of the first acquisition of their land for an Irrigation project and subsequently for a railway line expansion in Nayagarh district, where they were yet to get land right over the land they have been allotted 15 years back during the first displacement. It will be challenging to compute the benefit of two times compensation as per provisions of sec 39 of the RFCTLARR Act when they were not declared the rightful owner of the allotted house site in the absence of continuous Khatian (RoR) in their name during the first displacement. The law promises for making the required changes for the displaced families in the new Act; still, people fear for it, is now clear from such examples. The involvement of administration loses spirit after the land is acquired, and possession is given to the user agency, and the team engaged for the post-acquisition compliances lose their priorities in government.

In most cases, employees were diverted to alternative responsibilities by the superior as the government's priority changed. The old displaced members of the family of MCL coal mines enlightened that after the project implemented, they did not find a dedicated government authority in the district who was responsible for monitoring their issues and addressing their grievances nor they finding a dedicated team of the representative of the company who continued to look to their long-standing issues as promised in RPDAC. The priority was lost soon after they were displaced. Their grievance was addressed as a general grievance, and the system viewed their case as an ordinary case. The loss of livelihood indicated to be taken care of through employment and compensation was 99% failure since the person who has been given compensation to the tune of few lakhs/crores does not know how to manage the money and most of the money was spent by the family members in a non-productive expenditure. The younger generation within the family put lots of pressure to seniors of the family to spend in the dream luxury, which they were denied when they owned land. The owning of the landed property kept the man confident as a fixed asset with future growth escalation and was a strong point to keep himself at the helm of all family member with social dignity and respect within the family even if they were having a low level of income and expenditure basing on his income criteria.

4.1 Dedicated Institutional Mechanism

Till 2020 few states have notified a dedicated R&R administrator, state-level R&R Commissioner, district wise LARR Authority, and change team to cater to the need for a new LA Act. In the current scenario, a land acquisition office should be operated by a land acquisition officer, one R&R officer, a social scientist, a civil engineer with the power to execute the R&R colony plan with the required supporting team and IT professional for web-based grievance redress. Still, the districts are staffed by one land acquisition officer as was during old Act, and it is the sub-divisional Magistrate/SDO of the subdivision of the district is notified as additional in-charge of R&R administrator and district judge as LARR authority. They are burdened with their routine responsibility for which they were delaying disposal of LA cases. Hence new Act has the provisions of independent authorities has not got its due importance as envisaged in law. In that context, the law is made with new rules, but implementation continues with the same old spirit. Hence the change visibility expected is not coming up. As a result, the new Act and rules cannot create trust in the investors' minds or trust in the mind of land losers. The delay perception, the livelihood loss fear that was there in the mind of people which was capitalised by Abhay Sahu leadership against POSCO in the year 2005 is continuing in the mind of current investors and the impact of new land acquisition act trying to mitigate such apprehensions through provisions of law is looked sceptic with so much people consent provisions.

4.2 Common Property Resources Acquisition and Disguised Stakeholders

At some corner of the mind of the land losers, the compensation for the loss of common property resources (CPR) and natural resources existing within the territory of the village used by the affected population that stand either in the record of government or forest is not considered in the provision of new land acquisition Act. There is no compensation for the necessary amenities and common infrastructure facilities created by villagers or Government support over the years. The traditional rights are not also recognised though the loss of livelihood. It dealt only with the legal titleholders and the market value for a quantifiable commodity is the basis for compensation. Though statistics of displaced people centre around 80% displaced belong to the informal economy and few with legal rights of the land. The loss of CPRs, the psychological trauma of post displacement, the breakup of community, institutions and separate structures are ignored in the first schedule and second schedule calculation in the new Act. Compensation in each area is decided according to the market price at which the land is being registered, but it is a general practice that the land acquired involves both tangible and intangible cost during the sale transaction. So the cost computation of compensation for land at two times in Urban or four times in Rural is not the exact valuation and has no scope to capture the hidden price. The compensation amount is paid only on tangible cost. The expectation on two times in urban and four times in rural as compensation is yet to be understood as a challenge during implementation since raise in land compensation is not alluring to the landowners as the gap between the existing livelihood and the speculative livelihood after displacement is having missing links which new land acquisition Act though claims to have covered is still to be tested on the ground. The public hearing after SIA study with the intention that landowners and people in the locality will make of the required corrections on the six-point on which SIA study is made is given a platform to deny the project, a platform to express the strong resentment against the project, where the people who are not having any loss of livelihood or loss of land have got a strength to speak. In projects' public hearing disguised stakeholders, who neither have livelihood loss nor land loss but being influential in the locality and independent with power and/or interest over the project, take over the decision for the public by either threatening to speak against the project, or motivate the landowner whose mitigation formula are not developed against the project with agenda to create a stake of employment, logistics, construction and business partnership. While framing the law, it is presumed that such disguised stakeholders are having least say or no say whereas the practical experience shows that they may be few are a severe threat to the clearance of the project even if the project affected people (PAP) are ready for receiving the compensation as per the Act both for land as well as R&R.

Conclusion

The RFCTLARR Act 2013 has already made a journey of five years, with many ups and downs. The switchover period from old Act to new Act, the euphoria, apprehensions and legacy with transit from the UPA government to the NDA government, saw the beginning of the implementation of the Act in many states with the framing of the rules u/s 109. The amendment at the level of India's union government of Sec. 105, i.e., the compensation calculation's applicability in the list of 13 Acts of enactment, rate of negotiations and R&R took almost two years after the law is made applicable. However, the most crux of transit from the juvenile state of the Act and move to adulthood requires re-thinking for provisions of employment guarantee on livelihood loss and compulsory creation of statutory posts in all state at least in the district where major mining and industrial activities, as well as land acquisition for the irrigation project, are going on. In such districts, R&R administrator and LARR Authorities' position should be created independently, and communication is created for awareness of all. Both project proponent and the government should create post and space for experts in the team involving social scientist, land acquisition experts and other support staff with adequate infrastructure to handle the landowners' grievance. A committee should be formed at the level of government to examine if the employment to be created for displaced people can be clubbed to the vacancies of the states in respective government where the project proponent will be asked to deposit money against the posts to generate interest and treat as a backup for salary payment and the displaced person be given employment guarantee in the government sector. Such arrangement will help infuse confidence among people who are mostly unskilled and did not find the confidence to work in an industrial project of high-tech nature and that fear of losing a job is no match to the requirement. The assurance of compensation to the livelihood lost through negotiate employment in government sector will undoubtedly be a strength to the person to migrate from his traditional livelihood with loss of land and the project proponent who has expertise in their technical field can at least come up with a deposit of amount against employment for salary with the government for the displaced families and focus on a competitive market for productivity. It is observed that people who got a job in lieu of land loss are the biggest adversary of Land Acquisition as they lost their self-esteem in the company when they are recruited in a lower post compare to what they were enjoying as the landowner. In a developing country like India where most of the industries and mines are needed to be commissioned within the specified duration of execution to obtain mandate of cost competition in the market should be facilitated by government in the process of land acquisition even if the clause of consent and fair price is mandatory under the law. The change law needs to address the public hearing for land acquisition should be separated for environment clearance, and the participants should be confined to the affected persons and the affected villages instead of the affected area (5 kms/8 km radius). So that the land acquisition process will not be delayed for non-compliance of the public hearing and the disguised stakeholders of vested interest whose interest is not able to be fulfilled during the public hearing as the project is not sure whether it can come or not at that stage for any other statutory and financial and loan compliance.

Nevertheless, being an influential person and having power and interest over the area can delay or vitiate the public hearing, which will delay the whole process. The very purpose of keeping the public hearing provisions is not fulfilled with such influential community who are not supportive of constructive change suggestions and facilitate for smooth acquisition and project commission. The people whose land is acquired or livelihood is affected, or even the villagers whose common property is disturbed should have a say in the public hearing so that the public hearing could be meaningful with right suggestions with mitigating measures that obtain support from the project proponent to recommend the project for a public purpose. The amendment for such above suggestions should come up with parliament approval to make the RFCTLARR Act more meaningful and practical and create trust among both the land losers and project proponent for which the change law is envisioned.

References

The Gazette of India Vol 40, New Delhi Ministry of Law and justice The right to Fair Compensation and Transparency in Land Acquisition, Rehabilitation and Resettlement Act 2013 (Act no 30 of 2013)

The economy grew at the slowest rate in a decade in 2013 – Business Today year 2013 Roundup.

The Parliament Library and Reference, research, Documents and information service(LARRDIS) for member's Reference service Reference Note (No.5/RN/Ref./2013)

Discenza, R. & Forman, J. B. (2007). Seven causes of project failure: how to recognise them and how to initiate project recovery. Paper presented at PMI® Global Congress 2007—North America, Atlanta, GA. Newtown Square, PA: Project Management Institute.

India Spend (2014). Tribal's account for a third of community displaced by large projects, June 17, 2014

Jena, Manipadma (2006): Orissa: Draft Resettlement and Rehabilitation Policy, 2006, Economic & Political Weekly, February 4: 384-87.

Jenner, Stephen. (2015). Why do projects 'fail' and more to the point, what can we do about it? The case for disciplined, 'fast and frugal' decision-making. PM World Journal-IV (III)

Meher, Rajkishor (2008): Development or Livelihood Insecurity: A Study of Displaced Families by Three Public Sector Plants in India, Paper Presented at the Annual Meeting of the Society of Applied Anthropology, Memphis, US, March.

Merrow Edward W: Industrial Megaprojects (Concept, strategies, and Practices for Success)

Mishra, Banikantha. (2010) Agriculture, Industry and Mining in Orissa in the Post-Liberalisation Era: An Inter-District and Inter-State Panel Analysis, Economic & Political Weekly, XLV (20)

Mishra, Binod Chandra (March 2016) Journal of Management Special Issue on Land Acquisition, resettlement and Rehabilitation; Vol.45 No 1,

Mishra, Binod Chandra (2014) (Author ID: 2110054) ssrn.com, FDI in India and Its Impact on Land Acquisition & Involuntary Displacement – A case study on POSCO Project at Paradeep in Odisha,

Mishra, Binod Chandra (2013) ssrn.com, The In and Outs of Niyamgiri Gram Sabha for Mines of Vedant Alumina Ltd at Lanjigarh in Odisha

Obadia, Bett. (2018) Why do projects fail? Project Management Journal, Vol-1 (1000): 7 – July 2018

UNDP Status Report (2008). Land rights and ownership in Odisha

About the Author

Sri Binod Chandra Mishra is a Post Graduate and M.Phil in Life Sciences and MBA in Human Resource Management & Marketing. He has 32 years' experience in Land Acquisition in Government and Tata Group in India. He has published nine articles relating to Land Acquisition in Social Science Research Network, New York to (http://ssrn.com/author=211054). His article on Gram Sabha was also published in LA special in Vol 45 No 1 March 2016 publication of Journal of Administrative Staff College of Hyderabad. He has written a Book on 'Land acquisition case studies in Odisha and provisions of RFCTLARRR Act' and is Published by ALIVA press and is available in Amazon.